The Royal Navy Lynx

1982, The author (right) with Flight Commander Bob McKellar and CPO Tug Wilson, plus Lynx Mark 2, XZ 722 'ARFA', heading south from Ascension Island to join the Task Force. (*Author*)

The Royal Navy Lynx

An Operational History

Larry Jeram-Croft

Pen & Sword
AVIATION

First published in Great Britain in 2017 by
Pen & Sword Aviation
an imprint of
Pen & Sword Books Ltd
47 Church Street
Barnsley
South Yorkshire
S70 2AS

Copyright © Larry Jeram-Croft 2017

ISBN 978 1 47386 251 7

The right of Larry Jeram-Croft to be identified as the Author of this Work has been asserted by him in accordance with the Copyright, Designs and Patents Act 1988.

A CIP catalogue record for this book is available from the British Library

All rights reserved. No part of this book may be reproduced or transmitted in any form or by any means, electronic or mechanical including photocopying, recording or by any information storage and retrieval system, without permission from the Publisher in writing.

Typeset in Ehrhardt by
Mac Style Ltd, Bridlington, East Yorkshire
Printed and bound in India by Replika Press Pvt. Ltd.

Pen & Sword Books Ltd incorporates the imprints of Pen & Sword Archaeology, Atlas, Aviation, Battleground, Discovery, Family History, History, Maritime, Military, Naval, Politics, Railways, Select, Transport, True Crime, and Fiction, Frontline Books, Leo Cooper, Praetorian Press, Seaforth Publishing and Wharncliffe.

For a complete list of Pen & Sword titles please contact
PEN & SWORD BOOKS LIMITED
47 Church Street, Barnsley, South Yorkshire, S70 2AS, England
E-mail: enquiries@pen-and-sword.co.uk
Website: www.pen-and-sword.co.uk

The views and opinions expressed are those of the author alone and should not be taken to represent those of Her Majesty's Government, MOD, HM Armed Forces or any government agency

Contents

Foreword		vi
Author Profile		viii
Acknowledgements and Thanks		ix
Introduction		xi
Chapter 1	The Military Need	1
Chapter 2	Design and Development	3
Chapter 3	The Lynx HAS Mark 2 – The Early Days	21
Chapter 4	The Falklands War	37
Chapter 5	The Lynx HAS Mark 3 – Beefing Things Up	148
Chapter 6	The Gulf – 1980 to the Present Day	157
Chapter 7	The Lynx HMA Mark 8 – the Final Version	207
Chapter 8	There But For the Grace of God Go I …	215
Chapter 9	Rescue	237
Chapter 10	Around the World	256
Chapter 11	The Author's Story	271
Appendix I: Glossary of Terms		277
Appendix II: Naval Lynx Variants – Performance Specifications		283
Appendix III: A Dummies Guide to Flying a Helicopter		284

Foreword

BUCKINGHAM PALACE

I am delighted to introduce this book written by Larry Jeram Croft. The Lynx Helicopter has a long and illustrious history within the Royal Navy, as is demonstrated by its outstanding operational record.

Reading this book I am reminded of the flexibility of the aircraft as it has covered a much wider range of roles and capabilities than it was originally designed for. I was fortunate to fly the aircraft during my Service career as a Flight Pilot, Flight Commander and as Senior Pilot of 815 Naval Air Squadron and therefore experienced first-hand its strength, reliability and effectiveness.

In recording and celebrating the invaluable work of the Lynx aircraft, I am certain that this book will be an inspiration for the next generation of pilots as well as ensuring its proud place in Naval Aviation history.

HRH Prince Andrew, Duke of York, KG, GCVO, CD, ADC

As I moved from the venerable Wasp HAS Mk 1 (just why would anyone fly a Mk1 anything?) to the Lynx HAS Mk3, my aviation world suddenly looked very much more comfortable. Having all that Lynx power and speed was an extraordinarily step up the ladder of capability. And it had doors. And the spare engine definitely helped, so I very gradually weaned myself off waiting for the undemanded downwind engine-off at 400' at night over the sea...

My modest (nearly) 500 hours was a sheer pleasure, even if Larry is right, and the Lynx did rattle and leak a bit. But, compared to almost everything else we flew, it was a dream. Though we lost good friends in accidents, and we will never forget them, it never let me down. I'm grateful for that.

This is a wonderfully full record of the venerable contribution of the Lynx, and I'm delighted Larry has had the time to pull it off. Delve and enjoy!

Admiral Sir George Zambellas, GCB, DSC, DL FRAeS

Author Profile

Larry Jeram-Croft spent thirty years in the Royal Navy. He trained as an aircraft engineer and then as a helicopter pilot. He was awarded a Queen's Commendation for search and rescue duties and flew the Lynx off HMS *Andromeda* during the Falklands War. Retiring from the Royal Navy in 2000 as a Commander, he worked in industry for seven years before retiring for a second time. He then bought a yacht and lived in the Caribbean with Fiona, his wife, before returning to the UK to write books. He now lives in Somerset, where apart from writing he continues to fail to hit a golf ball with any skill whatsoever.

Apart from this book, he currently has eleven novels available on Amazon. Seven of these are the 'Jon Hunt' series that have been described as the 'British Top Gun' and cover the career of a modern naval officer in current times starting from the Falklands and covering events thereafter. Based on his own military experience they are regularly praised for a degree of authenticity rarely found in military fiction.

Acknowledgements and Thanks

Many people have helped me produce this book. Indeed it would not have been possible without them. Individual contributors have already been given acknowledgement against their respective articles. However, I would like to thank all those who have given their time, dug out old photos, and trawled through their records to remember things that happened, in many cases quite a long time ago. Apart from those contributors, I would also like to acknowledge the particular input and help I received from the following:

AgustaWestland Ltd:
Dave Gibbings, Colin Hague.

The Lynx Wildcat Maritime Force:
Commanding Officer, Commander Louis Wilson-Challon
The Force Warfare Officer, Lieutenant Commander Chris Yelland.

815 Squadron:
Commanding Officer, Commander Philip Richardson
Senior Observer Lieutenant Commander Matt Boulind
Operations Officer, Lieutenant Commander Alex Sims
Air Engineer Officer, Lieutenant Commander Brett Gilliss
Flight Commander and Heritage Officer, Lieutenant Rich Bell

The Fleet Air Arm Museum: Barbara Gilbert

The RN Flight Safety Centre:
Commanding Officer, Commander Ben Franklin
Lieutenant Commander Polly Hatchard
AET Stuart Donovan

x   The Royal Navy Lynx

Royal Navy Media Communications Staff at Whale Island for approval to use articles from the RN 'Cockpit' and 'Flight Deck' magazines.

Finally, I would like to apologize to all those who flew this marvelous aircraft and whose stories I have not been able to include. In such a long period of time there would be far too many anyway. Hopefully, those I have chosen provide sufficient evidence as to what a fantastic machine the Lynx has been.

Introduction

There is a well know saying that if 'something looks right then it probably is right'. I got my first glimpse of a Lynx on the runway at the Royal Naval Air Station at Portland in the summer of 1977 and it looked right. Up until then we had the large boxy Sea King, the rather humped Wessex, or the ungainly Wasp to choose from. This machine looked sleek, fast and modern, because it was all of those things. Two years later, when I was flying Sea Kings from HMS *Hermes*, another Lynx came on board. This time I was able to get a better look; and now that I was a qualified helicopter pilot myself, I could really appreciate what I was seeing. It looked even sleeker, faster, and up to date. So, it was with great delight that I was informed that my next appointment would be to 702 Squadron to learn to fly one.

The squadron had just formed out of the Intensive Flying Trials Unit (IFTU) at RNAS Yeovilton and the atmosphere was brilliant. It was a melting pot of aircrew: Stovies (Fast Jet), Pingers (Anti-Submarine Sea Kings), Junglies (Commando Wessex 5s) and Small Ship's Wasp Jockeys. Mix this experience up with a twin engine aircraft capable of one hundred and fifty knots, with its own radar and sea skimming anti-ship missile system as well as the ability to carry anti-submarine homing torpedoes, depth charges, or nuclear depth bombs, and we were in aviation heaven.

I had just finished my first front line tour on Sea Kings. They were relatively lumbering and old fashioned. My first flight in a Lynx was a revelation. With a rotor head made of solid titanium, the aircraft literally handled like a fast jet. In fact, the Lynx was one the world's first truly aerobatic helicopters. Not that we were allowed to exploit the fact (at least not officially). It was designed from the outset to cope with small ship operations. The undercarriage was so strong it hurt my back when my instructor dropped it onto the tarmac from ten feet. The hydraulic deck harpoon system meant that as soon as we were on deck we were secure; that, and the fact that you could actually reverse the pitch on the main rotor and push the thing down onto the deck with over half the power of the engines. Tactical operations were another eye opener; flying at fifty feet over the sea, flat out, at one hundred and fifty knots, in close formation with another Lynx and then splitting off and pulling 2g to ensure that when we fired, we could put eight Sea Skua missiles, at four different skim heights, into a target from ninety degrees apart. Wow.

xii The Royal Navy Lynx

Alright, it did vibrate a bit (actually rather a lot at full speed) and the engines had a nasty habit of failing after only a couple of hundred hours. Oh, and when you shut it down the ground crew had to clip little buckets to the engine exhausts to catch all the oil leaking out of the rear seals. Then there was the tail rotor that really hated the relative wind coming from the right, to the extent that you could end up with full rudder pedal and nothing happening, which could make deck landings interesting to say the least. So what? We knew all these things would be fixed in time and they were. As the Maintenance Test Pilot at Portland in later years I was able to make my contribution.

But then, early in 1982, everything changed. Many of the ships of the fleet now had Lynx Flights and a total of eighteen ended up being deployed 8000 miles to the southern hemisphere. The Royal Navy was about to fight a war it was very definitely not designed to fight, a very long way from home and any support. The Lynx, like everything else, was pitched into the fight with very little preparation. That it performed so well is a tribute to its designers and the men who maintained and flew it. What it didn't get – was much publicity. It didn't operate from the two big carriers with the press on board and it didn't fly over the land battles much. Nevertheless, its contribution was significant; from mundane tasks like delivering mail around the fleet to more glamorous missions like Naval Gunfire Support – spotting the fall of a ship's 4.5 inch shells and inserting Special Forces troops. In the absence of any real Airborne Early Warning aircraft it was regularly sent up-threat to listen out for the telltale radar of an Argentinian Super Etendard jet which had to be turned on to launch an Exocet missile. The first sea skimming missile fired during the conflict was a Sea Skua fired by a Lynx against an Argentinian patrol boat. Many more followed, even though technically, the missile system wasn't even accepted into service at that point. Although the submarine threat was actually quite low, there was the ever present threat of the two modern Argentinian U-boats and the Lynx flew many anti-submarine missions. When the Argentinian submarine Santa Fe was intercepted off South Georgia a Lynx was there. There were several encounters with enemy fast jets and surface-to-air missiles, but no Lynx were shot down. Several of the aircraft were fitted with active I-band jammers designed to seduce the homing head of an Exocet. The whole system had been cobbled together in weeks and proved to work against a real missile on a UK test range. These are just the headline stories about an aircraft that has never really had its praises sung. After that, a mere further thirty-five years of service has taken the aircraft to every theatre of operations. During nearly all that time there has been a Lynx deployed in the Gulf. Its performance during Operation Granby (First Gulf War) was outstanding; two aircraft effectively destroyed the Iraqi navy in just two days of attacks.

Introduction xiii

It has sunk more enemy ships with its Sea Skua than any other naval system, dropped torpedoes, caught drug smugglers and conducted rescues all around the world. In fact, it would not be unfair to claim that *it has been the most successful weapon system deployed by the Royal Navy since 1945.*

This book, based on the accounts of those who operated it, seeks to tell its story and put the record straight.

The Author – flying his Lynx – beating up his ship. The best aircraft in the world for that particular activity! (*Author*)

Chapter 1

The Military Need

After the end of the Second World War, military development continued apace not the least because of the continued threat from the Soviet Union. Submarines continued to increase the range from which they could attack and ships continued to increase the range they could detect the submarines from. It was a technological game of cat and mouse that continues to this day. Unfortunately, for the ships, it was soon realised that although a submarine could be detected, there was now no way of attacking it. One of the solutions was to develop a small helicopter that could operate from the tiny decks of Frigates and Destroyers and carry a weapon out to the target.

The system became known as MATCH, (Manned Anti-Submarine, Torpedo Carrying Helicopter) and the aircraft was known as the Wasp, a development of the Scout that was being built for the Army, it had a single turbine engine and a crew of one pilot. It could also carry a crewman for secondary roles. As a first generation ship-borne helicopter it was a great success and it allowed the Royal Navy to take a lead in small ships aviation.

A Wasp landing on a Leander-class frigate. The flight deck is barely bigger than the aircraft. (*WHL*)

2   The Royal Navy Lynx

However, the Wasp was limited. With two homing torpedoes slung underneath, it only had a few minutes endurance. Even with no weapons it struggled to fly for more than an hour. One description was that it was on a twelve mile piece of elastic around the ship. It soon became clear that a replacement would be needed. So, in the mid-60s, a replacement was planned. Given the designation WG 13, it would be twin engined and revolutionary in design. Westland helicopters were given the task of designing and developing it as part of a three aircraft production programme with the French. Westland would produce the Lynx, whilst Aerospatiale would produce the smaller Gazelle and larger Puma helicopters.

Then, on 21 October 1967, while the aircraft's specification was being firmed up and initial contracts were being awarded, the stakes were dramatically increased. Israel and Egypt had just fought the Six Day War and an uneasy truce was in place. The Israeli navy were operating the destroyer Eilat off the coast of Egypt. Eilat was launched in 1942 as the Royal Navy Destroyer HMS *Zealous*, but had subsequently been sold to Israel. Both sides disagree about what happened next. The ship was off Port Said, and according to Egyptian accounts, well inside their national waters. Whatever the rights and wrongs of the matter, two small patrol boats left the harbour and attacked as soon as they were clear of the breakwater. From a range of about ten miles, the first patrol boat fired two P-15 'Termit' missiles at the Eilat. These weapons were Soviet and known to NATO as 'Styx'. They were designed as anti-shipping missiles with a range of fifteen miles and could be fitted to any ship from a tiny patrol boat upwards. Despite seeing the incoming missiles, turning away, and increasing speed, the Eilat was hit by both. They hit amidships, one penetrating the engine room, and the ship started to burn and sink. An hour and half later, another patrol boat fired two more missiles. One malfunctioned, but the other hit the sinking ship's stern and finished her off: fifty-seven men died and ninety-one were wounded.

The incident sent shock waves around the world's navies. The Eilat may not have been the most modern warship around, but the fact that a tiny patrol boat could inflict so much damage simply by slipping its lines and pointing its nose out of harbour was something to which there was very little defence. The only weapon in the Fleet Air Arm helicopter inventory at the time was the AS12 short-range, wire-guided missile fired from the Wasp and it had neither the range nor the accuracy to take on this sort of threat. Something had to be done. One of the solutions the Royal Navy decided upon was to arm its new helicopter with a credible missile system that would be able to attack up to a Corvette sized target from outside their own defences. The Lynx would get CL 834, later named Sea Skua, a radar homing, sea skimming missile, with a range of over nine miles. Not only would the Lynx be used in the anti-submarine role like the Wasp, it would now have a credible attack role of its own.

Chapter 2

Design and Development

Much of the Lynx design was born out experience with the Wasp. (*Steve George*)

The Westland Aircraft Works, as a division of Petters Limited, was formed in 1915 to construct aircraft under licence for the First World War, and in 1935 became Westland Aircraft Limited. During the Second World War they took over Spitfire repair and overhaul when the Supermarine facility in Southampton was heavily bombed, and were largely responsible for developing the aircraft into the naval variant, the Seafire. In addition, they produced their own designs. The most successful was the Lysander monoplane, well known for taking agents into wartime France. However, their twin engine Whirlwind fighter might well have made a difference in the early years of the war as it was fast, it would leave a Spitfire standing, and armed with four 20mm cannon which would have outgunned any aircraft during the Battle of Britain. Unfortunately, problems and delays in procurement of the Rolls-Royce Peregrine engines, plus other issues, meant it entered service too late and saw little action. Just after the end of the war, the company produced the Wyvern, a heavy, fast naval fighter with contra-rotating propellers powered by an Armstrong Siddeley Python gas turbine. In all, eight naval squadrons operated the aircraft and it saw service during the Suez crisis, but its performance was overshadowed by the introduction of early jets. It also had problems with its technology, particularly the engine, which had an unreliable propeller control system and a habit of flaming out on take-off due to the accelerations of a catapult launch.

Above: The Turbo Prop Wyvern, the Royal Navy's last propeller driven fighter. (*WHL*)

Left: The Westland Whirlwind, nicknamed 'Crikey' because of its unusual appearance. (*WHL*)

Once the Second World War was over, Westland made a decision to concentrate on rotary wing aircraft. It was a brave decision, but not universally approved and the Chief Designer, W. Petter, left to form the aircraft division at English Electric. Amongst his post-war designs were the Canberra, Lightning and Gnat aircraft. Westland made several unsuccessful proposals for new helicopters in various categories, but in the end made an agreement with Sikorsky in the United States to build some of their designs under licence. These included the very successful Wessex and Sea King helicopters, which were heavily re-engineered versions of the originals.

In the fifties, there were a large number of aircraft manufacturers producing everything from long-range bombers to fighters. Because of the growing threat from the USSR, and other conflicts like Korea and Suez, the British Government continued to sponsor new designs. It was a golden age for the British aircraft industry. Many innovative ideas that are still being used today sprang from this time. Britain was a world leader. However, the country was almost bankrupt and by the mid-fifties something had to be done. The government commissioned a White Paper to review the situation. It was led by the then Minister of Defence, Duncan Sandys.

The report was instrumental in forcing fundamental change, although some of its assumptions, for example, that manned aircraft would not be needed in the future as missiles would replace them, were more than a little premature.

On the commercial side, the report concluded that many of the aircraft companies should merge. The incentive to do so was that only these groups would be liable to receive further government contracts. Consequently, by 1960, the British Aircraft Corporation (BAC) was formed out of English Electric, the Bristol Aeroplane Company, Hunting Aircraft and Vickers Armstrong. Hawker Siddeley took over de Havilland, Blackburn and Folland having already taken over Armstrong Whitworth, AVRO, Gloucester and Hawker before the war.

Rotary wing aircraft, although in their infancy, were starting to be developed by several companies. Westland, cash rich from their Sikorsky licence, were seen to be the main lead and so they took over Saunders Roe, Fairy Aviation and the helicopter division of the Bristol Aeroplane Company.

One of the projects that Saunders Roe took with them to the new premises in Yeovil was the Saunders Roe P531, a small single turbine-engined helicopter. It first flew in July 1958, but when Westland re-engineered it, two versions emerged, the Scout for the army and the Wasp for the navy.

The Design

Several years after the industry rationalisation, there was a proliferation of helicopters operating within the services. There was the large twin rotor Belvedere, as well as the Wessex, Sycamore, Wasp, Scout, Whirlwind and Skeeter. Westland proposed they should be rationalised with four replacements:

WG1 – a 35,000lbs All-Up Weight (AUW) machine to carry three crew and thirty-three military personnel, or perform ASW/heavy lift duties.

WG3 – a squad carrier with two crew at 8,000lbs AUW.

WG4 – a Wessex replacement at 17,000lbs AUW to carry twenty-four troops.

WG12 – a four seat light observation helicopter at 2,500lbs AUW.

The WG 3 soon turned into the WG 13 and thence the Lynx. Its original design criteria were:

1. Simple to maintain and reliable.
2. High speed (160 Knots).
3. Easy to manoeuvre on the ground and turn around.
4. Air transportable; particularly in a C130 Hercules.

Armed with these basic criteria, a prolonged debate took place with the MOD. It soon became clear that the aircraft could simply be modified to replace the Wasp with the exception that the rotors were too large. It was also becoming clear that the original intention to fit the T700 engine would not be acceptable, as it did not have the potential to have its power output increased sufficiently. Rolls-Royce then proposed using the more powerful, but untried, BS 360 engine, later to be called the Gem. Despite the risks inherent in mating a new aircraft to a new engine, the decision was taken to go ahead.

By 1966, under political direction, the Lynx was to be developed in conjunction with the French under a three aircraft agreement, where Aerospatiale would develop the Puma and Gazelle, and Westland would lead on the Lynx. It is interesting to note that these three aircraft broadly fall into the categories identified by Westland years earlier (above), with the exception of the large heavy lift aircraft, and of course it wouldn't be many years before the Chinook was procured for the RAF.

Design and Development   7

By this time the overall requirement for the naval Lynx had firmed up; so in addition to the original requirement it was to be:

1. Highly manoeuvrable.
2. Be versatile with an all-weather performance.
3. Be capable of operating from a ship with minimal need for the ship to have to change course to recover it.
4. Operate in three primary roles of: ASW or Anti-Submarine Warfare, Surface Search and after the Eilat affair, ASUW or Anti Surface Warfare.
5. Operate in secondary roles of: troop transport, day and night search and rescue and Vertical Replenishment (VERTREP).

About the only one of these requirements that wasn't fully met in the final RN version was a night SAR capability, as it was never fitted with a sufficiently sophisticated night hover system. However, in order to meet certain of these requirements, some innovative design was going to be needed.

And in the days before email, the internet and mobile phones, there were many in the Royal Navy who saw the primary role of any ship's aircraft slightly differently.

'What time you gettin' the mail Sir?'. (*RNFSC*)

8   The Royal Navy Lynx

Highly manoeuvrable

Very early in the WG3/13 programme there had been an aspiration to simplify rotor head design. Up until then there had been two main basic concepts. Bell were using a teetering system using two blades rather like a see saw. It was simple and effective, but had several major disadvantages, not the least an unfortunate tendency, when abused, to part company with the aircraft. Fully articulated rotor systems, where the blades could flap up and down as well as lag around hinges with bearings, were safer and could be used on larger machines, but were complicated, costly to maintain and limited the aircraft's manoeuvrability.

Westland were not the only company to pursue this goal, but it was not going to be a design solution without its pitfalls. In the United States, Lockheed were developing the Cheyenne attack helicopter, which was revolutionary in design in that not only did it have a rigid rotor, but it also had a pusher propeller at the rear and stub wings, making it more of a compound aircraft than a pure helicopter. It never made it into service; the original contract was cancelled due to vibration issues with the rotor head and other programme slippages, although there is also a school of thought that it was crossing boundaries with air force requirements for a ground attack aircraft – which eventually became the A10 Warthog.

In Germany MBB produced the BO105, which had a bolted together, hingeless titanium rotor head and was a great success and predated the Lynx by several years. However, when Aerospatiale attempted to adapt it for the Gazelle helicopter they were forced to abandon the idea due to high speed instability problems.

In Westland, there was a desire to make a rotor head out of one piece of material that itself would bend in the appropriate places. Initially, it was hoped to make the flexible sections quite soft, but once the design phase was reached it was clear that it would have to be stiff in order to minimise air and ground resonance issues. This had the advantage of making the aircraft very manoeuvrable, but at the cost of increased vibration levels. The material chosen was titanium as it has an excellent resistance to fatigue damage. As a trial, a smaller version was built and fitted to a Scout helicopter, which showed the idea had potential. However, one thing this trial showed was that lag dampers needed to be fitted to ensure that resonance issues were avoided. Unlike conventional helicopters, these dampers had no effect on the aircraft in flight, as lag compliance was achieved through the stiffness of the titanium section. Although quite revolutionary in concept, it is a reflection of Westland's confidence in their design that when the MOD offered them money to produce an alternative articulated rotor head, they declined on the basis that it would offer an easy way out if things became difficult.

The following diagram shows the final configuration of the production head; although earlier versions consisted of various parts bolted together.

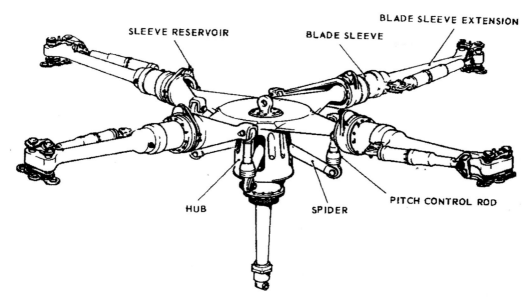

Schematic of the Lynx Monobloc production rotor head. (*WHL*)

Another feature of this design was the use of a 'spider assembly' to control the pitch on the blades rather than the more conventional swash plate arrangement used on most helicopters. The flying controls operated on the bottom of the spider, as can be seen, and up on to the pitch control arms. This was similar to the system used in the Wasp. The net effect of all these design features was a very compact and very effective, simple system.

As well as the innovative rotor head design, the rotor blades also needed to be light, stiff and strong, and consisted of aluminium sections that were glued together to form the main spar and a honeycomb rear section to make up the rear part. Later on in the service life of the aircraft these blades were replaced with composite ones that were the result of the British Experimental Rotor Programme (BERP).

The result of these design issues was an aircraft that was one of the first truly aerobatic helicopters in the world. Not only was this good for flying displays, but it saved the crew of at least one Lynx during the Falklands War, as will be narrated later.

There was also another major advantage. As the blades were attached via a solid piece of metal rather than a hinge, it was possible to reverse their pitch when on the ground. In fact the aircraft could generate almost half its torque through the rotors downwards, which was a major factor when operating from small ships as will be described later. It also accounts for the unusual aspect the aircraft has when shut down, as the blades, instead of drooping down as with most helicopters, actually do the opposite, almost seeming to defy gravity.

However, nothing comes without a cost and the downside of the design was that airframe vibration levels were high. Various palliatives were tried and will be described later, but the aircraft was never the smoothest, especially at high speed.

A truly aerobatic helicopter. (*WHL*)

Fit in a C130 Hercules and ship's hangar

In order to ensure that the height profile of the aircraft met MOD requirements for air transportability and to be able to fit into a small ship's hangar, it was clear that the gearbox would have to have a low profile if the cabin was to remain large enough. The gearbox would have to reduce the input from the engines at 6000 rpm to those of the rotors at 318 rpm and cope with powers of 1800 horsepower. The solution was to use a new type of gear profile.

Normal gear teeth have a convex shape and the point of contact rolls along the face of the tooth as it meshes. Westland designed a 'conformal' gear which was concave in profile and was able to transmit more power for a given size and had better lubrication properties. The net result was a very compact and simple gearbox that met all the requirements. Unlike the gearbox in the Sea King it could even operate for a significant time without oil pressure, which was very reassuring for the aircrew.

It did, however, have one downside. It was noisy, making a very noticeable high frequency whine which could be distracting to the aircrew and very good for alerting the enemy of its approach.

The Lynx Monobloc rotor head with the low profile, conformal gear and gearbox. (*WHL*)

Minimal effect on Ship operations
The Royal Navy and Westland had built up an enormous amount of experience operating the Wasp, from a great variety of warships, in all weathers, around the globe. This was put to good use when 'marinising' the design of the WG13.

The core design of the Lynx would ensure that, compared to the Wasp, the aircraft had good endurance, weapons and sensors. However, for a small ship's aircraft it needed additional features to ensure it could operate in all weathers, day and night, and also minimise the need for the ship to alter course to launch, recover and range it.

As already mentioned, the rotor head and blades of the aircraft gave it an incredibly high degree of manoeuvrability. When hovering alongside a warship in rough weather this gave the pilot the ability to get the aircraft on deck quickly when a quiescent moment arrived. However, at night, with no natural horizon, it could actually make things more awkward. This was because the only external visual reference was the ship, which was moving, sometimes quite significantly. If the pilot 'followed the ship' the controls were so sensitive it was almost impossible to hold a stable hover. The only

12   The Royal Navy Lynx

way to counter this was to look inside at the instruments, particularly the Attitude Indicator, which was not always the best thing to do when hovering a few feet away from a large lump of gyrating steel. All that said, the knack was soon acquired and night deck landings were, and still are, routinely and safely accomplished.

One area that did cause issues at first was the tail rotor. Westland released the aircraft to service with it effectively going around the wrong way. The reason for this stemmed from the original high speed design. At very high speed, the coning angle of the tail rotor could be sufficient to make the tips of the tail rotor blades get too close to the tail pylon if they rotated in one direction so the system was designed to avoid this. In the end the speeds achieved were not high enough for this effect to be significant, but it was too late to change the design and meet introduction into service dates. Consequently, with the blades rotating in the 'wrong' direction, the airflow interaction with that of the main rotor caused problems, and the net result was that in the hover, with winds from the right from about 30° to 90°, the aircraft could literally run out of rudder pedal. Having said that, it was a reasonably benign effect, unlike what could happen in the Wasp where a rapid flare to the hover could result in the well-known 'P2 death spiral'. This was a stall effect on the tail rotor that meant the aircraft started to spin uncontrollably and in all but one occasion resulted in a ditching. (The term 'P2' alludes to the fact that it normally happened to inexperienced pilots and those were often the second pilot or P2 of a ship's Flight.)

In the mid-eighties the company redesigned the tail rotor and reversed its direction. The problem was solved.

So initially, the requirement for the ship to be unhampered in manoeuvre to launch and recover the aircraft was in part compromised by this limitation and care had to be taken to ensure that the relative winds were in limits before approaching. However, for take-off it wasn't so much of an issue because of another design feature – that of the undercarriage.

A tricycle undercarriage was chosen with a wheel on each sponson and one under the nose. The oleos were very strong. The whole undercarriage was designed to take the impact of a fully laden aircraft landing at seven and a half feet per second (a significant thump!). On deck, the nose wheel could be hydraulically castored through ninety degrees and for normal use the main wheels were toed out at thirty degrees. This meant that the aircraft could swivel around on the deck and face into the relative wind for launch. This could also be used after landing cross deck, which mitigated the tail rotor issue somewhat. The wheels didn't have brakes as such, they had hydraulic sprag wheel locks to ensure they were either free to rotate or solidly held. The only time this became an issue was when landing ashore on one engine when there was a need to run the aircraft on with forward speed. With the main wheels toed out, the friction of the scrubbing tyre acted as an effective brake as long as the pilot remembered to disengage the wheel locks first!

One feature the Wasp had was a deck 'tie down' that could be released by the pilot, enabling him to spot turn the aircraft into wind on deck securely for take-off without the need for lashings. However, this could not be re-engaged on landing. The Lynx would go one better with a hydraulic deck harpoon that could be engaged or disengaged into a grid on the deck by the pilot. As an addition, as has already been explained, the rotor system was capable of pushing the aircraft down on deck with negative thrust, thus adding another level of security when the aircraft was about to launch or had just landed.

A Lynx of the German navy secured on deck in rough weather with chain lashings, and the harpoon connected to the deck grid which can be seen just to the left and behind the nose wheel. The aircraft may also be using negative pitch as the angle of the blades is well below normal, and with such a large wave about to hit – who can blame them! (*WHL*)

And so: On a pitch black and stormy night, in some ocean, miles away from anywhere in a radio and radar silent environment. Having been glued to instruments in the cockpit for two and a half hours and been over a hundred miles away from the ship. With the aid of the observer and the aircraft's own radar, the crew could find that tiny little green light in the wilderness and fly down the glideslope with power in hand.

Then they could hover alongside their home and as soon as it stopped leaping around for just a second, slam the Lynx down on deck and be immediately secure.

Meanwhile the ship was able to get on with its business.

Over forty years on and there are very few aircraft in the world that are as good at this as the Lynx.

Mind you there was always a feeling that on occasions the surface ship navy didn't appreciate their aircraft quite as much as they should.

'Here he comes – starboard 30.' (*RNFSC*)

The Powerplant

As previously mentioned, the engine selected for the Lynx was the Rolls-Royce Gem, previously known as the BS 360. The 'BS' was because the original design was from Bristol Siddeley and inherited by Rolls-Royce when they took over the company in 1966. When Westland were looking for an engine, they soon realised that their original power estimates were too low and a more powerful engine with 900hp would be needed. Rolls-Royce offered the Gem as the solution. In some ways it was a brave move for both companies.

Westland had not wanted to risk developing a new aircraft and engine at the same time, but in reality there was little choice, especially after the guarantees supplied by Rolls-Royce, who knew that the engine was a legacy design and was very immature and complicated for its size.

The engine's gas generator has two spools, the slower one with an axial compressor and the faster with a centrifugal one. A two stage free power turbine produces the power which is led back out of the front of the engine. This layout is extremely compact and allows the engine to be mounted behind the main gearbox. In addition, the engine was designed as a set of seven modules that could be interchanged when needed at the service's second line facilities. This led to some debate between the company and the services as to what constituted an engine rejection. The services considered that any time an engine had to be removed from an airframe then it had failed. Rolls-Royce originally tried to insist that as long as only a module was replaced, then the engine itself hadn't failed. However, this was an argument they were not able to win, not the least because all front line RN Lynx were deployed away on small ships with no module replacement capability. The only way to repair the aircraft if an engine failed was to replace the whole unit with a spare, if the ship was lucky enough to have one.

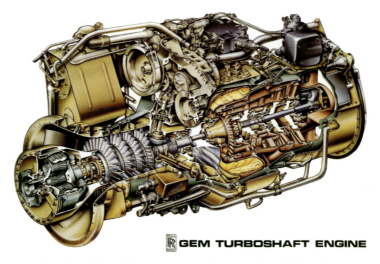

A cutaway drawing of the original, compact, but complicated Gem 20 engine. (*RR*)

However, there were many problems with the early engines. It took some time to get them to deliver sufficient power, and oil consumption was high. During the development phase of the aircraft, Westland's fears were realised as Rolls-Royce were not able to provide enough to maintain the flying programme and a year's worth of development time was lost. At one stage engines were being transferred between the development airframes on a regular basis just to keep some airborne. By the time the aircraft entered service there were still issues.

The engines were mounted on a slight nose-up slope and the rear oil seal required air pressure from the engine to work. Consequently, when the engine was shut down, oil poured out of the exhaust. Despite Rolls-Royce putting additional capacity in the oil system scavenge system, to this day this has never been fully sorted out. The ground crew had to rush out and clip small catch cans to each exhaust once the engines were stopped. They also had to make sure the exhausts were well wiped clear of oil before they were next started up, or the whole aircraft could disappear in a cloud of white smoke.

The mean time between failure of the engine was contracted to be 800 hours. In reality, in the early days, it was more like 200. There were several reasons for this; the primary causes were internal oil leaks or loss of power as the hot and fast part of the engine degraded too quickly. Also, the oil pressure gauging system was unreliable and could give an indication that the engine had lost oil pressure, when in fact it was perfectly fine. This caused more than a few heart stopping moments for aircrew, especially at sea when a long way away from the ship.

All this said, the engine rarely let the aircrew down in flight and rejections were based on accumulated data rather than a loud bang. After the Falklands war, Rolls-Royce and the MOD made strenuous efforts to sort out the engines issues and were in the main successful, particularly after the introduction of a more powerful Gem 42 to power the later Mark 3 and Mark 8 variant of the aircraft.

Development

Taking an unproven and revolutionary design and turning it into a safe production machine is no easy task. Issues that had to be considered right from the start of the development phase included:

1. Westland would be the design authority for the aircraft. However, there needed to be an agreed production work share with the French. This was initially agreed as a 35/65 split, with Westland taking the larger share. The French would build and develop the attack variant that they were looking for as well as the rotor head, tail rotor blades and hub, deck lock harpoon and participate in the naval variant for the capabilities they were looking for. For example, the French naval aircraft would have a dipping sonar, whereas the British one would not. Unfortunately, in September 1969, the French cancelled the attack

variant, which meant a further revision of the workshare was needed and they were given extra responsibilities for the naval undercarriage sponsons, the folding tail of the naval variant and much of the role equipment. From the outset this arrangement put considerable strain on the programme due to the need to deal with potential suppliers in two countries, with different procurement processes and a variable exchange rate.
2. The development and supply of major subsystems in time to meet the programme, for example, the flight control system. These were sub contracts from Westland.
3. The provision of Government Furnished Equipment (GFE), such as the radar and weapon systems in the correct timeframes. These were separately contracted by the MOD and then supplied to Westland.
4. Identification of 'high risk' areas that would need extra development work and could be critical paths for the programme.

By 1967 the programme was ready to commence. There would be sixteen development aircraft and a number of ground rigs which would allow development of aircraft systems such as electrics, hydraulics, the transmission, fuel system and rotor system, as well as airframe fatigue rigs. These rigs were particularly targeted against the identified high risk items such as the rotor and gearbox. In all, twelve static rigs were used.

The number of aircraft was reduced when the French pulled out of the attack variant. This put extra strain on the other machines, as all airframes had a common dynamic structure, and so the remaining aircraft would have to take the share of the common testing originally planned for the attack prototypes.

In the end, thirteen development Lynx were built along with two modified Scout aircraft which flew a scaled down version of the rotor head. There were six basic prototypes, one of which was used for engine testing, one Army utility, two French Navy, two Royal Navy and two general naval prototypes.

One of the two modified Scouts fitted with a scaled down rigid rotor. (*WHL*)

18 The Royal Navy Lynx

A decision was taken early on to paint all five of the basic prototypes in different colours. The reasons for this are lost in the mists of time, but apparently it was useful for the flight crews when spotting returning aircraft. Someone was heard to remark that when parked up they looked 'like a box of Smarties'.

The Westland 'Smarties' – XW 835 – yellow, XW 836 – grey, XW 837 – red, XW 838 – blue, WX 839 – orange.

So, on Sunday, 21 March 1971, eight months later than originally scheduled due to problems with the early engines, the yellow XW 835 was flown for the first time by Ron Gellatly. Preparation for the flight had been extremely thorough. The rotor system had already been extensively tested on the two Scout aircraft. A simulator at RAE Bedford had been used to prepare the aircrew and there had been a large amount of running on the various test rigs, especially that for the engines. Roy Moxam, OBE, the co-pilot, summed it up quite simply, 'the aircraft flew as predicted'. In fact it flew two short trips on the first day. Despite the fact that these flights were severely limited by the underpowered engines, the development programme was underway.

It took four years to develop the naval version of the Lynx. The first major problem common to all variants was that of high vibration. The rigid rotor head and the proximity of the rotor blades to the airframe meant that on the early flights vibration levels were unacceptably high.

After significant flight testing with various stiffening beams fitted to the aircraft, the final solution was to stiffen the rear cabin mainframe and engine decking and put two support rods across the tail. Unfortunately, because the naval variant had a folding tail pylon, this last solution wasn't possible and much larger castings to the tail fold area had to be fitted. Although these solutions produced acceptable levels of vibration when the aircraft were new, managing vibration has been an ongoing activity throughout the life of the aircraft.

As already mentioned, the engines were also a major problem in the early days because they failed to achieve their declared life and Rolls-Royce had trouble meeting the requirements of the development programme. At one stage engines were being transferred from airframe to airframe just to maintain the flying programme.

Another innovation in the development of the naval variant was the use of a moving platform based at RAE Bedford. Not only was it used to assess the aircraft's ability to land on a moving platform, but also proved useful in assessing deck operations such as removing and attaching lashings and carrying out maintenance.

Unfortunately, in November 1972, XX469, the first naval prototype, suffered a catastrophic accident. The tail rotor driveshaft coupling had been over-greased, so that when the tail pylon had been spread, the splines that coupled the drive were not fully engaged. Whilst in a low hover the drive failed and the aircraft crashed. Both crew survived with mild injuries, but the loss of the aircraft had a significant effect on the programme.

The sad remains of XX469. (*Louis Wilson-Challon*)

Notwithstanding all the programme issues, on 8 July 1976, the first production aircraft, Lynx XZ 227, was delivered to the Royal Navy.

Chapter 3

The Lynx HAS Mark 2 – The Early Days

All Shiny and New. (*RNFSC*)

When the Mark 2 aircraft became operational, it had a wide suite of sensors and weapons, much more so than any other aircraft of its type for the time. That said, not all were fully mature at the time of introduction into service. However, outlined below is the definitive Mark 2 list:

Avionics

Radar

The most important sensor in the Lynx was, and still is, the Ferranti Sea Spray radar. Fitted in the nose cone of the aircraft, and with the display in front of the observer on a small TV screen, it gave the Lynx several important capabilities. Firstly, when locked onto a target, it became the aiming mechanism for Sea Skua missiles, which would fly down the beam onto the target. Unfortunately, the radar only operated through 180°, which meant that when the missiles were in flight, the aircraft could only turn away from the target by a maximum of 90° at the most (in practice this was more like 80° to maintain missile lock). However, this generally wasn't a problem, as the missile could be fired well outside the self defence of most of the targets it was fired at.

It also became very important to most of the ships that the aircraft operated from, that they themselves carried long-range surface-to-surface missiles such as Exocet or Harpoon. The problem the ship had was that it couldn't identify targets at the ranges it could detect them. The Lynx could go ahead, identify targets, and provide targeting information for the ship. This was known as OTHT or Over The Horizon Targeting. And of course, the radar often proved invaluable in getting the aircraft back to the ship, particularly when the ship was operating under radio silence.

By modern standards the radar was fairly basic. To track targets, the observer had to place a small plastic screen on top of the radar screen, place a chinagraph grease pencil dot on the target, and then wait three or six minutes and see where the targeted move to. When practising this technique in the English Channel with tens, if not hundreds of potential targets, it proved quite difficult. However, in a tactical environment where the number of targets was limited it proved surprisingly successful.

Particularly in the early days, the radar had problems with reliability, often because of high vibration levels in the aircraft. The system consisted of seven black boxes and often the only way to get the radar to work was to continually change box after box until the system came back online. This meant a large number of units being returned for repair and no-fault being found with them.

Electronic Surveillance Measures (ESM)

Until the Orange Crop ESM system was introduced to the Lynx fleet, naval helicopters had virtually no way of detecting either enemy or friendly radars. There was a small handheld device in service, but it was of a very limited performance.

The Orange Crop display unit was fitted on top of the aircraft's dashboard and could be operated by either crew. It consisted of four bands of LEDs each representing a particular radar frequency band. Six aerials were fitted to the aircraft and provided 360° coverage. When a radar was detected, LEDs would light up on the bearing, the number of LEDs giving an indication of signal strength. A cursor could be placed over the signal and other parameters measured. In addition, an audio tone could be heard over the aircraft's intercom system. The system gave sufficient information to identify targets from their radars providing sufficient intelligence was available. It could also easily identify parent ship systems and help the aircraft to return to its 'mother'.

It was a revelation to aircrew at the time. Suddenly a whole new world of capability was opened up. During the Falklands War, the system was used extensively to search for the attack radar of the Super Etendard aircraft that the Argentinians used to launch Exocet missiles.

Magnetic Anomaly Detector (MAD)

The Lynx was never originally intended to have a method of localising a submarine target and hence attacking it without outside help. However, many of the ships it was going to operate from were going to be fitted with the new towed array sonars. These sonars could detect a submarine at enormous distances and could get reasonably accurate bearings, but were very poor at getting an accurate range. Consequently, if the aircraft could fly down the bearing and localise the target, the overall system could be highly effective.

One piece of equipment that was fitted and trialled to several of the early Mark 2s for this purpose was a Magnetic Anomaly Detector. The kit was developed from early magnetometers used by geologists to detect large masses of ferrous material, which by their nature have a measurable magnetic field. A submerged submarine falls well into this category. The equipment used was an American system bought off the shelf and for the Lynx a MAD 'Bird' was fitted to the starboard sponson and, when in use, it was trailed behind the aircraft on a long wire to get the detector well away from any of the aircraft's own influences. The aircraft would then fly to the approximate position of the target and conduct a search looking for a 'MAD mark' as it overflew the submarine. Once detected, a cloverleaf profile was flown to establish the target's course and speed before a weapon was dropped.

The trial, which was concurrently conducted with Sea Kings as well, was deemed successful, but in the end it was decided not to proceed with a fleet fit of the equipment, possibly because of the very tight accuracy limitations needed to successfully drop a Mark 46 torpedo at the time. That said, several ended up deployed for the Falklands War and were used. At one time there was a plan to fit an internal MAD system into the tail boom of the Mark 8, but that was cancelled as a savings measure.

A Mark 2 Lynx in the process of recovering the MAD 'Bird' during trials. (*Dick O'Neil*)

24   The Royal Navy Lynx

Navigation and Communication

Like the Sea King before it, the Lynx was fitted with a downward looking Doppler radar. The system could detect the aircraft's movement from the surface of the sea or land. In the Lynx, this data was fed into the aircraft's Tactical Air Navigation System (TANS). Much easier to use than previous systems, even a modern day GPS user would recognise how it worked using waypoints and providing navigation steering data. When navigating to a waypoint the system could drive a needle on the pilot's attitude indicator giving him direct steering information. It could also drive the crosshairs on a moving map display for the observer. Even nowadays, these systems have their use because the system is integral to the aircraft and does not rely on outside systems such as GPS satellites, which can be jammed or turned off.

So that the aircraft could be seen and identified on friendly radars, it carried two types of radar transponder. IFF (Identification Friend or Foe) was the system used with civilian and area radars and is fitted as standard to many aircraft. In addition, the aircraft had an I-Band transponder specifically to work with naval ship's radars. This was particularly important as the aircraft was made of a large amount of composite materials and although 'stealth' technology was in its infancy, the aircraft, more by accident than design, was actually very hard to see on radar. The initial system fitted used two little 'shark fin' antenna on the nose of the aircraft. Unfortunately, they were fleet fitted before it was found that the system would not work satisfactorily. As a consequence, the original 'baked bean can' aerial from a Wasp had to be fitted. The only place it could go was on the tail, which meant that when directly approaching a ship, the aerial was masked by the bulk of the airframe. A call of 'chin up' would therefore often be heard over the radio, at which point the pilot would pull up the nose of the aircraft and allow the ships radar to see the transponder aerial.

Radios consisted of a PTR377 U/VHF radio and a Collins longer range HF system. The main problem with both these systems was that, although reliable, they were used only in plain voice. When operating in a tactical environment there was often the need to transmit data that the enemy really shouldn't hear. It wasn't until much later, with the Mark 3, that radios which could encrypt their transmissions were introduced.

Weapons

With effectively two primary roles – anti-submarine (ASW) and anti-surface warfare (ASUW) – the aircraft would have to be capable of carrying a variety of weapons.

For the ASW role it would carry the American Mark 46 homing, anti-submarine torpedo, which would quickly be replaced in service by the all British Stingray torpedo.

These weapons have their own active sonar, and when dropped in the vicinity of a submarine can attack it autonomously. The MK 46 had to be dropped quite close to the target and had several limitations, not the least, that if the target was too shallow, it could mistake the surface for the target and leapfrog in and out of the water in 'surface capture' mode. In addition, it had a small internal combustion engine for propulsion. In order for the fuel to work in such an engine enclosed inside the weapon, it had to use a fuel that contained its own oxidant. In the Mk46 that was called 'Otto Fuel' and it was extremely dangerous. The Stingray, which remains in service to this day, is a quantum leap ahead in technology. The accuracy requirements for dropping it are much less demanding and it has a much bigger suite of attack modes. It is powered by salt water activated batteries and so is inherently much safer.

The Mod 3 Mk 11 Depth Charge is almost identical to the weapon used extensively in the Second World War and remains in service in all RN ASW helicopters to this day. Simple it may be, but it can still cause damage. The Argentinian submarine Santa Fe was disabled by two of them dropped from the Wessex Mark 3 aircraft from HMS *Antrim* during the Falklands War. Just as importantly, it makes an enormous amount of noise. Any submarine commander relying on passive sonar information to make an attack is going to be significantly distracted if someone is dropping them – even quite far away.

Until 1988, the WE177a Nuclear Depth Bomb was also carried. This device was used both as an ASW weapon by helicopters, but also a ground attack bomb dropped in a variety of modes by fixed wing aircraft. Its efficiency as an anti-submarine device was much more limited than might be thought as the attenuating properties of water to shock waves is very high. That said, and like the conventional Mk11, any submariner in the vicinity of one detonating near him was definitely not going to continue with his attack. There was also a school of thought that it was just as dangerous to the aircrew as anyone under the water. This was not in fact true, and trials in the sixties showed that the blast did not actually breach the surface (at least that was what we were told!). Trouble for the enemy it may have been, but the administration and certification procedures to stow it in ships and load it onto aircraft, probably made it more trouble for those given the thankless task of deploying with it.

With the exception of MAD, the Lynx had no way of localising the position of a submarine sufficiently accurately enough to drop any of these weapons. So, in the role of 'Pony', all would be dropped by the Lynx under tactical control of either a surface unit or another helicopter such as a Sea King that had ASW sensors.

The Stingray active homing anti-submarine torpedo, two are loaded on a Mark 8 Lynx. This British weapon replaced the earlier American Type 46. (*WHL*)

The Mark 11 Depth Charge, virtually unchanged since the Second World War, a light blue practice variant is loaded to the port weapon carrier. (*WHL*)

For the ASUW role it would carry four Sea Skua radar homing, sea skimming missiles. Fired from a minimum of two hundred feet, they had a range of nine miles. The missile could have four different skim heights pre-set, depending on the type of target. It relied on the Sea Spray radar being locked onto the target when it would use the reflected radar signal to home onto its prey as described in the section on radar earlier on. Each missile weighs 150kg, with a 30kg warhead, and flies at high subsonic speeds. It has sunk or damaged more enemy warships than any other British naval weapon since 1945.

In addition, the Mark 2 was capable of carrying 4.5inch flares for target illumination. This was a legacy from the days of the Wasp, where it was necessary to do this to be able to fire an AS 12 visually guided missile. This process was known as a DIDTAC, which for aircrew, translated into 'Death in the Dark Attack', and they were not referring to the enemy!

Sea Skua – the aircraft's (and Navy's) most successful weapon. Here, four are loaded to HMS *Alacrity*'s Lynx whilst undergoing a rotors running refuel. (*WHL*)

28   The Royal Navy Lynx

First steps – The Intensive Flying Trials Unit (IFTU), 700(L) Squadron

When a new aircraft enters RN service it is put through its paces initially in an Intensive Flying Trials unit or IFTU. These units are always given a squadron number of 700 followed by a letter in brackets designating the aircraft. Consequently, in 1976, 700 (L) Squadron formed at Yeovilton. In fact, this was a joint venture with the Dutch navy, who contributed two aircraft to the squadron's numbers.

The purpose of an IFTU is to train maintainers and aircrew on the new aircraft, start assessing its operational capability, and develop tactics and assess other factors such as maintainability and reliability. In terms of its technology, the Lynx was far more advanced than any of its predecessors and many lessons would have to be learned before it could go operationally to sea. Also, the Sea Skua weapon system was still in development and would not be available for several years.

Below is an article written by the commanding officer of 700(L) that was published in the Fleet Air Arm flight safety magazine, Cockpit. It gives a good insight into what was thought of the aircraft in its early days.

By Lieutenant Commander Geoff Cavalier commanding officer 700 (L) Squadron:

'*The Lynx has been operating at RNAS Yeovilton since the end of September 1976 and has now amassed nearly 3500 hours flying. I think it is time therefore to sound a few cautionary words on its flight safety aspects.*

'*Foreign Object Damage (FOD) is a potential hazard to all helicopters and the Lynx is no exception. Although the Gem engines are mounted above the cabin and well clear of the ground they are immediately aft of the cabin door guttering and an ideal channel for bits of loose locking wire et cetera. There is, however, a stainless steel mesh fitted around each engine intake to alleviate the problems of FOD ingestion, but this has to be removed in potential icing conditions.*

'*A further FOD problem could well be the amount of down wash created when true negative pitch is applied during a deck landing. Something like 60% engine torque is used (the same power required to fly at 120 Knots!). The blades drop a good twelve inches, noise increases dramatically and anything close by but not secure has a good chance of moving fast. So future Lynx FDOs you have been warned. Add to this the potential FOD hazards of the flight deck grid and you will require thorough briefing of all ships personnel on a very regular basis.*

'*Flight safety does not of course only concern FOD and I shall therefore briefly mention further points that could interest all those who may come into contact with the*

Lynx (not literally I hope). For perhaps the first time in the history of RN helicopters, the aircrew manual clearance will be well below the aircraft's potential performance, with the consequent temptation to exceed laid down limits: but let us all be very aware why these limits were imposed. The Lynx is an expensive beast with a lot of stretch and it will be required to fly for a considerable number of years. So please don't let our future Lynx crews inherit a dangerous helicopter in ten years' time because we haven't been responsible or disciplined enough to keep within specified limits. Gone are the days when we could fly only for fun. It is now very much a serious, expensive business and if the sortie profile of the aircraft does not require a certain manoeuvre then it must not be attempted. (Yes it can roll but despite everything you've heard, it is a very difficult and dangerous manoeuvre, the entry criteria are extremely tight and it could, at the very least, strain the airframe or at worst damage it.)

'The Lynx is highly sensitive to control and pilot induced oscillation, particularly in the pitching plane and this can ruin a smooth ride. It is also very fast (for a helicopter) and it is noticeable how quickly things happen when you've been used to struggling along at 90 Knots (apologies to Gazelle pilots). It is therefore not surprising that it doesn't particularly want to slow down and one should allow plenty of time for this manoeuvre when approaching a ship or any other landing area. A fast stop is relatively easy to execute but visibility over the long nose is almost totally lost and sideways glances at ground or sea are necessary with consequent disorientation problems. Visibility from the cockpit is generally good but there is a blind area abaft the beam (thank you Fish Heads) caused by the main control frame, so a very careful lookout is required at all times.

'Due to the rigid rotor design, auto rotations are difficult to carry out accurately. Sudden rotor rev increases or decreases with changes in speed or in turns can be quite dramatic and considerable control anticipation is needed if limits are not to be exceeded. A careful look at the future training syllabus is being made and will question the philosophy of practising any form of advanced autorotation in a twin-engine helicopter that will spend the majority of its operating life over the sea (has anyone in Sea King or Wessex Five ever done a 360 auto after both engines have failed?).

'Much has been mentioned with regard to the crew fatigue problem due to noise and vibration in the Lynx. I think it fair to comment that at the normal operating speed of a 140 Knots (later increased to 150 Knots) in-flight monitoring of noise levels has shown that it is no worse than other current RN helicopters, although tests at higher speed ranges and with the new bone domes have not yet been carried out in-depth. Subjectively the gearbox noise can become somewhat intrusive after a four hour period but not to the extent that it affects the cruise operational effectiveness. Similarly, vibration levels caused by the rigid rotor design are noticeable, but in the normal speed

range with a well tracked aircraft, far better than had been expected and not bad enough to cause excessive fatigue to aircrew. Much thought has gone into isolating the aircrew from the more extreme vibrations at high speeds and this has been achieved by the use of sprung mountings on the seatback and seat pan. Add to this correct lumbar supports and a properly contoured seat dinghy pack (the rigid PSP) complete with lambswool cushions (ducky) and you have an environment that should prove to be more comfortable than the majority of previous helicopters.

'In conclusion, the Lynx is a tough helicopter designed specifically to operate in a tough environment and considerable emphasis has been placed on reliability and ease of maintenance. Its sophisticated avionics fit (Sea Spray radar, Tactical Air Navigation System, ESM, IFF, and I band transponder), twin-engine reliability, high speed, good range and endurance and unique deck landing capability, give it very significant advantages over its predecessor, the WASP. It is easy and pleasant to fly, but due to its enormous potential it must not be mistreated.

'Careful consideration for this cat could keep its claws closed!'

Another, probably more pragmatic perspective, of the IFTU is provided by Don Chapillon, who was a Chief Petty Officer Watch Chief on the IFTU:

'The first aircraft, XZ 229, was received into service on 16 September 1976, followed by XZ 230 on 19 October. The last of the five RN aircraft, XZ 232, was received on 4 March 1977. Two Dutch aircraft were received into the unit between 15 November and 16 December 1967.

'The personnel who formed the IFTU came from various backgrounds. The aircrew were predominantly from the rotary wing world, whereas the maintainers were a mixture of fixed wing and rotary wing experienced personnel. The key senior rates had started their careers on fixed wing (Sea Vixens, Scimitars, Buccaneers, Phantoms and Gannets), but by the time they joined the IFTU they had all served spells on various rotary wing aircraft (Whirlwind, Wessex, Wasp and Sea King.)

'In May 1976, key senior rates, depending on their trades, were sent for various courses at Westland Helicopters, and in July 1976 they were sent to Rolls-Royce for the Gem Engine courses.

'On 1 September, they all came together at RNAS Yeovilton and the IFTU was formed. It was not until 16 September that the first aircraft, XZ 229, was received and the work to test and prove the newest addition to the Royal Navy helicopter fleet began. Westland had obviously carried out development flying but had not subjected it to the rigors of operational flying. The first aircraft did not have Sea Spray Radar fitted but had what was referred to as 'Blue Circle' Radar (a concrete block in its place). This proved a problem when carrying out vibration test flights as it was imperative that the concrete block was tightened down. In these days we were still using the Askania for vibration testing. Although past it's sell by date it did still prove useful in identifying various early problems, especially with tail rotor problems which made Westland do a quick rethink on static and rotary balancing.'

(Authors note: The Askania was a clockwork driven device that put a needle on the place to measure vibration and produced a simple paper trace. Not sophisticated, but surprisingly effective in expert hands.)

'Once the first aircraft had been through its acceptance checks the intensive flying began, the IFTU's claim to fame was that it always had an aircraft airborne outside the control tower waiting for the airfield to open (only inclement weather stopped this happening). This meant the watch chiefs and their maintenance personnel putting in some late nights and early mornings, and quite a few 'Red and Green' entries to allow flying with acceptable defects to achieve this.

'One major engine issue (other than oil leaking from the back end) was engine oil pressure problems. This was in the first instance put down to a pressure transmitter malfunction until one night we had run out of transmitters and it looked as though we were going to miss our early morning slot (could not even carry out robbery action). I realised we were not carrying out SOAP (Spectrographic Oil Analysis Procedure) samples and the oil filters did not have a removal life as was the case on all the other aircraft I had previously worked on. We did have a filter available so we changed it and the problem disappeared. The offending filter was sent for analysis to Naval Aircraft Technical Evaluation Centre (NATEC) and lo and behold it was blocked. SOAP samples were introduced and filter changes were introduced at fifty hour intervals until a history was built up. I mention this example as just one of the problems we solved by operating the aircraft intensively rather than its operations during development flying.

'Part of the task of the IFTU was to prepare the aircraft and personnel to form the first Flights ready to embark the aircraft and prove the aircraft at sea. On 4 July 1977, I became the Senior Maintenance Rate (SMR) of Sirius Flight (the first Flight to form) with Tim Brookman as Flight Commander and John Harvey as Flight observer. We did not remain Sirius Flight for long; in fact we never actually embarked. This was because HMS *Birmingham* was guard ship for the Queen's Silver Jubilee Review and Phoebe Flight were embarked with one of the

32   The Royal Navy Lynx

IFTU aircraft. After the revue, the Commanding Officer, Captain Kerr, made a case to the MOD for a Flight to be embarked permanently. He won his case; therefore, on 8 August 1977, we became HMS *Birmingham* Flight. Ironically, Captain Kerr and I had served together on 899 Sea Vixen Squadron when he was a lieutenant observer and I was a young naval air mechanic. We had some pretty hairy moments in those early days, a couple of which are documented below.

'One day I took off with Nick de Hartog to do a maintenance check test flight. After about twenty minutes I noticed that gearbox oil temperature was rising quite rapidly. We decided to abandon the test flight and return to base. With the temperature still rising we called for an emergency landing. On our training course at Westland, they told us they had run a gearbox on the test rig for a period with no oil and had found no damage at the end of the exercise, but we were in an aircraft with the oil temp gauge showing max temp, which we were not too happy about. (Although the oil pressure was constant and had not reduced which made me feel a bit more confident.) On landing, the aircraft was quickly shut down and moved to the hangar. On removal of the gearbox oil cooler, it was found that the quill drive shaft had sheared and the oil cooler was seized. Westland advice was to drain the gearbox oil and send an oil sample to NATEC, fit a new oil cooler, refill the gearbox and carry out an extensive ground run. Post the ground run we sent another oil sample to NATEC (who were pretty quick in getting back to say the sample was OK). It was with a bit of trepidation that Nick and I got back in the aircraft to do the test flight, but I am glad to say we had no further problems and the aircraft passed. The oil cooler was sent back through the 760 defect reporting system, but to this day we have never seen a follow up report. Unfortunately this happened with a lot of items.'

(Authors note: The Lynx gearbox could run for at least half an hour with failed oil pressure, which was a quantum leap over the Sea King which had a maximum of three minutes. Personal experience confirms this as I went for a swim in the Bristol Channel one sunny afternoon when exactly that happened in an 814 Squadron aircraft.)

'When we received an aircraft, we carried out the mandatory receipt checks and acceptance test flights. The test flights were all carried out in the Yeovilton area with no over the sea flying. Later, of course, this became important as part of developing the aircraft's tactics. When going over the sea we had to make the Emergency Services Safety Break (ESSB) switch live. This switch makes all the services such as the explosive winch wire cutter and flotation gear live and clearly needs to be active when over the sea. However, the first time XZ231 coasted out and the ESSB was made live, both emergency flotation bags inflated. The aircraft was recovered to Portland where it was impounded until I arrived. When I arrived, it was surrounded by every man and his dog all waiting to see what was wrong with the new addition. Having done my homework on the flight down, I realised that unless there was a major electrical problem, the only other problem must be with the salt water immersion switch, which was designed to fire the flotation gear if the aircraft entered the water. I crawled underneath and got access to the switch. I found a 2BA bolt lodged in the switch, which had obviously been dropped in there on the build line. This meant that as soon as the ESSB was made live the salt water immersion switch activated and the aircraft was flying along with two very large bags. The bags were removed, put in the cabin and we returned to Yeovilton.

'The footnote to this story is that on carrying out acceptance checks on the aircraft, on XZ229 we found a spanner on the transmission platform and on XZ230 we found a file in the avionics bay.

'Teething trouble aside, the feeling of all the people on the IFTU, aircrew and maintainers alike, was that we were involved in introducing what was going to be a world beating helicopter. We found and solved a lot of problems in the sixteen months of the IFTU, but we were still solving problems when I left 829 Squadron fourteen years later.'

It is interesting to contrast these two accounts of the IFTU. It could be said that Lieutenant Commander Cavalier's *Cockpit* article is a little optimistic, but it was for public consumption. Don Chapillon takes a more pragmatic view as he was involved in many of the grass roots issues. In fact the aircraft did have high vibration levels, particularly as the airframes aged, which caused many problems not just with the airframe but with the plethora of avionics on board. It would be many years before the engines met their original planned life. Although the noise from the gearbox was deemed acceptable, many Lynx pilots have suffered from noise induced, high-frequency hearing damage. Another facet of the aircraft was that for the first time maintainability was incorporated as a factor in the design. For example, all the hydraulic system components were mounted in one place and could be easily accessed. However, especially in the early days, the spare parts ranging and scaling did not necessarily reflect this concept. So instead of replacing a complete hydraulic pack, only individual items were available, which meant difficult repairs had to be conducted at the front line. Once again, time and experience with the aircraft gradually overcame these issues.

34   The Royal Navy Lynx

Another peculiarity was that because it was part of an Anglo-French program, it was decided that all the aircrafts units of measurement would be metric. Unfortunately, the original design had been in imperial units. The result was that many of the numbers that the aircrew had to remember were quite strange, as they were the metric equivalent of an imperial measurement. For example, the maximum load that could be carried underslung was 3000lbs. However, this translated into 1364kgs.

Notwithstanding these issues, the aircraft was a revelation to the aircrews who were lucky enough to be selected to fly it. The late 70s was a time when the navy fixed wing community were being decimated by the loss of the big carriers. Consequently, a number of fixed wing aircrew converted to the Lynx. Other aircrews came from the WASP and Sea King communities. This melting pot of differing aviation skills was just what was needed to develop the tactics for the new aircraft. Despite the Sea Skua system still being in development, the weapon's capabilities were well known and two aircraft coordinated attack procedures were quickly developed. Once operating at sea, there was also the need to educate the surface navy into the capabilities of the new machine. It was an exciting time for everyone. Little did anyone realise but many of these tactics were going to be exercised to the full in only a few years' time.

At this time, the aircraft was also generating a great deal of interest in Europe – with the German and Danish navies in particular. Martin Manning was one of the first Flight Commanders and recalls a visit to Denmark which was successful in singing the aircraft's praises in a roundabout sort of way

Lynx Talk at Royal Danish Naval Air Station Værløse

'In May 1979, having just formed Avenger Flight with a brand new Lynx, we went to Norway and then on to Denmark to demonstrate the Lynx landing on board KNM *HORTEN* and HDMS *HVIDBORNEN* (Polar Bear Classes). Just before our return to the Danish Naval Air Squadron Base at Værløse, I was asked if I could give a talk on the Lynx to the squadron members.

'We duly arrived on 3 May and I went into the briefing room to set up my lecture and was flabbergasted to see it already full up with admirals downwards sitting in smart uniforms waiting for me. Not having my slides in order yet, and feeling rather scruffy still in my goonsuit, I had to ask them to stand up and have a cup of coffee and a chat while I got my slides in the carousel – and my ducks in a row.

'The talk went well and I emphasised the many new and exciting aspects of the Lynx. There were many questions, as the Danes were keen to buy the aircraft.

'One question was, "what is the spares support like?" This was the killer really, because in the early days there were many shortages for us. I said, "Well, for us it is pretty poor still, but it will get better and, for overseas customers, it is now much better and you tend to get priority." Afterwards, one of the two-star admirals came up to me and said that they were well aware of the spares situation and that if I had not answered the question as I had, they would not have believed a word of what I had said.

'I thought no more about it until our return to Yeovilton. Whilst still taxying in, a message came over channel one; "Flight Commander, report to Commander Air IMMEDIATELY". I was then given a huge bollocking about my denigrating Westland to foreign customers. Unbeknown to me, there had been a Westland man in the audience who had passed the message all the way up to his chairman, who had spoken to the First Sea Lord and it had come all the way down to me. I told Wings that I would not accept this as I had done UK a good deal, telling him about the Danish admiral's comment. Wings said; "Consider yourself bollocked but well done. Off you go."'

When the IFTU completed its work, it transformed into 702 Squadron which, for the next thirty-six years, was the training squadron for the naval aircraft. As the numbers of aircraft entering service grew there was a need to separate training and operational activities. Consequently, in 1981, 815 Squadron was commissioned and, along with 702, both moved from Yeovilton to the Naval Air Station at Portland.

The numbers of Lynx continued to grow and so in 1986, at the same time that the WASP was being phased out, its parent squadron, 829, also converted to the Lynx.

The three squadron crests.

36   The Royal Navy Lynx

The Lynx fleet was slowly expanding. Sea Skua was about to be fully released into service and was already being fitted to some aircraft. The electronic surveillance system, Orange Crop, was also being fitted. A steady program of maturity was underway when everything changed.

In April 1982 Argentina invaded the Falklands.

Chapter 4

The Falklands War

HMS *Andromeda*'s Lynx 'ARFA'. (*Author*)

The Falklands War was a wake-up call for the whole Royal Navy. Not the least because the Fleet was not configured to fight the sort of war it was about to be involved in. Up until then, open ocean warfare and resupplying Europe from America with the attendant submarine and air threats was the order of the day. The Falklands War would require ships to operate in a landlocked environment or close to the islands themselves and thousands of miles away from any support.

However, the Lynx was probably one of the more well configured weapon systems in the Royal Navy's arsenal. It had been specifically designed to attack small fast patrol boats and submarines, both of which were seen as potential threats. On top of that, it had the flexibility to take on a great deal of extra roles ranging from naval gunfire support to delivering the mail.

38   The Royal Navy Lynx

The fact that it performed so well, yet little has been written about its contribution, is probably down to the way that Lynx Flights operate even to this day. The Flight on the ship is an individual unit in its own right and although the men are appointed to the ship they are also part of a squadron back ashore. Each Flight had different experiences, but there was no way of comparing notes as there would have been on a large squadron on a carrier. So, when the individual ships and therefore Flights returned, their stories were never put together in a coherent manner.

Lieutenant (later Captain) Chris Mervik summed up the situation rather well:

'HMS *Penelope* sailed for the Falkland Islands on 10 May 1982, arriving back in Devonport on 10 September. A further post-war deployment to the Falklands began the following January, returning in June 1983. In the short period between those deployments, the hectic comings and goings of other ships' Flights meant there was little opportunity to share and compare experiences of the Falklands War with other aircrew; those events that were discussed back at 815 Squadron's new headquarters at RNAS *Portland*, served to demonstrate that, for single aircraft Flights in frigates and destroyers, the flying on operations was a uniquely individual experience – for that reason alone, the accounts in this book should make for interesting reading, if only for those who were involved in those extraordinary times.'

The aircraft that went to war was the Mark 2. It had an all-up weight of 4220kg and a maximum speed of 150 knots. Its endurance was up to two hours forty minutes, although this could be extended to over four hours with an internal fuel tank. The standard aircraft could carry four Sea Skua missiles or two Mark 46 anti-submarine homing torpedoes. Some of the aircraft were modified to carry the latest Stingray torpedo. In addition, Second World War Mark 11 depth charges could be carried as well as 4.5 inch flares for illuminating targets. Nearly all aircraft were fitted with Orange Crop ESM. In addition several aircraft were MAD fitted. Some aircraft were given or acquired additional kit, for example, several thermal imaging systems were used. In addition most Flights had CHAFF. This was designed to produce extra radar echoes to confuse the radar picture; particularly for incoming missiles. It consisted of thousands of small slivers of aluminium foil, the exact length dependant on the frequency of radar it was designed to confuse. Later on in the aircraft's development this was deployed from special launchers mounted outside the aircraft. For the Falklands, the aircraft observer would carry small cardboard canisters which he would deploy by simply chucking them out of his window. The ever present danger was that the cardboard container would break up before fully leaving the aircraft and fill it up with the stuff, causing major problems, not the least the possibility of shorting out electrical systems. All that said, it was very effective and is still used to this day on occasions.

Another more active way of confusing an enemy missile, particularly an Exocet, is to jam its own seeker radar. A jamming system was hastily removed from a Canberra bomber and shoehorned into a Lynx. It was successfully trialled against a live missile (see the author's account from HMS *Andromeda* later) and then fitted to several of the aircraft in the Task Force. Simply known at the time as 'the I-band Jammer' it was later given the designation 'Hampton Mayfair'.

One of the capabilities the Task Force lacked was that of Airborne Early Warning (AEW). This capability had gone when the Gannett AEW aircraft were retired with HMS *Ark Royal*. Because of the Orange Crop system, it was possible for the Lynx to operate up-threat of the task force and listen for the attack radar in the Argentinian Super Etendard aircraft which it had to switch on to launch an Exocet missile. This was probably the single most important role that the aircraft was given during the conflict. That said, as will be seen from the individual accounts, the aircraft was used in a large number of ways for which it hadn't ever been designed.

Finally, there was probably not one Lynx Flight that didn't break peacetime rules on more than one occasion. It is testament to the quality of peacetime training therefore that no aircraft were lost due to aircrew error.

So, this section of the book tells the story of most of the Lynx Flights deployed to the war, in the words of those who were there. They are individual accounts written by those involved. Editing these accounts has been limited as much as possible so that the reader can not only hear their stories, but get a feeling of how people felt in each individual Flight. However, because of the passage of time and fading memories, it has not always been possible to account for all the personnel involved.

HMS *Glasgow*

Flight Commander – Lieutenant Commander Andy Lister
Flight Pilot – Lieutenant Dick Ormshaw
SMR – SMR: CPO Devonald, PO Brinkley, PO Paterson, PO White, LAEM Bayliss, AEM Martin, AEM Taylor.

Aircraft – XZ 732, XZ 247, XZ 696. (XZ 732 was exchanged early on with Fort Austin, as XZ 247 was Sea Skua capable. XZ 696 was taken back to UK and XZ 247 went to Ambuscade in late May.)

XZ 247 launching; armed with Sea Skua. (*Andy Lister*)

Like several other ships, HMS *Glasgow* was participating in Exercise Springtrain off Gibraltar when the Argentinians invaded and was ordered south on the 2 April. On 1 May, along with *Sheffield* and *Coventry*, they were the first warships to enter the total exclusion zone (TEZ). As the Flight was airborne conducting an HDS at the time, they can claim to be the first British aircraft to fly inside the TEZ. On the night of 2/3 May the Lynx was scrambled and things got interesting, as Andy Lister recalls:

'Dick and I were really fired up because there was intelligence that we could be opposing the three Exocet-armed French-built Drummond Class (Type A69) corvettes, *Drummond*, *Guerrico* and *Granville*. There had been concern that the Argentinians were preparing a pincer attack which would include these ships. After the event, we were informed that in fact two armed tugs, the *Commodoro Somerella* and the *Afrez Sobral* had actually been in the area.

'What we didn't know was that after *Belgrano* had been sunk that afternoon, all the opposing ships had immediately run for shallow water! So our adrenalin was still flowing.

'That evening we and *Coventry's* aircraft had been tasked with a surface search. *Coventry* found what could have been a fishing vessel but there was no sign of the Corvettes. The weather was getting very bad and it hadn't been possible to make a positive identification. So we both returned to deck. However, a Sea King subsequently went to investigate the *Coventry's* contact, who made the mistake of declaring his status by opening fire on the aircraft. The call came to scramble the Lynx.

'After getting airborne in under seven minutes the aircraft suffered a UHF radio failure. We had to hold off while Coventry Flight was guided by the Sea King and fired at the target into wind, over a heavy sea. We saw an explosion, and on the ship jamming of HF frequencies suddenly stopped. According to Argentinian reports, one missile made it to the target and hit a backstay/HF aerial, destroying a sea boat, causing one minor injury and no serious damage. Although at the time it was thought the target was sunk. The captain, Lieutenant Commander Sergio Gomez Roca, ordered all non-essential crew below.

'We had been ordered to close the position in case any survivors could be rescued, even though it was blowing a steady 45 knots by now. It was with some surprise, therefore, that a radar contact was quickly seen, followed by anti-aircraft fire. We very quickly pulled clear and reported back to the ship who ordered us to engage with Sea Skua. We then repositioned and fired two missiles along the swell from eight miles using medium skim height settings. The missiles impacted the bridge and superstructure immediately beneath very efficiently, with little wasted explosive energy. The captain and all on watch in that area were killed and several others wounded. The bridge was blown away, but the twin 20mm gun remained functional. Although ordered to carry out a damage assessment we were so low on fuel by then we had to return to the ship.

'Later that morning the ship again fired on the original Sea King that had found it the previous night and managed to eventually limp back to Argentina.

'After the event, Coventry Flight was awarded the *Somerella* as a kill and *Glasgow* the *Sobral*. There was bitter disappointment at it not having been a Type 69! And only later was it discovered that in fact only one ship, the *Sobral* was attacked. *Somerella* saw out the war alongside in Argentina.

'It is of interest that the remaining bridge structure of *Sobral* is kept as a monument in the Naval Museum in Tigre, Buenos Aires Province.

'As an end piece, I did take a certain attitude regards being invited to approach a live target, which had supposedly been destroyed. We were very close and, if it had been a Drummond, we would not have survived!'

For the next few weeks the ship and aircraft were tasked with escort and shore bombardment duties. On 12 May she was attacked by two flights of A4 jets and one bomb hit the ship but didn't explode. This incident could have had long and unexpected repercussions as Andy Lister recalls:

'After we were hit by the bomb on the twelfth, I went below to examine the damage with the Marine Engineer Officer. While I was there, part of the arming vane was found. As an ex Buccaneer Observer, I was able to recognise it immediately as part of a British ballistic bomb tail unit. Subsequently, since the enemy was using a 'Laydown' attack with a ballistic bomb, which is not the best way of doing things, I was able to explain the Argentinian's shortcomings and why the bomb had not exploded. This information, by default, gave instructions on how easy it would be, with a bit of knowledge, to make the bomb explode immediately after leaving the aircraft (dangerous to the pilots, but lethal in this fudged mode of attack). This information was passed by secret signal to the Flagship – duty done.

'A couple of days later the BBC World Service read out my signal to the world while I was having a cup of coffee in the wardroom! The air turned blue, a signal left *Glasgow* immediately but the damage was done and advice had been passed to the Argentinian armourers. I remain haunted by the fact that almost immediately the bombs started working and in the case of *Coventry* in particular, the very same attack profile had such devastating results.'

Authors note: The BBC came under severe criticism for this and several other gaffs, including announcing the attack on Goose Green twenty four hours in advance.

The Falklands War 43

Glasgow being attacked by A4s. (*Andy Lister*)

The result – the exit wound. (*Andy Lister*)

Because of the damage to the ship, temporary repairs were made and she returned home on 26 May with the Flight eventually disembarking on 16 June.

Andy Lister and Dick Ormshaw were both awarded a Mention in Despatches for their efforts.

44   The Royal Navy Lynx

HMS *Coventry*

Flight Commander – Lieutenant Commander Alvin Rich
Flight Pilot – Lieutenant Bertie Ledingham

Aircraft – XZ 700, XZ 242

Coventry was another of the ships taking part in exercise Springtrain when hostilities broke out. On 2 April she headed south. Once past Ascension Island she rendezvoused with RFA *Fort Austin* and swapped XZ 700 for XZ 242 as it was Sea Skua capable. The ship and aircraft was on general tasking, but on 3 May things became more interesting.

As described in the previous entry for *Glasgow*, at about 0400 hours, the Lynx was scrambled along with *Glasgow's* Lynx to attack a target that had fired on an 826 Squadron Sea King about seventy miles to the north of the islands. *Glasgow's* aircraft suffered a radio failure, so under the direction of the Sea King, *Coventry's* aircraft found the target and achieved a lock on with the Sea Spray radar. Two Skua were successfully fired and explosions were seen. The target was reported as sunk. By now *Glasgow's* Lynx had regained its radio and so both aircraft were tasked to look for survivors. As previously described the ship had not been sunk and then opened fire on *Glasgow's* aircraft, who then fired two more Skua at it.

After this incident, things settled down and the aircraft was tasked with ESM patrols and other routine duties. On 6 May another contact required investigation, and in poor weather, along with *Arrow's* Lynx, a search was made. Two Sea Harriers had already been lost in the fog investigating the contact, but in the end it turned out to be the hulk of HMS *Sheffield*. (See entry for HMS *Arrow* later).

Because of her Sea Dart missile system, *Coventry* was regularly used in the 'missile trap' position with a Sea Wolf armed ship to the north of the islands attempting to intercept Argentinian aircraft resupplying or attacking the islands. In fact, the ship had some success in this role. On 25 May she successfully destroyed two A4B Skyhawks with her Sea Dart missiles. Unfortunately, later in the day, she was bombed by more Skyhawks and was hit by three bombs. The ship started to list, and by 1850 hours that evening she was abandoned. Unfortunately, it had not been possible to launch the aircraft in time and XZ 242 went down with the ship. All members of the Flight were recovered.

Al Rich and Bertie Ledingham were both awarded Mention in Despatches for their efforts.

HMS *Brilliant*

Flight Commander – Lieutenant Commander Barry Bryant
Flight Pilot – Lieutenant Commander John Clark
Flight Pilot – Lieutenant Nick Butler
Observer – Lieutenant Paul McKay

SMR – CPO O'Hara, CPO Elmer, CPO Vickery, CPO Peach, PO Grant, PO Ross, PO Dunford, AEM Turner, AEM House, AEM Goodall, AEM Nelson

Aircraft – XZ 692, XZ 729, XZ 721, XZ 725, XZ 254, XZ 723, XZ 322, XZ 732

Like HMS *Broadsword*, *Brilliant* was large enough to operate two aircraft, and the reason for the number of different ones operated was that they were swapped on occasions due to the equipment fit in each one. For example, XZ 721 was the first Sea Skua capable aircraft to reach the Islands and was used by several Flights on occasions. This entry covers the Flight's involvement in the recapture of South Georgia at the start of the war.

Nick Butler provided the following extract from his ships diary:

HMS *Brilliant* Flight Diary

'HMS *Brilliant*, equipped with two Lynx HAS Mk 2s and an augmented Flight comprising two crews and sufficient personnel to run two watches of deck crew was one of the first ships to head for the South Atlantic, departing Gibraltar on 2 April.

'On 22 April, *Brilliant* detached from the high speed group heading south towards the Falkland Islands to join the HMS *Antrim* group and Operation Paraquat, relinquishing the task group command to HMS *Sheffield*. XZ721 (fitted with Sea Skua) was exchanged with *Sheffield's* aircraft, as the expected role was anticipated to be trooping and surveillance (Radar & ESM).

'Two significant developments marked the Flight's preps for operations. The first was the construction of an interim General Purpose Machine Gun (GPMG) mounting for the Lynx cabin floor. This modification was necessitated by the early dispatch of the ship, no access to an official mounting and the possible gunship role for the Lynx.

'The chosen design consisted of the metal section of a ship's office swivel chair, upturned and mounted on two lengths of angle iron and fitted to either of the Lynx's common weapon carriers by two pip-pins. The GPMG was attached to the frame via a brass mounting constructed from a valve rod gearing joint (as used in ship's pipework), and was able to move in azimuth and elevation controlled by the gunner. Arbitrary safety stops in azimuth, to prevent shooting at the airframe, were fitted by wire strops between the gun and the frame and in elevation by a webbing strap between the butt and the cabin grab handle above the door. The gun was locally 'cleared' for use by the two Flight observers and trained Royal Marine gunners. The distinct advantage of this modification was that it could be stowed internally without taking up space and easily fitted to the port or starboard carrier, whether or not torpedoes or Sea Skua were also carried. The winch could remain fitted and usable and there was no confliction with the Sea Skua missiles.

'The machine gun was flown attached to the weapon carrier on most Operation Corporate sorties. The gun was used operational in the attack on the submarine *Santa Fe* in South Georgia (as described later) and a number of subsequent actions in the Falklands. On each occasion the mounting itself proved entirely effective and the gun easy to control, the only difficulty being the production of a suitable pouch for collecting spent cartridge cases. In fact, when used operationally only a few cases fell inside the cabin and the majority fell well clear below the aircraft, at all airspeeds.'

Simple and effective.
(*Nick Butler*)

'When the 'legal' mounting finally arrived, it was found to be cumbersome and extremely restrictive on other roles. It was not fitted due to these restrictions and the original design remained ready for use until the end of the conflict. The mounting is now held by the Fleet Air Arm Museum, where it took pride of place in the main Falklands display for many years.

'The second significant development was the construction of a gravity bomb. The Lynx helicopter was blessed with an array of impressive weapons, including depth charges and torpedoes, Sea Skua anti-ship missiles, and now a machine gun, but what was lacking was the means to launch a weapon that could cause damage and casualties amongst land targets or ships operating close to the land where missiles were ineffective.

'Thus the creative juices flowed and the expertise of the ship's Demolitions Officer, Lieutenant Chris Sherman, who happened to be a Mine Clearance Officer and thus practiced in handling explosives even in his sleep, was sought. The result was an extremely threatening device which resembled a beer barrel; because it was in fact an aluminium Courage Sparkling Bitter (CSB) beer barrel packed with about 30lbs of plastic explosive, and then filled with as much "shrapnel" as we could pull together from the engineering workshops and elsewhere in the ship that looked as if it would cause harm. It was then topped-off with a timed fuse in three varieties depending on how long you wanted to wait for the bomb to go "bang" after the fuse was activated. Thereafter, it was a simple matter of finding a willing Royal Marine to hold it between his legs in the back of the aircraft, fly around until we found a target, and then launch it manually through the side door from a pre-calculated altitude that would result in it detonating at the desired moment, hopefully on or close to the target.

'The crews did subsequently use the weapon over the Falkland Islands against Argentinian held vessels at night, but after-action damage assessment was never a priority and so were never really certain how effective it was.

'So by the evening of 22 April, the Flight was prepared in all respects for the invasion of South Georgia. This is an extract of her Lynx Flight's diary of events during those busy days:'

Operation Paraquat

25 April:

0830. Having rendezvoused with the *Antrim* Group, one aircraft (Bryant/Butler) launched to search the north coast of South Georgia (possible Fast Patrol Boat threat).

48   The Royal Navy Lynx

0855. Antrim Wessex III sighted and attacked submarine *Santa Fe* with depth charge.

0905. *Brilliant* Lynx 341 (Bryant/Butler) joined the Wessex and launched Mk 46 torpedo attack against surfaced submarine (the submarine captain later disclosed hearing Mk 46 circling below). The submarine remained on the surface because of the torpedo threat. The Lynx continued attacking with GPMG, and one brave soul on the submarine fin bravely returned machine-gun fire which forced the Lynx to climb to about 1,000ft and literally pour 7.62 rounds out of the GPMG and 9mm from the pilot's 9mm pistol onto the poor soul.

Having reversed course to return to Grytviken, *Santa Fe* abandoned the fin and continued navigating by periscope.

Unfortunately, during this sortie, the box of chaff stowed in the back of the Lynx became detached and exploded. A cloud of chaff went throughout the aircraft, which then left the aircraft at height and was initially called as an enemy aircraft by the ever-vigilant HMS *Brilliant* Ops Room! The Lynx returned to refuel, re-arm and a plea for a large vacuum cleaner.

0930. Second Lynx 342 launched (Clark/McKay) armed only with GPMG. HMS *Endurance* Wasp achieved hit with AS12 missile on submarine fin. Both Lynx continued strafing as the submarine continued in towards Grytviken.

1015. *Plymouth's* Wasp carried out AS12 missile attack with some success.

1100. *Santa Fe* alongside, damaged, oil escaping and smoking. She appeared to be settling in the water as the crew escaped. 342 recovered and role changed (to trooping), whilst 341 carried out search along the coast for possible Fast Patrol Boat threat in very poor weather conditions. 342 re-launched to *Antrim* for assault briefing and 341 recovered shortly afterwards at 1300.

1430. 341 (Bryant/Butler/Edwards) launched from *Brilliant*. 342 (Clark/McKay) from *Antrim*; and joined *Antrim's* Wessex III (Stanley/Parry) for assault on Grytviken. After being led in by the Wessex, the two Lynx carried out a high-speed troop landing of SAS and Royal Marines. Meanwhile *Antrim* and *Plymouth* conducted heavy and effective gunfire support around the enemy positions.

1715. Declaration of surrender of Argentine Forces ashore in South Georgia. Both aircraft continued trooping and VERTREP ashore until 1930.

2100. Lynx 342 (Bryant/Butler) launched to carry out surface search to seaward to counter possible surface threat. Found only icebergs in very poor visibility – after second low-level probe on a high-level iceberg, conditions became too treacherous to continue and the Lynx recovered at 2330.

By the author: There has been significant publicity regarding the recovery of Special Forces members from the Fortuna glacier by Antrim's Wessex III and rightly so as it was an outstanding piece of airmanship. However, what is not so well known is there was another 'rescue' mission that took place on the 26 April by Bryan and Butler, for which they both received a Mention in Despatches:

26–28 April: PARAQUAT consolidation:

'After an interesting few days trashing the *Santa Fe* and recovering South Georgia from the Argentine forces, there was a degree of tidying up to be done, quite a lot of VERTREP, prisoners-of-war transfers, and just shifting stuff around. As darkness fell on 26 April, there came a call from a troop of SAS who had been ashore for some time (pretending to be SBS), originally to reconnoitre the whaling stations, but then just trying to survive and preserve their valuable kit in the appalling weather conditions. They had finally reached a narrow strip of beach near Stromness station and requested urgent evacuation. There was, in short, only one option.

'After a cursory brief over the air, we headed into Stromness Bay to see what we could see, which was nothing. We groped our way in under radar just about able to see the breakers hitting the cliffs in the 40kt+ winds and not relishing getting very much closer to the coast. We then saw a couple of torch flashes and edged into the beach to find about a dozen troopers with huge bergens, a Gemini dinghy and a load of kit. The sloping beach was less than a rotor-span wide and landing was out of the question, so we adopted about a 30ft hover and prepared the rescue winch to lift the guys out of the surf. Hardly daring to look at the clearance between the rotor tips and the cliff edge, up came a succession of smelly, exhausted men and bergens, until the back of the aircraft was absolutely topped up and that was only the first half. We headed back to *Antrim* flying completely blind, relying on radar to keep clear of the several islands in the bay and leaning between the front seats to operate the tube while trying to keep order amongst the troops. Finding *Antrim*, we flopped on the deck and just threw the cargo out before returning to the beach. This time, the adrenaline was replaced by a more natural caution having got away with it the first time. Never ready to let an opportunity pass, the remaining troops indicated that they would really appreciate the recovery of their beloved Gemini as well. We just happened to still have the VERTREP strop attached, so down we went into the flying foam to attach the boat, winched up the remaining soldiers, and began once more to search out the ship, this time going very slowly with the Gemini spiralling wildly underneath. The other abiding memory was the smell. These guys had been living off compo rations for some time and whether it was the relief of the rescue or the altitude (maybe all of 200ft), they were farting for England! We were much relieved to dump the Gemini and our guests on *Antrim* before getting back to *Brilliant* after a sortie lasting 6 hours 40 minutes.

'In all we flew over thirty-five hours in the four days during Operation Paraquet, with *Brilliant's* other Lynx and our Wessex III colleagues in Antrim Flight and the Wasps of *Plymouth* and *Endurance* proving equally busy. Little did I know that thirteen years later I would return to the beaches of Stromness while in command of the new *Endurance*, only this time it was in brilliant sunshine and the only occupants were elephant seals – but at least they smelled better!

'As a final postscript, the officer in command of the SAS troop unit spotted Nick Butler on a list whilst both were serving in the US on exchange. He contacted Nick almost ten years to the day after the rescue to thank us for saving their skins. He reported that all the lads were on their last legs and at the end of their tether and so had never been so pleased to see a navy Lynx. He went on to eventually be the chief of staff at HQ Special Forces in London. When Nick next met him he was treated to a fine and memorable dinner in the SF Club. We were reunited again in 2007 at the twenty-fifth anniversary – the so called 'Falklands Heroes Dinner' – at Greenwich.

'Finally, on the 27 April, *Brilliant's* Lynx, XZ 725 (Bryant/Butler), carried out what is believed to be the first landing of aircraft type on a Type 12 (HMS *Plymouth*). Champagne gratefully received. VERTREP continued with the prospect of detaching the next afternoon to rejoin the main Task Force.

'The two aircraft flew a total of fifty-six hours in support of Operation Paraquat 25–28 April, often in appalling conditions, without missing one sortie or take-off time.

'Then off to rejoin the Task Force and take part in the war for real.'

This certificate was handed to Nick Butler the day of the final attack on Grytviken. After the surrender, his aircraft landed at the town and a very professional looking person marshalled them onto a landing spot. The person turned out to be the captain of the submarine *Santa Fe*, who had trained in the UK. His training included completing the RN Flight Deck Officers course. Not only was he completely unfazed by meeting the crew of an aircraft that had been recently trying to kill him, but later in the day he handed them this certificate along with a case of brandy and some other presents for the ship.

John Clark, Barry Bryant and Nick Butler were all awarded a Mention in Despatches for their efforts.

815 Squadron HQ Flights operating from various ships

Detachment Commander – Lieutenant Commander Dick O'Neill
Pilots – Lieutenant Commander Rick Sear
 – Lieutenant Al Harper
Observer – Lieutenant Dick Murphy
 – Lieutenant David Edwards

Aircraft, XZ 240, XZ 242, XZ 247, XZ 700, XZ 720, XZ 725, XZ 730

No. 815 Squadron was tasked with providing aircraft from the outset of the conflict, which initially deployed in Hercules aircraft to Ascension Island and then onwards in various ships, including both of the carriers.

Dick O'Neill has provided the following extract from the squadron diary as well as his own individual recollections of a busy and demanding time:

'Deployment: 815 Squadron was first warned off for a possible deployment on 1 April 1982, with Flights to be at twenty-four hours' notice for deployment by Hercules. At that time the destination was not widely known.

'On 2 April, at 1000 hours, two Flights were to be ready for deployment by 0800 the next day. However, over the next eight hours this requirement grew to three flights plus two extra crews to be ready by 0500. The aircraft needed to be both ESM and Sea Skua capable. Individuals were sent home to pack, to include plenty of cold weather clothing.

'At 0500 on 3 April, the first Hercules arrived and they continued to arrive at two hour intervals with a two hour turn around. The tasking was to go to Ascension Island and rebuild the aircraft. Further tasking would be sent in due course.

'After an uncomfortable eighteen hour flight with very little seating room, the first Hercules arrived at Ascension Island, being only the second aircraft to land, having been preceded by a Hercules with a UKMAMMS team and Hercules spares.

'It was interesting over the next couple of days as we rebuilt the aircraft in blistering temperatures with no tropical kit or hangars to get out of the sun, and also receive two Wessex V helicopters and crews by *Belfast* under the command of Nick Foster. Most work was conducted at night when temperatures dropped. We had bought cold weather clothing and had not expected to work in tropical temperatures. There were various meetings with the personnel based on Ascension Island, including the Administrator, the USAF Base Commander and members of the BBC and Cable and Wireless to discuss the future. The main question was how many people would be coming to the island as they were concerned that they had little fuel or water as they were only resupplied every four months and the next ship was due shortly. My only reply was that I did not really know, but maybe a couple of hundred. Little did we know that within a couple of weeks there would be thousands in the area! We embarked in Royal Fleet Auxiliary Fort *Austin* during the evening of 6 April with three aircraft and spares to head for South Georgia and rendezvous with HMS *Endurance*, just as a full staff began to arrive.

'Having both SAS and SBS teams on-board, and since we had been conducting an exercise with the SBS the week before we deployed, much time was spent briefing for possible tasking. The SAS team were keen to practice free fall parachuting despite the fact that the Lynx had not been cleared. After much signaling with the UK, we were told that we could conduct a trial, but to take care! A successful trial was carried out from 10,000 feet, falling into the Atlantic, the only problem being that just as they left the aircraft a pod of whales appeared right in the drop zone. Luckily no whales were harmed in the conduct of the trial.

'HMS *Endurance* was due to take part in Operation Paraquat, the liberation of South Georgia (see the entry for HMS *Brilliant*), and once Fort Austin had replenished her we turned round and headed back to meet the main Task Force. The transit periods proved invaluable for conducting briefings and training, particularly with the new Sea Skua system now fitted to all three aircraft.

'Aircraft were now exchanged with *Arrow*, *Coventry* and *Minerva*, as it was deemed necessary that they have the Sea Skua capable aircraft. Back at Ascension one modification that was made was to produce a cabin mounted GPMG. This was done in a similar fashion to that made by HMS *Brilliant*, using the parts from an office swivel chair. Once again it was successful and all observers and aircrew men fired 200 rounds each.

'Fort Austin then joined the Main Task Force in the Exclusion Zone and took on a role as a floating Lynx Support Unit as well as operating her own aircraft. For example *Alacrity's* damaged aircraft was sent over and swapped with XZ 700 whilst it was being repaired on board.

'On 17 May the Fort Austin Flight was split up with one Lynx each going to *Hermes* and *Invincible* to operate in the ESM and anti Exocet roles – these aircraft were fitted with the I band Exocet jammer on 23 May. XZ 700 was transferred to the *Atlantic Conveyor* on a one flight only basis for storage and was lost when the ship was attacked and sunk on 25 May.'

It was on this day that Dick O'Neill was caught up in the raid and recalled a particularly interesting sortie:

'At 1945 on 25 May we were on alert when Air Raid Warning Red was called. We scrambled, and just as we got airborne and the jammer was coming on line we saw a puff of smoke from *Atlantic Conveyor* as she was hit by an Exocet. We took up station 600 feet above HMS *Hermes* as she was steaming west, to the north of *Atlantic Conveyor*, with inch chaff rockets going off all round us. Meanwhile, HMS *Invincible* was steaming east and crossing behind us. The next thing I heard was the pilot, Al Harper, shouting that *Invincible* had fired large flares at us (which quickly changed to missiles), as we appeared as a pop up contact in the rough direction of the threat! Luckily, with all the chaff around and the fact that we were probably within their minimum arming range, they missed, with one going above and the other going below us, to explode about 400 yards beyond us.'

XZ 240 and XZ 720 then stayed with *Hermes*:

'From 26 May until I left, we remained at Alert 5 throughout daylight hours with the jammer in case of Exocet, launching whenever Air Raid Warning Red was called. The main problem with the jammers was that, because they were very old and valve driven, they needed about five minutes to come on line once rotors were engaged. Thus we were invariably very late in the attack before the jammer came on line. Added to this the fact that at Air Raid Warning Red all I band radars went unrestricted, hence it made it much more difficult to identify the Exocet radar in the very short interval (if any) we had between the jammer coming on line and the missile finding its target.

'Overall, I believe that the Lynx proved itself to be a highly effective aircraft during the conflict. Despite the shortage of spares and long supply chain, the maintainers proved their expertise and dedication many times in overcoming problems through temporary repairs and robbing other aircraft, all made easier by having our own Air Engineer Officer (John Ackerman) in theatre. Despite the Sea Skua having to be rushed into service and training having to take place on a very ad hoc basis, the system proved itself and was a very effective addition to our armoury. The fact that the airframes were flown out to Ascension and then over the three month period were readily swapped between ships and Flights, frequently at very short notice, also showed the flexibility and effectiveness of the Fleet Air Arm system for the provision of ship's Flights.'

HMS *Broadsword*

Flight Commander – Lieutenant Commander Rick Jones
Flight Observer – Lieutenant Charlie E Thornton
Second Observer – Lieutenant Mike Chirnside
Second Pilot – Sub Lieutenant Ray Middleton

Aircraft – XV 298, XZ 240, XZ 691, XZ 728, XZ 729, XZ 732, XZ 736

Bombs can come from odd directions. (*R Jones*)

The two, Type 22 Frigates, *Broadsword* and *Brilliant* had enlarged hangars and flight decks and could operate two aircraft. The reason for the large number of aircraft operated by *Broadsword* was that they were swapped with HMS *Invincible*, *Alacrity* and *Brilliant* at various times during the war.

In March, *Broadsword* had two Lynx embarked which between them had MAD, Sea Skua and Orange Crop. The second pilot and second observer joined the ship. On 5

56   The Royal Navy Lynx

April she was heading to Naples on the way to a Far East deployment when she was recalled, and on 8 April she joined the Task Force heading south to Ascension. Below are extracts from the Flight diary written by the Rick Jones, the Flight Commander:

'Early April, Ascension Island. Went ashore, moved eight Sea Skua to *Hermes* and *Broadsword* for later sorting out. Moved the spare Lynx to *Hermes* (with jammer) and collected second Lynx (with MAD). We now had one Lynx with MAD and Skua, the second with a Hele Tele sight working in infrared.

'Late April – with the Task Force, most sorties long-range surface search with ESM and radar.

'1 May, HMS *Broadsword's* MAD fitted Lynx was spotted on deck with three Skua missiles on, expecting to launch on a surface search in a couple of hours. HMS *Brilliant* – in a separate group some ten miles away had a sonar contact very close to some of the surface ships and was engaging the contact (innocent dolphins as it turned out) and requested a MAD fitted helicopter to check out the contact. The order to launch was given, though the aircraft was not specifically at any alert state. All involved rushed around as expected, the aircraft started and launched. The reason for mentioning was that the lashings were removed before launch – apart from the starboard aft lashing which was hidden by the MAD bird which came down to some eight inches from the deck and thus hid the lashing. Despite the temptation for an 'over the shoulder' launch to cut down the time to the scene of action, a normal cautious launch was executed. The lashing was felt at the same time as the Flight Deck Officer saw it. Later, no incident signal was raised – we were at war, most of the Flight were later injured and three Lynxes suffered cannon, shrapnel and bomb damage and the incident seemed minor.

'21 May, Invasion. In the early hours we sailed into Falkland sound. We flew the spare Lynx at dawn to test the Skua system – still not working. Landed back on to await the day's events. In a line of seven ships: north to south: *Argonaut, Brilliant, Broadsword, Antrim, Ardent, Antelope* and *Yarmouth*. Many air attacks against frigates: saw ships being hit. We had two LMGs on flight deck and the GPMG on a shock mat on the starboard forward side of the flight deck. First attack from port – the picture appeared in *Time* magazine. Diagonal line of shells took out hangar by hitting the door (sprayed aluminium through hangar) and side wall. I emptied an LMG magazine at aircraft and later found a shell had missed my foot by six inches by going through ships side into the laundry. Lynx hit and we had to defuel it over stern to remove fuel danger. Second attack from starboard side; again I emptied a magazine from LMG. I watched a bomb falling, but it splashed into the water just short of the ship – then I was hit and thrown onto the deck. The cannon shell hit starboard aft corner of hangar and I was hit in my arm, leg and through the chin. I went to the temporary sick bay in the wardroom to be checked and patched – I was still there during a later attack (you could tell because the 40/60 Bofors could be heard firing). I then went back to the flight deck. Later air attacks made me nervous! In the evening a Sea King lifted me and SMR to *Canberra*, which sailed to South Georgia that night. I was given a jab and looked at. I went across with no warning so had no kit. I was just dressed in green trousers, roll neck with green jersey and a goon suit (waterproof flying kit) on top. We got a survival bag, a towel, toothbrush, razor and soap. I was in a ward with eight SAS survivors from a Sea King IV that had crashed into the sea and looked after the remains of Ardent Flight. Others in the ship: *Ardent* survivors, *Sheffield* survivors, some wounded Argentinians.'

The gun sight picture from the strafing A4. (*R Jones*)

'23 May, at South Georgia, we went ashore to see the whaling station and the Argentinian submarine leaning against the jetty, where it went after being hit by missile from *Endurance's* Wasp. The survivors went to *QE2*. *Canberra* took on

Welsh Guards, Scots Guards, and Ghurkhas (5 Brigade). A briefing was arranged by the RN captain for 5 Brigade officers. I gave a lecture on air attacks and what they could do. When I had finished the CO turned to his intelligence officer and said 'that won't be a problem, most of their aircraft have been shot down'. However, as we sailed from South Georgia, I noticed they had five machine guns per side manning the ship. Later they forgot all this in Bluff Cove.

'2 June, a Sea King lifted me back to *Broadsword*. There was a hole in the flight deck and the nose missing from one of my Lynx. John Acherman (the roving air engineer officer) was in my cabin – he had come with a couple of maintainers to assess the Lynx.

'Sorties were now mostly ESM to hear enemy Etendard radar – we went to seventy miles out, then went to low-level (the Etendard radar looks down) and put the electronic radar warner to max time (ten seconds) so a radar sweep would give us ten seconds to analyse it. Then you make an appropriate radio call (climb rapidly to gain UHF contact). Next scan quickly with the radar down the bearing of the enemy so they think they have a Harrier on their nose.

'When the Lynxes were fixed (we took the tail off one to replace the tail of our first lynx) the remains (one with no tail – borrowed – and no nose – bombed) were airlifted to *Hermes* and tail flown internally in a Lynx to another ship.

'After the surrender and some brief repairs, *Broadsword* took over as escort for HMS *Hermes* with whom they sailed on 3 July to return home.

'23 July, HMS *Broadsword* returned to Devonport.'

A rather unusual internal load. (*R Jones*)

HMS *Ambuscade*

Flight Commander – Lieutenant Phil Henry
Flight Pilot – Lieutenant Alan Bucknall

Senior Maintenance Rating – CPO Paul Pedrick, M1 Bill Powell, M2 Fez Parker, M3 Pete Dodds, L1 Keith Hartley, L2 Kev Murkin, R1 PO Caldwell, R2 John Fehley.

Aircraft – XZ 696 until 25 May, then XZ 247, nickname 'Gonzo then Gonzo 2'.

Just another Day in the South Atlantic. (*P Henry*)

By Phil Henry:

'30 May 1982, the start of another day for HMS *Ambuscade* and her Flight in the South Atlantic Task Force, we joined the Task Force area on the 20/21 May via a circuitous route having re-ammunitioned at Gibraltar and two days as Ascension Guard ship on the way.

60   The Royal Navy Lynx

'By the thirtieth we were well and truly in the groove, spending our days as the north-west part of the carrier screen, with the ship using her UAA1 ESM equipment tasked against the Super Etendard/Exocet threat and us in the helicopter some eighty miles up threat using our ESM searching for the same threat and using the radar for surface search; at night we left the Task Force and the ship closed the Falklands to whatever gun line was active. In those ten days and nights Al Bucknell and I flew some fourteen sorties and went through two air attacks on the Task Force. This included the Exocet attack on the twenty-fifth, during which the ship detected the release aircraft radar and missile transmissions on our UAA1 and subsequently detected the aircraft turning away and the missile closing on the radar. The missile locked on to us initially, but we managed, through manoeuvre and use of counter measures, to break its lock, but unfortunately the missile reacquired *Atlantic Conveyor* and hit her, resulting in her ultimate loss.

'So back to the morning of the thirtieth, the start Al and I thought of as another routine day, but at the brief for our ESM/ASV search we were told that we would not be returning to *Ambuscade,* but instead to land on HMS *Avenger* for other tasking. We knew that *Avengers'* aircraft had sustained some tail rotor damage from an OPDEF (operation deficiency) signal received the night before, but not how, so we spent some of the flight wondering what we were in for.

'On completion of our task we started our recovery to *Avenger*, threading our way through the Task Group, and having identified her started our recovery, to have it interrupted by an air raid when we were short finals to land. With the experience of a previous air raid, when we were airborne, we held in a low hover off the stern of *Avenger* in her missile and weapon dead range. This gave us a grand stand seat to the ensuing action, punctuated by various war cries on the radio and missile trails and guns going off all around us with the highlight being an A4 exploding a mile or two to the north.

'When everything calmed down we landed-on, to be met by the Flight SMR and the off watch PWO, who told us that the captain (Hugo White) wanted to see us on the bridge as soon as we were happy with the security of the aircraft. Arriving on the bridge, I was expecting to get some initial information on our future tasking, but Hugo was more interested in our professional opinion on some wreckage that they had just fished out of the water after the air raid. It was bits of an ejection seat with part numbers and labels that identified it as a Martin Baker seat fitted to an A4. The brief was to come a little later in the day.

'We got a bit of an insight of what was to come when we got back to the hangar. The reason we were there was because *Avengers'* aircraft had inadvertently put

The Falklands War   61

her tail rotor into a sand dune on the previous night extracting some Special Forces from North Falklands. This explained the twenty-odd people crashed out in various spots in the hangar and office spaces and the piles of small and not so small arms dotted around the place. The penny dropped and we realised that we were going to be doing some interesting flying in the near future.

'Before that could happen we had to solve a bit of a logistic problem. We were fitted with four Sea Skuas which needed to come off, and the aircraft's cabin had an overload tank fitted which needed to come out. The tank was easy, but the missiles were another problem, as *Avenger* had no missile trolleys. The problem was solved by the novel use of four camp beds and tie down lashings! That done, we joined the captain and the officer commanding the SBS detachment – which we had found in the hangar – in the captain's cabin to be confronted with a table strewn with charts and maps of the north-east corner of the Falklands.

'Our task was to infiltrate twenty SBS and four NGS spotters to a location inshore from which they would deploy forward to spot for fire support operations leading up to and the retaking of Port Stanley. With the number of men and the large amount of weapons and stores they carried, this was going to involve at least five Flights. It was going to be interesting, as there was no moon and the sky was overcast. We had no Night Vision Goggles (NVGS), and even if we had, we were not trained in their use and we needed to fly about two miles inland to their desired drop off point. Hugo left us to it, asking to be briefed on our plan with any options within the hour.

'We studied the maps and found a beach hut/building marked on a beach in our drop off area with a small lagoon on the other side of the sand spit from it, with a water course leading inland. From the contours, we reckoned we would be able to get enough contrast using the aircraft's radar to be able to attempt some simple yacht type navigation inland to a suitable drop off point which the OC was content with. With very little in the way of light, Al was going to have to fly mainly on instruments, using the Barometric and Radar Altimeters to keep us at a safe height, with me conning him at slow speed along our chosen path. Having flown together for nearly two years in places all over the world, and in some pretty adverse weather conditions, we thought it was going to be a challenge, but well within our capabilities. We duly briefed Hugo White, who was happy with the plan and the risks involved and for good measure decided he would fire over the top of us as we went in, with the shells landing in a safe area to help mask our rotor noise, even though we thought the chance of detection was going to be low.

62 The Royal Navy Lynx

'As night fell, we proceeded inshore to our start point about two miles off shore. As we transited, an air raid warning red was called. As we stood-to on the flight deck, I had a thought that any attacker from the stern was in for a shock, as in addition to the ad hoc GPMG that the Flight had rigged around the flight deck, the SBS guys pitched up with an assortment of heavy machine guns and Stinger ground-to-air missiles. The ship's transit proved uneventful and we went to flying stations as we approached the drop off point. The marines and spotters were split into sticks and we briefed everyone of escape procedures. We were, in turn, told that if we went down ashore to grab the back of the nearest marine and follow him.

'As we launched, the ship started its bombardment, and on closing towards the beach I turned on the radar in sector scan on the lowest range scale and adjusted the brilliance and contrast to get the best picture. Sure enough, the beach hut stood out like the proverbial and the water beyond and stream bed were well defined. Conning Al in, he kept an eye on the Bar and Rad Alts. I dropped a navigation waypoint as we "on-topped" the beach hut and we hover taxied over the beach and water beyond, and then followed the winding stream inland for about two miles. At the drop point, I inserted another waypoint and we came to a low hover and dropped the stick of troops off. The return to the ship was pretty straight forward and we landed on to get the next stick. The next four runs were more of the same, with the drop off being a little easier, as the marines provided us with a small red light "T" using angle torches. The last drop off complete, we were about to lift when one of the Marines threw a large lump of turf and gorse so that we could prove that we had landed on the Falklands. The return flight was straight forward, with the whole evolution lasting one hour and forty five minutes, but it seemed a lot shorter, I guess that's what adrenalin does for you!

'Mission complete, *Avenger* made ground to the north for her next mission and we took a break while *Avenger's* maintainers reloaded our weapons and fitted the fuel tank in double quick time. Two hours later we were ready to depart to rejoin *Ambuscade*. We were briefed that she was returning back to the Task Force having completed her night run into San Carlos for her NGS on call mission. Off we set, with a rendezvous plugged into the nav computer and fingers well and truly crossed that the navigator had done his sums correctly. About thirty minutes later, using a few random sweeps on the radar, we found a surface contact in about the right place, and after a few short radio calls got them to transmit on their main radar for two sweeps. *Ambuscade* had a very distinct PRF signature which we detected on our ESM and after a challenge and authentication; we closed the ship and landed on. After briefing our command team on the mission, we got a few hours in the rack and were back to our routine tasking the next day.

'The main lessons I learnt from the mission was that the phrases "train hard, fight easy" and "train in peace the way you would fight in war", are very true and gave Al and I the confidence to carry out the mission. In addition, the time we had spent flying together all over the world in the previous two years gave us the confidence to push the envelope if we needed to, in the full knowledge of the risks involved.'

HMS *Alacrity*

Flight Commander – Lieutenant Commander Bob Burrows
Flight Pilot – Lieutenant Rob Sleeman

Aircraft – XZ 720 until 24 April; then XZ 736

Alacrity sailed on 5 April in company with *Antelope* with whom they worked closely. The aircraft was exchanged so that they had a Sea Skua capability. The following is a rather understated narrative by the pilot, Rob Sleeman:

> 'On 1 May, we were off Stanley, Naval Gunfire Support (NGS) spotting and as usual the ships weren't ready. So, whilst taking up position behind Kidney Island we spotted an Argentinian patrol boat and a fishing boat (which we thought was "local"). Our "schoolie" (ships instructor officer) was an ex TA machine gunner, so was on board to operate our cabin-mounted General Purpose Machine Gun (GPMG) and he opened up against the patrol boat and both of his 20mm guns were "silenced", although we found out that he didn't kill anybody, which we were happy about. Unfortunately, the fishing boat was not "local" and they fired at us with their GPMG and we had a few hits. One went through the windscreen in front of me. Fortunately we were turning left, and being a good aviator I was looking left, so it didn't go through the back of my head!

'Fortunately we were turning left, and being a good aviator I was looking left, so it didn't go through the back of my head!!' (*Rob Sleeman*)

The Falklands War   65

'We landed to check for damage and wait for ships to be ready for NGS. We had an SBS lieutenant on board who said "we have either a fuel leak from the ferry tank or a natural upwelling of Avcat" (or words to that effect). We didn't know it at the time, but another round went through the tail rotor drive shaft and both exhausts.

'As the ships were still not ready, HMS *Arrow's* Lynx was sent to replace us and we returned to our ship just as it was attacked by a couple of Argentinian Mirages. A few years after the war I had some e-mails from the captain of the Argentinian patrol boat who ended up being a judge! (See below). XZ 736 went to Fort Austin for battle damage repair and we had XZ 700 until 8 May. On 9 May, we were tasked to investigate a sonar contact and dropped one Mk46 torpedo. The weapon ran but did not explode, so it was probably a whale!

'On 11 May, *Alacrity* was used as "bait" down through the sound and the ship ended up sinking the Argentinian transport ship the *Isla de las Estados*. We had disembarked and dropped flares over the west Falklands and found out afterwards that they were in the process of setting up radar controlled anti-aircraft guns!

'On 25 May, when *Atlantic Conveyor* was sunk, *Alacrity* picked up a lot of survivors and the deck was unavailable when we returned from ESM search, so we went to HMS *Exeter* and ended up watching "hot gossip" (the dancers) whilst people were drowning not far from us. When we eventually returned to "mum" we found a lot of "Junglie" friends from *Atlantic Conveyor* on board. That was the end of the war for them.

'The ship left for home on about 6 June as the 4.5 gun was worn out!'

Bob Burrows and Rob Sleeman were both awarded a Mention in Despatches for their efforts. In 2007 Rob Sleeman received the following letter:

Puerto Belgrano, March 2007

Dear Rob,

I am very happy for having received your email. Unfortunately, during these last months, I have been work which has managed my times, that's why I can answer you only now. I'm expecting to get my retirement from the Navy just in these days. Although I retired in 2001, I was then reincorporated as a military Judge ranging my responsibility from Mar del Plata to Ushuaia.

Nowadays, I've just been made grandfather. Pilar Narvaes Molini, my first granddaughter was born on 22 January and now my only desire is to devote my life to her, my wife, my children, my friends, the Rotary Club and golf, which is the only sport I practice and I think I do it quite well actually. So my life programmed, I hope to have the chance of travelling to Europe very soon and of course to meet you and your family.

As you can imagine, in a few days here in Argentina, we'll begin to remember intensely the facts of the war. I'm often invited by civilian institutions to speak about what I had to face in the war. I'm besides summoned by Escuela Naval Militar (Military Naval School). Escuela de Guerra Naval (Warfare Naval School) and some others institutions in the Navy.

I tell you the truth, when I refer to the 'meeting' we had. I don't stop telling everybody that there was a group of very brave 'MEN' in front of me, because if we had a 12.7mm machine gun, I don't really know how the story would have been. Thanks God both of us can tell that story.

According to what you tell me about the activity you have at present, you are really a very good pilot. I didn't have any doubt about it at that moment either.

The 'FORREST' the ship I was then commanding, received the shots from your machine gun with the result of very many holes. Several glass panels were broken, including both belonging to my berth. The radio also received an impact, anyway it went on working. I remained standing on the bridge while I went on shooting my rifle. I didn't cover myself at all and while I shouted my orders to the helmsman I was thinking that a shot could hit me at any moment. It didn't happen. It was God's wish. Well, it was an unforgettable experience which only military men can understand in its real measure.

The most difficult moment I had to cope with was when the PREFECTURA Patrol Ship which had two 12.7 on board, left the place as I was told they had a seriously wounded man (a shot in his stomach). Thanks God he got over.

One of the so many doubts I have, as you can imagine, is that if you received any shots, I hope not to have hurt anybody. Another one is if the mission that the two helicopters were accomplishing, was as fire spotters for the ships that were, at that moment, performing their task over the aircraft runway.

Well I don't want to go on so long because although I've got some knowledge of English, I must have this mail translated.

HMS *Arrow*

Flight Commander – Lieutenant Phil Barber
Flight Observer – Lieutenant Chris Palmer

Aircraft – XZ 241, XZ 730 (XZ241was exchanged early on with Fort Austin as XZ730 was Orange Crop capable).

SMR – CPO Jim Longley, CPO Pete Gibbs, CPO Tom Jones, PO Bob Greenwood, PO Rob Crawford, AEM Chris Hughes, AEM Dave Charnley

HMS *Arrow* Flight in full action gear. (*Phil Barber*)

By Phil Barber:

'HMS *Arrow* Flight's Falkland experience starts in February 1982, with a period of disembarkation during which the aircrew were getting to grips with the new Orange Crop equipment, carrying out annual QHI checks etc. Orange Crop was not yet fitted to XZ 241. On 1 March the Flight re-embarked at Portland for a

68 The Royal Navy Lynx

period of Staff Sea Training in the Portland Exercise areas, prior to heading down to Gibraltar for Exercise Springtrain. The intention was that after Gibraltar there would be a return to UK waters, a visit to our affiliated city of Sunderland, before the ship went into a maintenance period.

'After an uneventful voyage to Gibraltar, we disembarked to North Front on 18 March. There followed flights from North Front in support of HMS *Arrow's* gunnery drills to the south-east of Gibraltar, which included VERTREP recovery of Chukka targets, some very valuable practice for what was to come.

'The 25 March saw the first omen that all was not well. The rumour was that one of the SSNs (Nuclear attack submarines) was to be dispatched to sea early by the C-in-C, apparently because of its crew's misbehavior ashore. However, Arrow Flight re-embarked in blissful ignorance on 26 March. On 1 April, it became clear from a flurry of staff transfer activity to the Flag Ship and changes to the operational programme that something was afoot. All was revealed on 2 April. There then followed a period of seven hours of continuous VERTREP save a short break for lunch, as we offloaded all our training depth charges, torpedoes and shells, to be replaced with our war complement from the ships heading back to the UK and loaded every useful store we could imagine which might be in short supply. We did not, of course, know how long we would be gone. As we headed south towards Ascension, there was much speculation as to whether or not we would be equipped with a new Orange Crop equipped aircraft. We would be sorry to see the departure of XZ 241, one of the first batch of Lynx which had been with HMS *Arrow* since the beginning, but despite her advancing years, she had been kept in concourse condition by the fastidious ministrations of the maintainers. A couple of weeks later an engine change was required, and then on 17 April we handed her over to Fort Austin and in the following days took delivery of XZ 730, Orange Crop equipped and with the white of the roundels painted out in black. XZ 241 would have looked better at a Fleet Review, but we had to admit that the newer XZ 730 looked suitably menacing in her warpaint.

'There was further storing at Ascension when we noted with some wry amusement the loading of pallets of frozen Argentinian beef. Also delivered was a 'Harry Tait' radar reflector, which resembled half a very large, heavy and definitely un-aerodynamic dissected biscuit tin. It was supposed to be attached to the weapon carrier – the idea being that it was optimized for the frequency of the Exocet missile homing head. The Lynx, with its enhanced radar signature, would fly over the top of the ship until the Exocet, detected by Orange Crop, had locked on, then the lynx would air-taxi astern, drawing the missile away from the ship until it duly passed underneath the aircraft without exploding and disappeared harmlessly towards the horizon. Neither the aircrew nor the ship were entirely convinced that this boffin's solution was likely to prove entirely effective and I do not recall that it was ever flown by us. Between Ascension and the Falklands, the Flight took the opportunity to practice their Naval Gunfire Support (NGS) spotting procedures and to carry out functional tests on the Sea Skua missile systems – seldom done in peacetime with a live missile. The aircraft and missile passed with flying colours. We were ready. On 1 May we entered the Total Exclusion Zone (TEZ). The aircraft was equipped to cover all eventualities carrying both Sea Skua and torpedoes. Following a short surface search sortie we got airborne with Captain Willie McCracken, Royal Artillery, to conduct NGS on the Argentine positions on Port Stanley. However, after about forty-five minutes and about a couple of miles to the west of us, we observed two Mirages crossing the coast heading for the ships. One was shot down by Argentinian 'friendly' fire, but the other continued. We forewarned the ship. However, the officer of the watch, having clearly not been paying attention during the Flight's recognition training quizzes on the way south, misidentified it as a Sea Harrier. Notwithstanding the very obvious differences, it clearly did not occur to him that an aircraft flying directly at the ship at wave top height in a war zone was unlikely to be a British aircraft whose pilot had suddenly thought it would be a good idea to do a fly by. Notwithstanding a second confirmation from the helicopter controller, the command decided to believe the OOW. Fortunately the 20mm gunner, who had been paying attention during the recognition quizzes, took matters into his own hands and opened fire, causing the mirage pilot to jink to avoid the stream of tracer, and his cannon shells buried themselves in the funnel, but not before one able seaman, who had wandered from his designated action station to admire the South Atlantic scenery, had received a piece of shrapnel for his pains and become the first British casualty. Arrow Flight was shortly recalled while the ships regrouped. NGS was incidentally conducted with the spotter in the observer's seat and the observer in the back leaning over his shoulder to operate the radar and TANS. There then followed a night NGS sortie. Judging by the volume of tracer, the Argentinians were clearly aware that we were around, but they were unable to see us to be able to dispatch any aimed shots. Our new Orange Crop provided added confidence that had any anti-aircraft missile system locked on to us we would know. Both the Flight observer and I were intrigued at the technique being used by Captain McCracken, which did not appear to be following the bracketing of the target technique taught to us. While we were both trying to work out the maths, at the sixth ranging shot, a magnificent firework display started with tracer flying in every direction to which Captain McCracken's response was, 'Oh! They don't like that; give them another dozen rounds – fire for effect'. He was clearly lobbing the shells around more or less at random until he got a reaction!

'The following day our sight-seeing able seaman was looking decidedly peaky after his encounter with the shrapnel and we were obliged to CASEVAC him to HMS *Hermes*. Two days later, HMS *Sheffield* was hit by an Exocet. We were the adjacent ship in the screen. A lengthy four and a half hour sortie was flown, interspersed with two role changes, one from surface search to CASEVAC and VERTREP to lift additional pumps onto *Sheffield* and one to CASEVAC the injured on-board. During the process and at a heightened state of alert, a submarine contact was gained and we were airborne again re-rolled in the ASW role with a Mk 46 torpedo which was released onto a contact. It may just have been a submarine, but was more probably a whale. No explosion was heard. On 6 May, the Flight were dispatched to investigate a contact to the south-west of the Task Force with *Coventry*'s Lynx. The adrenaline levels were high as contact had been lost with two Sea Harriers sent to investigate the same contact. It was not helped by very poor visibility and mist patches at the surface. However, we were reassured by the likelihood that with Orange Crop any hostile radar emissions or fire control radars would be identified in sufficient time to allow us to take appropriate action. Lest the contact was radar-silent, we adopted an intermittent occasional sweep radar policy and approached at very low-level – below 50ft. What we had not appreciated was that at very low-level, emissions from the radar altimeter would be detected by the Orange Crop, which gave us a few anxious moments while we ruled out a fire-control radar lock on. Eventually, out of the mist, at quarter of a mile, the profile of the hulk of HMS *Sheffield* could be seen and after a brief search for as long as our endurance would allow we returned to the ship.

'The next week or so was spent on surface/ESM search in the vicinity of the Task Force when it was hoped that Orange Crop might provide early warning of an Etendard attack with Exocet. On 15 May, *Arrow* was dispatched to land a stick of Royal Marine SBS on North Falklands by night, under the command of Captain David Heaver. We were not equipped with night vision goggles and there was no moon. Nor was it desirable that we should recce occupied territory in daylight and risk alerting the Argentinians to our intentions. We therefore selected a featureless cliff top for the insertion from the map,

The Falklands War 71

hoping it was free of rabbit holes and trees (a pretty sure bet on the Falklands). The intention was to air taxi under sea-spray radar control to the location and then establish a less than ten foot hover by radar altimeter, Doppler and instruments, assisted by opening the cockpit window to provide some visual reference – (no landing light use was permitted nor indeed any lights at all) at which point the SBS would leap into the darkness. To achieve this, it was essential that internal lighting was at an absolute minimum. Unfortunately, the ergonomics of the Lynx cockpit lighting left something to be desired. When the flight instruments were at absolute minimum brightness, there was still an infuriating and distracting glare from the corner of the engine instruments and they could not be dimmed independently. In the event, a variable chart table light was adapted, gaffer taped to the underside of the instrument panel coaming, shielded with cardboard to illuminate the flight instruments, allowing the aircraft's instrument lighting to be switched off in the hover. This Heath Robinson arrangement worked perfectly. The insertion comprised three individual sorties from the ship. After the first, we were rather dismayed to find a rifle trapped between the weapon carrier and the side of the aircraft. This was pointed out to the next stick of troops and it was duly reunited with its owner. Having gained in confidence, and not wanting to risk any broken ankles during the second insertion, we touched the wheels and on the third landed without incident. We were pleased to discover a few days later, in San Carlos Water, that all had accomplished their mission without injury. We heard this from Captain Heaver when he rejoined HMS *Arrow* briefly for a shower after the San Carlos Landings! The landings back on-board after the insertions were carried out without GPI, flight deck, or aircraft lighting, by using, in effect, a helicopter controlled Poor Visibility Approach (PVA) without flares, but using the ship's wake for visual cues. This could be accomplished because the Lynx had such reserves of power and control to get out of trouble when needed and was completely without vice to catch out the unwary.

'Following on from our success, someone on the staff on HMS *Hermes* thought it would be a good idea for us to repeat the operation inland somewhere rather closer to Port Stanley. This appeared to us to be an altogether more challenging assignment and one for which we were neither trained nor equipped. However, not wishing to appear in any way less than keen, a secure phone call was made to the flag ship. We found ourselves talking to the CO of one the commando squadrons, to whom we explained the situation and requested if we might borrow a couple of pairs of his night vision goggles for the sortie. The response was

72   The Royal Navy Lynx

something along the lines of; "You've been asked to do what? Roger, wait, out!" Five minutes later a signal arrived countermanding our instructions and both we and a stick of SBS lived to fight another day.

'Meanwhile, HMS *Arrow* had been suffering from a series of cracks in the superstructure which was a known problem with the class of ship, going back to the design stage when the Corps of Naval Constructors, piqued by the fact that Vospers had been allowed to design the ships without their input, started meddling and told them to remove what they regarded as unnecessary strengthening in the area to save weight. The cracks had started appearing the previous year and had been due to be addressed in the ship's forthcoming docking period, but they were now deteriorating further in the South Atlantic, so *Arrow* was sent to San Carlos Water to await repair. Fortunately for *Arrow*, she arrived the day after the attacks which put paid to HMS *Antelope* and *Ardent*. Notwithstanding, the ship came under heavy attack on a couple of occasions over the following days. The first attack occurred with the Flight closed up at Alert 5 on the flight deck. The commanding officer was in full flow, briefing the ship's company on the tactical situation which went something like: 'There are no known Argentine ship movements or aircraft within the TEZ – AIRCRAFT IN THE SOUND – AIR RAID WARNING RED!' I do not recall whether AEM Hughes managed to get any rounds away from the quarter deck mounted GPMG as an A4 passed over the quarter deck and a bomb dropped about 100 yards astern. I do recall that the aircrew, who for want of anything better to do, were considering the use of their 9mm pistols in the hope that an aircraft at that height might just run into the bullets, failed even to load them! It was quite apparent that the West London Shooting School technique of; 'Bum, belly, beak, BANG'! (for pheasants) was going to be inadequate for a 9mm pistol and an A4 jet. During future air attacks, the Lynx was sent ashore to a suitably inconspicuous valley as it was no use on-board during an air attack.

'During this period, the Flight was deployed mainly on surface and ESM search to the north of the islands. On returning to the ship on one occasion, a reflection was spotted from Western Falklands. It quickly became evident that it was deliberate and probably from a heliograph. It was acknowledged by a wing rock and the location reported back on board and an SBS platoon was subsequently recovered.

'On 31 May, *Arrow* and *Minerva* Flights were tasked with boarding the *Bahia Paraiso*, a hospital ship which was suspected of helping the war effort. *Minerva* Flight conducted the boarding while we provided top cover. Nothing untoward was found. On 3 June *Arrow* Flight, with Captain McCracken this time in the

The Falklands War 73

back and with the observer restored to his seat, conducted NGS spotting for HMS *Arrow* against Argentine targets in the vicinity of Fox Bay – approaching at low-level up the Sound from the direction of Port Edgar. Very light and sporadic small arms fire was observed. On 4 June, the Flight were tasked for a surface search sortie to attempt to identify the exact location of the land based Exocet missile system near Stanley. This was thwarted by poor visibility and the Argentine's Roland Air Defence Missile system, which was continually locking up, despite the deployment of chaff, evasive manoeuvres and very low-level approaches. Later in the day, XZ 730 required a tail rotor hub change and balance, which could not be conducted on-board, so this was attempted at San Carlos Airport (the newly constructed Harrier Forward Operating Base at the north end of San Carlos Water).

'On 7 June, *Arrow* departed San Carlos Water to rejoin the Task force to the east of the Falklands having been repaired by the simple expedient of welding/bolting two large I-beams down each waist. The Flight continued to fly surface search sorties in support until the surrender. *Arrow* was one of the first group of ships to depart for home on 18 June, disembarking to Yeovilton on 7 July having flow about 157 hours, a third of which were by night. In its first combat role, the aircraft had proved to be a thoroughly safe high performance and adaptable addition to the ship's weapons. If there was a niggle, it would have been the issue of vibration and the effect on the radar and radio components, but this could be substantially ameliorated by matching replacement rotor blades and punctilious attention to rotor tracking and balancing. In recognition of their efforts in the Falklands War the maintenance team, led so ably by CPO Longley, were awarded the Rolls-Royce Engineering Efficiency Trophy for 1982.

'Also, as I get older, I can now tell former Lynx observers from pilots by which ear they are wearing their hearing aids in! XZ 730 remained with *Arrow* Flight until Nov 1987, when she went to be converted to Mk3 with uprated engines and thence to 815 Squadron, and in 2007, 702 Squadron, when she became one of the Lynx Display Team aircraft. XZ 241 had a less happy end, being lost on the Weddell Sea Ice Shelf, while offloading supplies from HMS *Endurance*, fortunately without serious injury. A Lynx aircraft carrying *Arrow* Flight's number (326), and the aircrew's names remains as a gate guardian at the Royal Naval Air Station at Yeovilton.'

Phil Barber and Chris Palmer were both awarded a Mention in Despatches for their efforts.

74   The Royal Navy Lynx

HMS *Argonaut*

Flight Commander – Lieutenant Commander Alan Walker
Flight Observer – Sub Lieutenant John Davies
Flight Second Pilot – Sub Lieutenant John Hopkins
SMR – CPO Bernie Gould, CPO Mike Rendell, CPO Pete Muddiman, PO Pete Bennet, LAM Beaseley, AEM Tim Court, AEM Trev Cole

Aircraft – XZ 233, nickname 'Jason'.

HMS *Argonaut* – operating for a week with two, one thousand pound unexploded bombs in her. (*Al Walker*)

By Al Walker:

'The ship: Let's start with the ship – HMS *Argonaut* was (I use the past tense since she was scrapped in 1993) a Leander class frigate. As you can see from this picture our ship was not that big, but could deliver quite a punch if it had to, also the Lynx helicopter could extend the range of the weapons system by about 150 miles, so over the horizon attacks were very possible. Bear in mind that someone standing on the bridge at 21ft above the water sees a horizon which is only about fifteen nautical miles away. Fortunately the radar can see much further than that.

The Falklands War   75

'The build up to war: At the start of the Falklands campaign I was the flight commander for the ship and I was also the Squadron Aviation Officer (SQAVO) for the 7th Flotilla. Our Flight disembarked to RNAS *Yeovilton* on 14 April 1982 following our latest FOST encounter.

'Although we knew that there was a fight brewing down at the Falklands we had not been directly involved, much to our disgust. However, the weekend following our disembarkation, we were told that we were to embark on 19 April and that the intervening week end would be taken up with briefings on a new untested torpedo called the Stingray. Needless to say, the weekend was busy with briefings from the manufacturers on the new air-droppable torpedo which had not even been tested. We were to take four of them to the Falklands. At last we were being allowed to join in the fun! A lot of activity ensued as we got the Flight and aircraft ready for war and ready to embark. We also had to ready our families to the fact that we were off to fight, which at the time seemed somewhat surreal. I think we were all fairly excited to be going and to be having a chance to put into practice what we had been training for all these years. But we really did not appreciate just what we were going to – it all seemed like a big game, another exercise just like all the others but further away.

'The weekend prior to embarkation was taken up not only with preparing the aircraft for embarkation but also with the briefings relating mainly to the new torpedo. How it would affect the flight of the aircraft, what the dropping speeds and heights were etc. All things being equal, it was a fairly hectic weekend. We said goodbye to our families and embarked on to HMS *Argonaut* on 19 April 1982 and sailed for the first of our stops, which was Ascension Island.

'The Passage South: We had sailed in company with HMS *Ardent* and both my observer (Lieutenant John Davies, RN) and I were friends with the *Ardent's* aircrew and completed several cross deck training sessions with them as we sailed south. We also collaborated with them in the development of a draft FOTI (Fleet Operational Tactical Instruction) for the new Stingray torpedo, so that it could be used in the South Atlantic.

'As we continued south we still had a feeling that it would all be sorted by the time we got to the Falklands. Then, on 1 May, the captain made a broadcast over the tannoy that Port Stanley had been attacked and that three Argentine aircraft had been shot down. This was the first inkling we had that what we were going to was a real fight, not a game or an exercise. Then, on 3 May, the captain informed the ship's company that the *Belgrano* had been sunk. A slightly nervous cheer went round the ship. However, the cheers of the previous day became a distant memory when, on 4 May, we were informed that HMS *Sheffield* had been sunk with the loss of twenty of our colleagues and a Sea Harrier was also shot down over Stanley. This really brought home that we really were in for a bit of a shindig. There were quite a few slightly worried personnel on board following those announcements.

'We arrived at Ascension Island, re-stored, and two days later we sailed south again, now with the rest of the fleet containing the landing force. It was quite a sight to see so many ships together ploughing through the heavy seas of the South Atlantic Ocean. During passage south, we were buzzed a few times by a Russian Bear spy aircraft which was being hosted by Brazil. No doubt some intelligence was consequently sent to the Argentines as to what we were doing and how many and what types of ships were on their way. As a Flight we were tasked with flying between the ships of the Task Force so that various commanders could talk to each other face to face rather than on radios, which of course can be picked up by spy planes. We also carried out a delivery service between the ships of the fleet.

'On one notable occasion we were tasked to go ahead of the Task Force and conduct a surface search at night, to see if there was anything lurking out in front of us. As we left, we took the mandatory surface plot so we knew where our ship was in the formation. We did not find anything and at the end of the sortie we duly returned to our ship, or so we thought. During the sortie we were under a strict radio silence policy and consequently, unless there was an emergency, no unit was allowed to use their radios. Also, use of our radar was restricted to one sweep only. We had done our one sweep only and noted the position of our ship and my observer talked me back to it as I was flying purely on instruments since the ships were all darkened, that is no lights on at all.

'As you approach at night in darkened ship conditions the members of the Flight would listen for you and when they heard the noise of the rotor blades they switched on a device which helped to guide us down. The device is a light beam which is shone up what they call the red 165, that is at an angle of 165 degrees from the bow; there are three colours to show you that you are approaching at the right rate of descent – green means that you are on the glide path, amber means you are too high and red means that you are too low. Well, we did not see any such helpful light beam and assumed that the ship had said no to lights. My observer did a great job getting us to the stern of the ship only for us to realise very quickly that it was not our ship! What was so dangerous was that the normal method of approach was to come down to about 60ft above the sea, about 100yds behind your ship and then air taxi forwards up the port side of the flight deck and then land. However, the ship we had approached had a flight deck that was some 80ft above the sea!

'Following a few choice words from both of us, which I won't repeat here, it became apparent to us that the fleet formation had been changed whilst we were away, but we had not been informed that this would happen at the pre-flight briefing. So, we climbed to a safe height, which kept us clear of any masts and did a one sweep only, plotted all the ships positions and visited each likely one in turn until we found ours. On our return I went to see the captain and told him precisely what I thought. He did not like aviators in the first place. He liked them even less by the time I had finished.

'For the next few days, we continued our passage south towards the islands. The days were punctuated by various air raid warnings when we had to take cover in the hangar. It was on one of those occasions that I looked at my SMR and then at the many boxes we had stored in the hangar. He looked back at me and we both started to laugh. We were taking cover behind boxes of high explosives, ammunition and torpedoes. After that, we just stood at the hangar door and watched what was going on.

'On the night of 20 May 1982, we were told that the following morning at first light we would be commencing the landings in San Carlos water. However, just before my observer and I turned in for the night so that we would be ready for the morning, we were summoned to the bridge by the captain. They had a radar contact about 120 miles ahead, just 30nm outside San Carlos water and wanted to know what it was. We were to fly out to it and identify it in the dark, which meant that we would have to turn our landing light on to illuminate it and if it wasn't a fishing vessel, we would be shot down. The captain's response was, "well then I will know it is hostile won't I?" I did say that he didn't like aircrew, but we thought that was a bit rich. However, an order is an order and off we duly went. At a range of about 20nm, I flew the aircraft down to 30ft above the sea and at 150kts that tends to concentrate the mind somewhat, especially in the dark. The observer called out the range to go to reach the contact and at the right point I flared the aircraft into a fast stop so that we came to a hover at 50ft above the sea and just astern of the vessel and turned on the landing light.

'Fortunately, we only found a very surprised fishing vessel crew who could see that we were a military armed helicopter and promptly dived for cover. We turned out the landing light and in total darkness flew away from the fishing boat towards the islands and went back down to low-level again. There were two reasons for this, the fishing boat would think we had come from the Falkland

Islands and any shore based radar would not be able to pick us up. We then duly returned to our ship without incident.

'The Landings: Next morning the big day arrived and just before first light we all slipped quietly into San Carlos Water and started the landings, which went well in general terms. Our ship was tasked with patrolling the north end of the Falkland Sound to prevent any Argentine submarines from entering, so we were ploughing backwards and forwards across the entrance and this can get a bit boring for everyone. I was strolling idly around the flight deck – as my second pilot was flying the aircraft on a surface search – when I spotted an aircraft which I recognised as an Aero Macchi and I knew we did not have any so I shouted, "enemy aircraft to starboard" as loud as I could. At that point I could see what appeared to be flashes coming from the aircraft and shouted, "Take cover" to the rest of the Flight and anyone else who could hear. I also started to run towards the hangar since I was at the rear end of the flight deck.

'Just as I got to the hangar, I heard a sound that I can only describe as sounding like a despairing shriek which slowly got louder and louder and culminated in a series of extremely loud explosions and thumping noises. We had been rocketed and machine gunned. I looked at those members of the Flight who were in the hangar with me and we all realised that someone had just tried very hard to kill us. This very definitely was not a game or an exercise.

'The ship continued to crisscross the entrance to San Carlos water on submarine patrol and as we were proceeding towards Fanning Head at about 14kts we came under attack from six Argentine aircraft. The aircraft came in at low-level and dropped their bombs and two of them hit the ship but failed to explode. However, we felt the impact of both bombs even in the hanger. One entered well below the waterline and penetrated the forward diesel tank and went on into the forward magazine where it caused impact ignition of two Seacat missiles and it was this that killed two sailors. A mixture of diesel fuel and seawater fortunately put out the fire as the compartments flooded. The second bomb entered the ship's hull at the waterline and went into the port boiler room, which promptly flooded, causing the ships generators to fail. This caused the loss of all electrical power throughout the ship and the ship effectively "died" and became very quiet.

'Now at the time of the bombing we were progressing towards Fanning Head at 14kts and with no means of steering the ship we would end up on the rocks of the headland. However, as luck would have it, in a manoeuvre to attempt to fool the aircraft, the captain had ordered a turn to starboard just before the bombs hit, so we were in fact turning as the power was lost. Fortunately, we

The Falklands War   79

continued to turn as we lost speed and became static in the water unable to do anything.

'In the hangar we were somewhat isolated from the rest of the ship when all communications have gone, so we were not sure if we were sinking or not. All we could hear was water lapping against the outside of the hull, or was it inside? We didn't wait to find out so we started to prepare to range the aircraft so that if we were sinking maybe I could get airborne in time to airlift some personnel off the ship. As we were starting to move the aircraft a voice shouted from the hangar roof, "we are not sinking, leave the aircraft in the hangar". At this point there was a lot of activity within the ship. The Marine Engineers, (commonly known as clankies), were trying to pump water out and the damage repair teams were trying to shore up the holes in the hull any way they could, but they were fighting a losing battle and eventually the flooded compartments were fully sealed off so that flooding did not spread. We sat still in the water like a sitting duck.

'Fortunately for us it was getting dark when all this excitement took place and by the time we all knew what was going on it was pitch black, so it was unlikely that there would be any further attacks that day. By now, the first lieutenant had appeared on the flight deck with a right angle torch in his hand. He went and stood on the starboard aft corner of the flight deck. He then held the torch up and pointed it directly aft from the flight deck. We started to think that he had cracked but soon found out why, as another ship (HMS *Plymouth*) came alongside about a foot away from our side. A very clever bit of ship handling. It was during this evolution that another of those amusing moments happened.

'The ship had triple torpedo tube launchers and they were located beside the aft end of the hangar and of course they were trained out over the side of the ship and locked in position in readiness for firing if required. The first lieutenant realised this as the bridge of *Plymouth* went past him and gave the order: "Stow the Torpedo tubes". A quiet unknown voice replied: "Aye Aye sir". Now *Argonaut* had a walkway all round the ship, *Plymouth* did not, so its bridge superstructure came right out to the side of the ship. As *Plymouth* moved further along our side there was a very loud metallic cracking and crunching sound as the tubes were unceremoniously pushed out of the way and some wag was heard to shout: "Tubes stowed sir!" *Plymouth* provided us with electrical power which allowed us to use our own galley and start to get control of the whole ship again. She also towed us into San Carlos water so that we were in with all the other ships out of harm's way, or so we thought.

'Bomb Alley: We spent about two weeks being bombed two or three times a day whilst resident in what became known as "Bomb Alley". We flew several sorties during that time, mainly EW listening for enemy radars and on one of those sorties we had to land on the nearest shore as an air raid took place. We watched the jets going in to attack the ships and then it was quiet and I noticed a movement outside the aircraft on the ground. On looking down, I saw a group of penguins looking up at me as if to say, "this is our beach, sod off you noisy so and so!" It's little moments like that when you realise that we humans are not as intelligent as we think we are.

'Whilst in bomb alley we watched HMS *Antelope* come in and anchor just 500yds from us with a UXB on board. I was on our flight deck the evening that she blew up and burned out. Over the next few days we watched as she burnt out, broke her keel and eventually sank. There were quite a lot of the ship's company on the upper deck when *Antelope* went down and for a few minutes nobody could speak. It was a very sad and poignant moment.

'We also had a major fire which devastated most of the forward compartments of the ship. There was a constant strong smell of diesel fuel throughout and most of the accommodation forward had been rendered unfit for use by the bombs and the fires. So, not surprisingly, a lot of us were pretty tired and it is not good for an aviator to be tired prior to flying.

'Whilst in bomb alley, my senior maintenance rating, "Bernie Gould", took the opportunity of putting his engineering skills to good use. The Lynx radio was not the most robust set ever to be invented and had a habit of frequently wandering off tune or just not working. It was manufactured as a sealed unit so that only the manufacturer could fix and maintain it. Bernie decided that he would set up his own radio repair shop in the hangar and quite a few ships Flight radios were refurbished using his knowledge and skill. Overall, we found the Lynx to be a reliable and useful workhorse which performed well. However, the only time we came to fire a Sea Skua it misfired and we had to return to the ship with a hang up. Sea Skua was generally regarded by us as an unreliable system because of its software.

'During our time in "Bomb Alley" I was tasked with going ashore to recover HMS *Antelope's* aircraft. I was to fly it back to HMS *Intrepid*. I believe that it was a great testament to the robust design of the aircraft that after approximately seven days out in the open and sitting at a slight angle on the side of a hill, I had no trouble starting it and getting airborne. During the transit, we checked as many of the systems as the current comms policy would allow and had an

The Falklands War   81

uneventful flight to HMS *Intrepid*. This was the only time we managed to get ashore whilst in the Falklands.

'We all continued to attempt to get the ship seaworthy again and tried to make her more habitable. We eventually got our electric supplies back on line and were then able to use our weapons systems, but we still could not move under our own power yet. Eventually, the engineers got the propulsion systems sorted out and we were able to sail out one night to carry out the burials at sea for our two comrades who were killed in the forward magazine. That was one of those very emotional moments of the conflict for all of us. However, the short trip also proved that we had got our systems back such that we could at least go out and get some repairs before going back to UK. Eventually, we sailed out for South Georgia to meet up with Stena *Sea Spread*, the repair ship. She gave us a temporary patch and we started to limp back to UK and, as we left, we heard over the tannoy that the Argentines had surrendered. We spent quite a bit of time cheering our army and marine colleagues at that moment.

'The return to UK: During the transit to UK the patch which had been welded onto the hull to keep us watertight sprung a major leak, so we had to slow right down and effect temporary repairs to allow us to reach UK without sinking. Needless to say, from then on we made very slow progress, but the Flight disembarked on 26 June 1982 whilst the ship was passing Ushant and the ship eventually arrived back at Plymouth on 27 June 1982. The whole affair ended on a sour note for the Flight because although the ship went into Plymouth to a rapturous reception from the public and families on the 27 June: we, by total contrast, arrived at Yeovilton to nothing. We even had to contact our own families to let them know we were back so we could get transport home. I didn't impress the Squadron CO when I told him what I thought about it – but significantly, he didn't argue!

'I have often been asked: "Were you ever scared?" And a truthful answer is yes. However, when an attack comes in you are too busy to be anything but efficient at doing your job, whatever that may be. Also, I feel very proud to have taken part in the conflict and done my bit for our country.'

Another perspective comes from the Second Pilot John Hopkins:

'I had only just joined the Flight only a few weeks before the war broke out, having had one of the fastest flying training courses on record, eight months in all: having been a commercial helicopter pilot on the North Sea with Bristows. I therefore got slung in at the deep end and can remember getting used to landing on some very heavily pitching and rolling decks on the way south, with which the Lynx, with its Harpoon system, coped admirably. We were also tasked with a large number of VERTREPS in heavy seas, but the Lynx, with its high maneouvreability, never presented a problem, though the shortage of power of the HAS 2 needed consideration.

'The first piece of real action occurred on the day of the landings on 21 May. That day dawned bright and sunny with excellent visibility with *Argonaut* patrolling the northern end of Falkland Sound quite close to Fanning Head and the entrance to San Carlos Water. All seemed very calm with little activity except for some Junglie machines doing their stuff. Our captain had it in his mind that the Argentinians would fire an Exocet into the ships down Falkland Sound, something we knew was impossible as the thing would never guide with all the land clutter, but he wasn't to be persuaded. A very agricultural Exocet radar decoy had been designed on the way down which consisted of steel plates of about a metre square which were welded together to form four sides of a cube and bolted to the weapons carrier. The idea was that you hovered, as I recall, about 400 yards off the stern of the ship at about 400 feet pointing in the threat direction, the idea being the Exocet radar head saw the decoy as a bigger target than the ship and headed for it, exploding under the helicopter rather than in the ship. It was fairly obvious that either way it was a suicide mission, as, if the missile didn't take you out, the first attacking aircraft would in your utterly exposed position. The decoy transformed the Lynx from the world's most manoeuvrable helicopter into a total sitting duck with a reduced Vne of 85kt. I wasn't even allowed to take the flight observer as there was only one of him, but our amiable flight winchman, the late PO Wiggy Bennett, volunteered to come along to man the GPMG mounted in the doorway. Sitting above the ship on this bright day with the Argentine air elements imminently expected reminded me of what Eugene Esmonde must have felt as he flew off to intercept the German battle cruisers in the Channel Dash – it was a one way ticket. That morning at Port Stanley, Lieutenant Owen Crippa of the Argentinian Navy took off on an offensive patrol to the northern coast of East Falkland (originally as a pair, but the other went u/s). Predictably the first thing he saw was a hovering Lynx, so he manoeuvred to attack it, thus becoming the first air action of that day. Our captain's determination to expose the Lynx in this way thus gave away where the task force had landed. On Crippas' run in, just before he squeezed the trigger to his cannon, he caught sight of *Argonaut* and decided to attack that instead, strafing with 30mm cannon and two inch rockets from his Aeromacchi 339. The first thing I knew about this was when an aircraft appeared in the chin apertures of the Lynx heading away, having passed underneath from directly behind and I could see the white smoke trails of his rockets. As the threat direction had been ordered as Port Stanley we had no chance to manoeuvre to see behind and of course Owen Crippa chose this naturally as the attack direction, which conveniently brought him broadside to the ship. At this point it seemed a good idea to test the Vne limit of the decoy and we dived away to seek shelter in a small valley on the headland opposite Fanning Head where a Falklands goose sat in a small pond calmly observing the goings on around.

'On returning to the ship I landed on and decided in my high rank of sub lieutenant to tell the captain directly from the hangar EMR exactly what I thought of his decoy plan and that it would almost certainly lose him his valuable Lynx if attempted it again. Water off a ducks back – what happened a while later – action Lynx with the decoy still fitted. What we didn't know at the time was that Owen Crippa had flown all the way through the anchorage and then back up to the north in close proximity to note the ships disposition on his kneepad, an action which subsequently got him Argentina's highest military decoration, the cross of Heroic Valour in Combat. This caused the main activity to be launched from the mainland bases and it was this that led to our second mission. The highest Lynx alert was Alert 5, but due to the circumstances on that day I had developed a procedure of switching everything on so that as soon as you hit the Master switch you were starting the first engine and I reckoned that one could be wound up and airborne in just over a minute. This proved to be highly valuable, as having just lifted to the side and transitioning I saw two Daggers approaching the flight deck at speed and very low, again broadside on, the first aircraft dropping a 1000lb bomb which hit the sea about four yards off the stern and almost took the tail off the Lynx as he passed. This turned out to be Nandu section, led by Capitaine Carlos Rohde, who later became head of the Argentinian Air Force. I therefore transitioned, staying at zero height, to my amazing Vne of 85kt and sought refuge in my little valley again, there seeming no point to play at Exocet decoy as it was obvious we were being bombed instead! I landed back about twenty minutes later to see *Antrim* pass across our bows into San Carlos having suffered damage in this raid with cannon and an unexploded 1000lb bomb lodged in the heads. Very little happened for a while, but finally the decoy was removed at long last and the aircraft put in Fly One so that the casualties from the first attack could be winched off. As soon as a Wessex appeared over the flight deck for this purpose it disappeared again as another raid was inbound. I took cover next to the stored Stingray torpedoes and Skua rounds we had strapped to the deck in their boxes at the back of the hangar! One could distinctly feel the two bomb hits as we were raided by six Skyhawks and the ship seemed to move sideways under the force. Fortunately neither went off, but they knocked *Argonaut* out of the war with serious damage. The rear bomb hit only just beneath where I was lying and lodged in the boiler room. The forward hit went in under water into the forward Seacat magazine causing some of them to explode, killing two sailors at their action station and starting a fire. It also ruptured the fuel tanks causing *Argonaut* to come to a hissing stop with no power of any sort. The Officer of the Watch, Sub Lieutenant Peter Morgan, subsequently got the DSC for leaping off the bridge wing and releasing an anchor to stop *Argonaut* running into the headland, all steerage having been lost with no hydraulics or generator power. We gathered on the waist but could see nothing as we were enveloped in smoke, but as it cleared we could see *Ardent* had not been so lucky and was burning heavily with the tail of its Lynx sticking at an ominous angle out of the flight deck. *Argonaut* and *Ardent* had been the two warships escorting the landing force south, so we had seen a lot of their Lynx flight, Lieutenant Commander John Sephton and observer Lieutenant Brian Murphy, but much as it looked at the time, it sadly transpired their luck had run out. HMS *Plymouth* came to our aid and took us in tow into San Carlos before the following daybreak, but it was a strange sensation being on a completely silent and dark powerless ship. We even went to have a look at the unexploded bomb beneath the boiler room hatch; it seemed a relatively safe thing to do after the goings on of that day! The rear bomb was quickly defused by Staff Sergeant Prescott, who was killed repeating the attempt on *Antelope* the following day.

'As I currently visit Buenos Aires in my job with BA, I have met with Owen Crippa and two of the Skyhawk pilots, Vincente Auterio and Alberto Fillipini. We have had a couple of great parties there with no ill feelings, gentlemen all. Owen always wanted to meet the pilot of the Lynx he was about to blast out of the sky as he couldn't understand why anybody would be so idiotic as to be hovering at 400 feet in Falkland Sound on such a day! I told Alberto Fillipini that one of the bomb disposal guys had said that out of the twelve turns required to fully enable the fuse of a 1000lb bomb, that they had gone in with eleven, so they were one thread away from detonating – he proceeded to tell me they had already wound them six turns before take off! We were told that other ships observing this attack on *Argonaut* thought she was a goner as she disappeared in a huge cloud of smoke and steam, a fact confirmed by the Skyhawk drivers as this was their departing impression also.

The Falklands War   85

'The day after the landings dawned very differently weather wise, so not much occurred in the low cloud and rain. However, *Antelope* was hit in the Sound and came in to anchor alongside us in San Carlos. As my home in the midshipman's "grot" had been destroyed in the forward fire I was sleeping on a camp bed in the flight EMR under the flight deck, which on a Leander had no real use once it received a Lynx in place of a Wasp, so we tended to use it as a crewroom. I was just removing my "goon suit" after dark when the whole thing shuddered like a big drum. This was *Antelope* exploding alongside and it was quickly back on with the "goon suit" and up on deck to see what was going on –quite a frightening spectacle. A couple of large Marine Landing Craft came alongside and managed to move the powerless *Argonaut* a little further away from the inferno.

'The following day the good weather was back and I was detailed with the Flight Observer, Sub Lieutenant John Davies, to carry out a surface search down Falkland Sound with two Sea Skuas strapped on. We tried to get some intelligence on where our forces and the Argentinians were, but none was forthcoming. John later told me that part of the idea of this sortie by the ships ops team was that if we didn't come back they would know a bit more about where the enemy was and their capabilities, particularly the defences around Fox Bay! We therefore proceeded at extreme low-level down the Sound feeling much better as we were able to exploit the Lynx manoeuvrability to the full, being free of the wretched Exocet decoy. As we weaved continuously I could see we were leaving our wake in the rather still water. We passed the remains of *Ardent* and later found a parachute washed up on a small island, which turned out to be that of Flight Lieutenant Glover, who had been shot down previously by the Fox Bay defences. Shortly after, we spotted a freighter which appeared in steam proceeding west to east across the Sound. This was an obvious Skua target as we had been told to attack anything we found, as it wouldn't be one of ours. As we set ourselves up the light sequence went Arm, Lock, but not Ready, so the missiles might not be guided if we fired them. This left us two sub lieutenants in a little dilemma, as we had got about eight or twelve of these brand new toys, but I recall the figure of £300,000 had been quoted for each one so we were a bit concerned that somebody might be quite upset if we wasted one. However, it was a big target so might they just hit anyway if we pointed them in the right direction? We decided to return to the ship and have this investigated as the freighter didn't appear to be going anywhere fast. In fact it wasn't going anywhere at all, having been attacked by Harriers the previous day and abandoned and was the *Rio Carcerina*. We were sent to *Broadsword*, who had some Skua experts on

86   The Royal Navy Lynx

the flight, to discover in the hasty Skua fit our Lynx had received before sailing south, that the little radar feed to the missile from the sponson (so it knows the frequency state of the radar it is expecting when it appears out front) had not been wired up. It is doubtful they would have guided, so I guess we saved a couple of Skua there. By the time this was remedied another flight had planted another two Skua in the *Rio Carcerina*, as the intelligence on the abandoned state of the ship had not been fed back.

'The following evening John and I were detached to a Marines FOB with the Lynx as the ship was evacuated whilst work progressed trying to extricate the forward unexploded bomb. We landed on a hillside in San Carlos and found a tent with a bed of heather and spent an uncomfortable and damp night. In the morning we had to return to the ship, but having been watching the continuous air raids for the past few days the Marines didn't envy us. A couple of nights later, on the 26 May, we were detached again, this time to HMS *Arrow*, she became a two Lynx fitted 21, I recall ours was stowed in the hangar and the *Arrow* Lynx was arranged in readiness on the flight deck. We thought this was to be highly civilised and peaceful as *Arrow* was undamaged, but on landing on and being met by Philip Barber and Chris Palmer, their Lynx crew, we were told that *Arrow* was going to provide Naval Gunfire Support all night as the battle for Goose Green got underway. Not having a gun on *Argonaut* it was a new experience as the ship reverberated to the continuous firing and we watched the starshell bursts and gorseline fires in the distance. Later in the night the gun jammed, so we did get a bit of sleep.

'After over a week immobilised in San Carlos during the worst of the air raids, the remaining bomb was removed and we sailed to the TRALA out to the east for repairs courtesy of one boiler and a propeller shaft they had got working. We later swopped our Lynx with *Cardiff* flight as I recall they had vibration problems and *Argonaut* was being sent home. I believe XZ 233 later had another close encounter in the hands of Chris Clayton, this time with a Dagger.

Authors note: Al Walker and John Hopkins make light of the fact that they sat in Bomb Alley for some time with two unexploded bombs in the ship, one in a missile magazine. The rest of the fleet knew all about it and had nothing but admiration for an incredibly brave crew.

Now that time has passed there had been plenty of time for people from both sides to meet up. John Hopkins regularly keeps in touch with some of the people who many years before could have shot him out of the sky:

The Falklands War   87

By John: The photo is of our last veterans meeting in Buenos Aires last October at the air force club whilst I was down on a trip. Mike Sear, who was 2 i/c the Gurkhas during the conflict, happened to be down there as he now works in airline safety, as does Juan Membrana, who was a Tracker pilot on 25 Mayo.

Left to right back row are:
Sergio Fernandez (now head of the Argentine Veterans association and retired general in Argentine special forces who was commander of forces in west Falkland), Ruben Zini (commander of Grupo 5 Skyhawks), Nicolas Karansew (only Argentine journalist on the islands and our interpreter for the meeting), Owen Crippa (pilot of navy Aeromacchi 339 that attacked *Argonaut* first thing on 21 May, holder of Cross of Heroic Valour), Juan Membrana (Tracker pilot 25 Mayo and now Safety Officer Aerolineas Argentina), Vicente Auterio (former Brigadier FAA and pilot of Skyhawk in port echelon of the raid that put *Argonaut* out).

Front row:
Alberto Fillipini (former Brigadier and leader of rear echelon of Skyhawks that hit *Argonaut* late in the day on 21 May), Mike Sear (2 i/c Gurkha Regiment), myself with Grupo 5 Skyhawk scarf that they presented to me.

HMS *Antelope*

Flight Commander – Lieutenant Tim MacMahon
Flight Observer – Lieutenant Gary Hunt
SMR – CPO Bob Shadbolt, PO D. Swayne, PO P. Hudson, PO A. Skelton, LAEM M. Beardmore, AEM P. Norman, AEM D. Marshall

Aircraft – XZ 723, nickname 'Norman'. *One story about the origin of this name is that when the aircraft originally embarked, the captain wanted to call it 'Bambi'. Thinking on his feet the flight commander explained that it already had a name and Norman was the first one he could think of!*

HMS *Antelope* shortly after being attacked. The bent mast was caused by being hit by an A4 which was subsequently shot down. A bomb hole in the starboard side of the ship can clearly be seen. (*Tim McMahon*)

By Tim MacMahon:

Preface: Prior to the conflict a series of Type 21 frigate refits were conducted which included modifications to the ASW weapons magazine (port side forward of the hangar) to accommodate Sea Skua missiles. *Antelope's* refit completed in early 1982 and the ship was on workup at FOST Portland when the conflict began.

'On the evening of Thursday, 1 April, following a Thursday war and other classic Flag Officer Sea Training (FOST) serials, when turning in was uppermost in our minds, the CO, Commander Nick Tobin, called the officers to his cabin at 2300 to tell us we were at four hours' notice to depart south. The effect of this thunderbolt, after decades of "cold war peace", hardly needs emphasising. We awaited clarification in Weymouth Bay overnight without sleeping a lot and at 0500 were called again to be told we would land remaining FOST staff immediately and proceed at best speed to Devonport to store ship and head south on completion. In the end, *Antelope,* and most other ships leaving UK bases, headed south early on Monday, 5 April. The extra days allowed time to change the aircraft for a Skua-capable model and on Sunday morning I departed from alongside to Yeovilton, where, in a few short hours we traded up to XZ 723, and the SMR and L1 did the fastest Sea Skua course to date. It also allowed one or two of us to say our goodbyes to families who had been able to get to Yeovilton. The departure from alongside in Devonport had been at high tide, but the afternoon return was at low tide against a steep dockyard wall with other ships now moored outboard – an interesting manoeuvre.

'The Task Force headed south, training hard, and after a pause at Ascension Island headed south again. Shortly after this departure, *Antelope* was detached to meet HMS *Antrim* and its Task Group heading north from South Georgia with prisoners of war and members of the British Antarctic Survey. We were ordered to transfer our Sea Skua stock to a destroyer heading straight to the Falklands, which prompted some understandable dripping, and led to suitable "goodwill" messages being written on the missiles for the receiving Flight.

'On meeting *Antrim* and RFA *Tidespring*, we transferred by Lynx, the infamous Captain Alfredo Astiz – erstwhile commander of the South Georgia forces – to *Antelope* for shipment back to Ascension. We also transferred Cindy Buxton and Annie Price of the British Antarctic Survey, plus various scientific samples including sundry ducks. Captain Astiz was kept under armed guard in a vacated cabin. The ladies shared another and the ducks and other samples lodged in the captain's bath! On arrival at Wideawake airfield on Ascension to land the POWs, everything was done to prevent them seeing any of the assets ashore. Consequently, they were landed at night and the Lynx flew into and out of a square landing site bordered by vehicles with headlights on main beam. This had the desired effect of blinding the POWs, but was no good for my night vision, so after each lift from Wideawake, I had to readjust to be able to land back on the ship for the next batch.

90 The Royal Navy Lynx

'The next day brought a stroke of luck, as on an HDS run into Wideawake with the supply officer on board, we spotted a recently arrived VC10 with four Sea Skua sitting on the open lateral cargo door as if waiting to be picked up. In the finest traditions of the RAF the crew had gone for lunch leaving a poor stores corporal to guard the aircraft. He was soon re-briefed on the meaning of a direct order and we set off back to the ship with four Sea Skuas underslung.

'One role for which the Lynx was perfect was the pickup of air-dropped stores, usually from a RAF C130. This required some planning. The Lynx would get airborne with low-ish fuel to maximise available payload, wait clear of the drop zone, and as soon as the load was in the water, close to attach the 80ft strop. This would be done by a swimmer from the ship, who got to the load either by sea boat, if conditions allowed, or was winched down from the Lynx. All this depended on the load floating as advertised and its weight being as declared, but if the watertight packing had been torn during the drop, its weight would rapidly increase, hence the need for speed. Once VERTREP-ed back on board, a large stores party would break the load down at high speed to clear the deck to recover the Lynx. On one occasion a curious killer whale decided to check out the load whilst the swimmer was hooking on. The observer gesticulated furiously to warn the said sailor of the danger, but he merely thought this was the Flight having another jape – until he too saw the whale and tried to shin up the strop.

'Approaching the Falklands, the Lynx was tasked, like others, to conduct EW patrols west of the Task Force. The idea, or hope, was that we might, with our new Orange Crop ESM equipment, detect an inbound Super Etendard should he use his Agave radar approaching the Task Force. We'd fit one overload tank and head west, for up to four hours, hoping not to be engaged by the Task Force during the return. These were long, lonely patrols and on the hour we'd briefly tune the HF radio to the BBC World Service to get the latest news. If I never hear Lillibulero again I'll be quite happy.

'*Antelope* entered San Carlos early on 23 May and was tasked as a picket at the entrance to the sound where *Ardent* had been sunk two days earlier. We had few illusions about the day to come, which was gin clear, though for a time all was quiet. The Lynx was then tasked to engage the *Rio Carcaraña*, an Argentinian freighter known to be conducting resupply between West and East Falkland. We had four Skuas, but chose to fire just two and conserve weapons for a re-attack if necessary, or for another mission. Skua worked exactly as in the manual – remember, none of us had used the system before so were reading draft Flight

Reference Cards. One particularly acute memory is how long 1.5 seconds, the time from release to booster ignition, seems to last when in the combat zone. Two hits were achieved. The target was seen to be on fire and we returned uneventfully to the ship.'

A long-range shot of the *Rio Carcaraña* on fire after the attack. (*Tim McMahon*)

'Later, we were tasked for a battle damage recce and on the way back up Falkland Sound were overtaken by three A4 Skyhawks, prompting the immediate unspoken question, "where's No4?" (They always attacked in pairs or fours). An instinctive hard turn right proved to be a wise move and the Skyhawks continued up the Sound to attack ships in San Carlos. To cut a long story short, this attack led to the eventual sinking of *Antelope*, although, before the unexploded bombs (UXBs) detonated later that evening, the Lynx ferried casualties ashore to the field hospital. It was whilst awaiting instructions at the field hospital talking to Surgeon Commander Rick Jolly that the first bomb detonated and we got airborne to see what help we could give. The fire was midships and the captain and first lieutenant had split the ship's company forward and aft to fight it, though with no power, communications, or firemain, it was soon clear this was a lost cause. On the flight deck, we were able to watch the SMR and the Flight's heroic emptying of the torpedo/Skua magazine. They moved the weapons to the aft end of the flight deck to postpone the inevitable. As the evening turned to night, we stayed airborne to give illumination for firefighting, trying to balance the benefit of our illumination against our own noise, which won't have helped. Once the ship had been abandoned, we searched for a deck for the night. It wasn't an easy job as we lacked the next day's communication plan, so after midnight it became strangely quiet. Eventually, we stumbled onto *Fearless* for the night.

'The following day, although the ship was lost, we had a serviceable Lynx so we moved ashore and co-located with 3 Commando Brigade Air Squadron (3BAS), conducting miscellaneous tasks in the Amphibious Operating Area before leaving XZ 723 in a field to be collected by another Flight in due course. With the Flight personnel we then embarked in MV *Norland* for the start of the long trip home.

'Postscripts: The deployment of Sea Skua to the Falklands was an inspired decision, but not without risk as the missile was still doing its development firing programme at Aberporth. As is known, it performed very well, but a contract is a contract, so in late summer 1982, after a spell of survivors' leave, the Flight detached to Aberporth to complete the official firing programme!

'In 1983, Westland persuaded MOD Defence Sales (DESO) to lend a couple of Falklands 'warriors' for a sales tour of the Middle and Far East. Off I went to tell the Lynx story, which was the start, among others, of the Korean interest in Lynx. My bonus is still in the post, I believe.

'During the campaign the Argentinian Aircraft Carrier ARA *Veinticinco de Mayo*, complete with air group, briefly put to sea and a lot of feverish planning went into countering the threat. I wasn't alone in considering whether, if it came to it, a Skua attack might be an option. Long before we had to consider it seriously, she returned to port with boiler problems. Decades later, I started going through my late father's wartime memorabilia. He served in the British Pacific Fleet as a communications officer and I discovered a photo of him on the deck of HMS *Venerable* in Hong Kong in October 1945. *Venerable* went on to become the *Veinticinco de Mayo*, so, thirty-seven years after my father's photo was taken I was considering how, and if, we might contribute to sinking his old ship.'

HMS *Exeter*

Flight Commander – Lieutenant Commander Ron Goddard.
Flight Observer – Lieutenant Charlie Devine.
Second Pilot – Lieutenant Phil Stonor, later Sub Lieutenant Derek Batty.

SMR – CPO Deryck Hiscox, CPO Steve Gibson (R1), CPO Les Smith (M1), PO Bob Ault (Wpns), LAEM Joe Kear, NAM Nick Jowett, W/L Simon Wheeler.
Flight Deck Officers – Lieutenant Hank Armstrong (Capt. Sec), MAA George McCormack.

Aircraft – XZ 733, Nickname 'Trigger'

Dedicated to the late Charlie Devine. (*Ron Goddard*)

94　The Royal Navy Lynx

By Ron Goddard:

'The story really starts in July 1980, when I was appointed to 702 Naval Air Squadron together with a bunch of aviators with mixed experience. My colleagues were fixed wing aviators and others with considerable helicopter flying experience and some "third prongers" – aviators straight from training. I joined with over 1,000 hrs in various aircraft which included the Chipmunk, Hiller 12E, Whirlwind 7, Sea King and the Wasp; it was a delight to be introduced to the powerful twin engine Lynx.

'Conversion went smoothly, I learnt new tactics, how to deploy the various weapon systems and above all experience deck landings in an aircraft with a wide operating envelope. At the end of the course, in January 1981, the Fleet Air Arm saw the formation of a new 815 Squadron; I was to join as the squadron Qualified Helicopter Instructor (QHI). During my time in 815, I was responsible mostly for the individual pilots flying standards, and enjoyed some exhilarating flying with Chris Waite from 702 Squadron as the Lynx display team.

'The QHI appointment was short-lived and on 11 July 1981 we formed HMS *Exeter* Flight with Charlie Devine as the observer and CPO Derek Hiscox at the SMR. We commissioned the Flight at the Exeter Air show, where we put on a flying display. The captain of *Exeter* was captain of the 5th Destroyer Squadron, so I had some responsibility for the other helicopters in the squadron, and the Flight was augmented with a second pilot, Lieutenant Phil Stonor. During the remainder of 1981 and the beginning of 1982, the engineers got XZ 733 up to standard by installing Orange Crop and Sea Skua equipment. We spent some time embarked and more excitingly we started to develop Maritime Counter Terrorist (MCT) tactics with troops from the Royal Marine's Special Boat Service. This involved being based at Lee on Solent, practising fast roping techniques both by day and night to land on targets before moving on to "attacking" HMS *Bacchante* and the *Europic Ferry* in the Channel. Mid–March 1982 saw us sail for a three month deployment as West Indies Guard Ship (WIGS). We did some whale counting off Bermuda, thoroughly enjoyed the colourful life in Key West, did some encounter exercises with some US Navy hydrofoils and generally slotted the Flight into being an essential part of the ship's weapons system. In April, *Exeter* participated in Exercise Redex; a multi layered US led exercise and shot down two drones with her Sea Dart missiles. The Lynx was given the task of recovering the downed drones by underslung hook and diver. Always a tricky manoeuvre, as the diver had to be dropped first to disengage the parachute and hook on the drone, then be recovered before the drone could be picked out of the water and returned to the target launching ship. This called for close cooperation between the observer and the pilot, who was unsighted and relied entirely on verbal commands.

'Besides the fun of WIGS, things became a little uncertain with the Argentinian forces going into South Georgia. A quick look at the map showed we were one of the closest naval units, but the decision was made to continue with our WIGS deployment while the fleet assembled and sailed from the UK. The report on 29 April that a "destroyer is sinking" prompted lots of phone calls to the MOD from anxious relatives of the crew of *Exeter*. The MOD issued a denial that we had been involved in any military activity. After Key West some challenging and interesting flying in support of the British forces in Belize, which involved landing on a mountain top observation post overlooking Guatemala. Then all hell broke loose when we were in Nevis and news of HMS *Sheffield* being hit by an Exocet missile was announced.

'Under sailing orders, the crew frantically unloaded most of their personal effects into huge containers on the jetty in Antigua. Then it was a high speed dash to the Falklands via the Ascension Islands. Under the watchful eye of a Russian spy ship, the Lynx loaded tons of stores, spares, mail and fresh produce in the eight hours before the long dash south.'

Trigger at Wideawake in Ascension. (*Ron Goddard*)

'During the passage, the crew were subjected to endless training exercises, including simulated "Action Stations". The Flight had its own training programme using Chaff "H" and various "unconventional" manoeuvres to try to outwit our own 1022 and 909 radars which would target the helicopter. We were acutely aware that in Portland, just a few years earlier, our own elite sea riders were training the missile crews of the two Type 42 destroyers we had thoughtfully sold to the Argentinians – our own weapons were likely to be used against us. On the way south we met with the survivors from HMS *Sheffield* in mid-South Atlantic, and Trigger was tasked to go and collect Captain 'Sam' Salt and a couple of the officers for a briefing on board *Exeter*. The Flight also had the chance for a chat with Brian Leyshon, *Sheffield's* Flight commander who, in a personal letter, advised us on some specific preparations, like keeping all your valuable and personal effects in your respirator bag, he also warned us that the war was 95% boredom, 4% fright and 1% terror, statistics which we were later to agree on. I still have that letter today.

'The ship and the Flight had a good war, which included the ship shooting down at least one and possibly two A4 aircraft during the last Exocet raid of the war on 30 May (See HMS *Andromeda* entry) as well as an Argentinian Lear Jet reconnaissance aircraft whilst anchored in San Carlos.'

Sea Dart being fired from HMS *Exeter* in San Carlos. (*Ron Goddard*)

'When we joined the fleet, the Flight spent hours delivering mail, stores and transferring personnel. During these transfers it was good to receive a cheery wave from our fellow fixed and rotary wing colleagues from the UK, who had done a fantastic job of getting the fleet down south.

'On one passenger transfer in thick fog, we managed to complete the task through the professionalism of Phil Holihead, who took control of the Lynx on his radar; and with the radar altimeter engaged at 20ft, so we could see the surface, drove us around an invisible fleet to the wake of an RFA, where, once we saw the stern, we were able to disengage the rad alt and climb up and safely deliver Lieutenant Rupert Nicholl and our other precious passengers.

'Whilst under air attack in San Carlos it was usual for the helicopters to "Scram", and we found a quiet bolt hole next to a 1,000lb bomb crater from where we could watch the air attacks in relative safety, while the Flight deck crew kept the enemy aircraft in their sights.'

Action stations with an ad hoc machine gun mounting. (*Ron Goddard*)

'Landing ashore was always a hazardous operation. Avoiding the indiscriminate Argentinian anti-personnel minefields was routine, but the Lynx tricycle undercarriage, while optimised for landing on a rolling pitching flight deck, was not exactly designed for landing on the Falklands. To protect the vulnerable underside of the helicopter, a "sloping ground" landing technique had to be carried out to prevent the narrow wheels breaking through the dry surface of the peat bogs and often a low hover with one wheel on a tuft of tussock grass was the only way to disembark passengers – a tricky manoeuvre at night!

'Being embarked on a ship has obvious advantages, and our captain was keen for us to "cross-pollinate" with the lads on land. We delivered a birthday cake to some colleagues ashore and a few bottles of whisky to our Ghurkha colleagues we met in Belize. Before setting off on most sorties, we would take a couple of sailors ashore to a neighbouring Rapier Battery and bring the soldiers on board for a shower, some clean socks, a change of underwear and a decent hot meal. Returning them at the end of the day was always amusing as the hospitality usually included a can or two of beer and perhaps even a tot!

'There were always lighter moments. On a quiet moment we took a photo of the Harrier which "slipped" off the temporary runway in San Carlos.'

The words "SOD OFF ARGIES" were subsequently removed by higher authorities. (*Ron Goddard*)

'I also recall, during a developing air raid in San Carlos, a small boat came rushing towards us full of press. They arrived at the Jacob's Ladder saying how relieved they were to get to the safety of a warship. One of the ratings told them not to be so f...... stupid as they had just arrived alongside one of the biggest targets. They soon left for the shore! We also took a photo of the "menacing" FPB that Chris Mervik and Nick Last used for Sea Skua target practice! (See HMS *Penelope* entry)

'Getting around the fleet and ashore, especially when returning from ESM barrier patrol, was tricky and sometimes dangerous. There were established corridors and speeds to be followed, but the knowledge that you were being illuminated by search and fire control radars by your own trigger-happy colleagues was at times unnerving. This problem was not just ours. One day, we were on routine patrol not far from the Falklands when we heard Bravo November, the only Chinook which had not gone down in *Atlantic Conveyor*, calling on the emergency frequency "guard". The aircraft had set off from the ships for San Carlos and was asking anyone listening for instructions on how to enter the heavily fortified anchorage. Charlie coaxed them to another frequency and after a "coded" conversation, BN continued safely to the islands and provide supreme support to the troops ashore.

'The Flight's war involved some exciting and demanding missions. They included:

'Exocet Decoy: Intelligence sources indicated that the Argentinian forces had cleverly taken some MM38 Exocet missiles from their ships, mounted them on a trailer and transported them to Port Stanley. The ships which regularly took up the NGS station at night to the south-west of Port Stanley were the target. It was decided to try to get the Argentinians to expend the remainder of the missiles using HMS *Exeter* as a decoy. The plan was for the ship to station outside of Exocet range to the south-east of Port Stanley with all her radars transmitting and the Lynx, fitted with a cube-shaped radar reflector, to fly within Exocet range (actually up to four miles from the coast) on the same bearing, at 500 feet, to try to entice the Argentinians to expend their missiles. This radar reflector was the ultimate in technology, it was three sides of a Rubik cube, about half a metre across, made of sheet metal and bolted to the starboard weapon station. It had the aerodynamic properties of a flying brick! So, while the rest of the aircraft were trying to reduce their radar cross section, we were deliberately making Trigger look like a surface ship. Orange Crop showed the aircraft being illuminated by various enemy radars, including

"Tanktrap", the Roland missile fire control radar, but sadly the trick failed to generate a missile launch.

'Recce of LSL route: The Flight was tasked for its first trip behind enemy lines to search for forces, radars and perhaps aircraft located on the islands to the south-east. So, with the ship under the safety of the Rapier umbrella and Charlie glued to the cabin mounted GPMG, we took off to investigate. We flew into Goose Green and saw the remains of the intense battle there and on to Lively Island where we landed and spoke to the Islanders and took their mail, then to Sea Lion Island where we had a game of cat and mouse with some types in army uniform who subsequently turned out to be our own Special Forces who had been landed the day before by *Avenger's* Lynx! Thence on around the south and up Falkland Sound to Fox Bay and back to "mother" in the dark, being careful to use the correct codes on entering Port San Carlos. Landing at night was always a challenge, and it was easy to misidentify "Mother"'.

Friendly faces at Sea Lion Island. (*Ron Goddard*)

The Falklands War 101

'Elimination of an Argentinian Observation Post: It was ascertained that an Argentinian OP had been established on Mount Rosalie to the north of Fitzroy and Bluff cove. This OP was responsible for calling in the air raid on *Sir Galahad* and *Sir Tristram*, resulting in the damage of both ships and the huge toll on the Scots Guards. The aircraft was fitted with a thermal imaging camera (operated by Special Forces in the rear cabin door!) and allowed a training sortie before the real thing. The training was a flight over Fanning Head, Dolphin Point, Many Branch Point and Port Howard to identify soldiers in the vicinity of where Captain Hamilton and his team had been ambushed. The actual sortie was hairy to say the least, we collected the SF from HMS *Intrepid*, and after some pretty interesting flying and being conned verbally from the back, the OP was finally identified. Apparently, the SAS subsequently sent in a land team to eliminate it. After the sortie, the Lynx landed to drop off the SAS on what we thought was HMS *Intrepid*, but was in fact HMS *Fearless*! As we were shutting down, we heard the voice of Eddie Featherstone, the ship's aviation officer, booming out, "what is that Lynx doing on my flight deck?" A hurried start and take-off ensued and we landed on the correct ship. I don't think Eddie really knows the identity of the "intruder" to this day!

'Simulated attack on Port Stanley: As a diversion to the major land assault on Port Stanley, *Exeter* and *Minerva* Flights were tasked, on 11 June, to simulate a night-time attack on Port Stanley. We took off from our respective ships in San Carlos and went north-east around the Falklands. The plan was for us to load up with Chaff "H" and to chatter on a series of different radio frequencies, while dropping the chaff to simulate a helicopter force approaching from the north-east. With one eye on the instruments, the other on Orange Crop, we made our approach and were soon illuminated by search radars, so we dropped altitude to get below the radar beam and continued until detected again, this time by Roland fire control radars. Eventually, we got too close for comfort at an altitude of 40ft and both Flights decided to call it a day before returning.

'We were also tasked, on one dark night, to approach Stanley and create a diversion, which we subsequently learned was tied in with one of the Operation Black Buck raids – the Vulcan raid on one of the Argentinian radar sites.

'Search and Rescue: The Lynx is not optimised for search and rescue missions, especially at night, and when loaded with two Sea Skua missiles. On 30 May we were tasked, as usual, up threat some 60–100 miles east of the task force when we heard Flight Lieutenant Jerry Pook (who went on to write a book about the Harrier in the Falklands) calmly telling the ship that he had been hit and was losing fuel. Looking up, Charlie and I saw the vapour trail and Charlie told him we were below and would stand by to assist. Shortly after, we heard the Mayday call, and some seconds later saw the huge splash of the Harrier ditching a few hundred yards away from us, then – silence. We waited and thought the worst – that the pilot had gone down with the Harrier – but a few minutes later we picked up the Search and Rescue Beacon (SARBE) transmission. Switching on the Violet Picture UHF radio homing equipment we followed the transmission but could not get a bearing, until I looked up and saw Jerry dangling in his parachute hundreds of feet above us and floating down towards the sea. Unable to pick him up from the water because of the Sea Skua missiles on the starboard weapon station, which prevented us from using the winch, we watched while a Sea King plucked him from the cold water. He had been immersed for less than ten minutes. On another occasion we were also tasked to try to recover Flight Lieutenant Ian Mortimer, who had been shot down over Stanley by a Roland missile. Being late at night with no hover capability it was a tough task, but despite flying as close as we could to Stanley we failed to locate his SARBE. He was subsequently picked up by a Sea King from 820 Squadron after ten hours in the water.

'No Lynx Flight article would be complete without mentioning the Flight maintainers. They were a fantastic bunch led ably by Derek Hiscox. They worked tirelessly to keep the aircraft serviceable, spent hours at Alert and worried for our safe return. Some innovative engineering kept the aircraft serviceable, which included an overnight engine change on the flight deck while the ship was darkened, the fitting of a piece of brass piano hinge to the starboard engine nacelle, and hours swapping printed circuit boards to try to keep the avionics working. They conducted hundreds of HDS transfers, refuelled visiting helicopters and provided the air defence for the stern of the ship. Above all, they were the ones put in danger when an incoming Exocet attack developed, as the tactic by the ship was to fire decoys and turn the stern towards the incoming raid! Trigger flew nearly ninety hours in May and Charlie himself clocked up over fifty hours in June.

'Almost forty-three years to the day after her predecessor entered Port Stanley after the Battle of the River Plate, HMS *Exeter* sailed into the same port. In the cemetery in Port Stanley are buried victims of the battle. The ship paraded a guard of honour which marched through Port Stanley. Trigger flew ashore with the some members of the ship's company and landed in a dense snowstorm at Stanley airport. Then the unthinkable happened, and a primary hydraulic failure due to a burst pipe forced the aircraft to be grounded. Frantic calls to the ship revealed no spare was held on board, nor was there another in the vicinity. The captain made his views clear that the ship was about to sail back to the UK and no matter what happened, the Lynx was to be on-board. Some frantic searching found a similar pipe in the ejection seat system in a damaged Aermacchi 116 and miraculously the threads matched, so the pipe was installed, the system was checked for leaks, and subjected to a test hover. In a short while, the aircraft was back on-board. The SMR was not wild about this piece of "creative engineering", but it was what war was all about. We gave him peace of mind with a signal to FOF3 (our command authority) saying that we intended to continue flying with the replacement until another became available (which was on final arrival several weeks later in the UK).'

The donor aircraft.
(*Ron Goddard*)

The pipe.
(*Ron Goddard*)

A happy team.
(*Ron Goddard*)

'After the war, *Exeter* returned to the UK in company with HMS *Cardiff* and HMS *Yarmouth*, arriving in Portsmouth to the inevitable "heroes" welcome!

'On 12 October 1982, HMS *Exeter* Flight was honoured to lead the helicopter part of the historic Falklands Victory Parade flypast over Mansion House, which was conducted under the watchful eye of members of the Royal Family, the Prime Minister and broadcast around the world. The seventeen aircraft flypast included Lynx from 815 Squadron, Wasps from 829, HMS *Antrim's* legendary Wessex Mk 3, Wessex Mk 5 from 845 Squadron, Sea Kings from 846, 826, and 706 Squadrons, Gazelles from RM Brigade Air Squadron, Scouts from the AAC and Chinooks from 18 Squadron RAF. The Operations Order was comprehensively written by Captain Jim Flindell with details of the various VIC formations, routes and communications. The rehearsal, on 6 October, went without a hitch, with Charlie Devine leading us all faultlessly on time and on place (without GPS!) over Central London. The actual flypast was a bit of an anticlimax, but generated the following signal from FONAC: "Falklands formation flypast over City of London was most impressive. Thank you and well done all concerned".

'In 1983, HMS *Exeter* returned again to the Falklands for a further patrol during which we enjoyed some exhilarating flying with our new P2, Sub Lieutenant Derek Batty. We undertook to take photos of nearly every "downed" aircraft site on the Falklands, many of which were reproduced in the book *Falklands – The Air War*, which is one of the authoritative books on all the aviation aspects of the conflict. During this second deployment Charlie Devine clocked up over 1,000 hours flying in the Lynx, most of them in Trigger.'

HMS *Cardiff*

Flight Commander – Lieutenant Chris Clayton
Flight Observer – Lieutenant P. Hullett

Aircraft – XZ 254, XZ 721, XZ 233

Cardiff was originally bound for the Gulf and Armilla patrol when the war started. She departed Mombasa on 20 April for Gibraltar and arrived at Gibraltar on 7 May. On 12 May she sailed and joined the Bristol Group heading south. At Ascension, spare parts for the aircraft were eventually received, which had caused it to be unserviceable for some considerable time until then.

The day after joining the Task Force, the Flight transferred to HMS *Brilliant* and swapped XZ 254 for XZ 721 as the original aircraft was not Sea Skua capable. They spent thirty-six hours on board *Brilliant* getting briefings on Skua operations. They then returned to *Cardiff*, retaining XZ 721 until 30 May when they got their old aircraft back. Tasking was generally ESM barrier work or HDS around the fleet. However, on 5 June, they were able to swap XZ 254 with *Argonaut's* Sea Skua capable aircraft XZ 233, as *Argonaut* was returning to the UK for repairs post being bombed. (See entry for *Argonaut*.) The aircraft had a few problems, not the least that the Sea Skua electronics were unserviceable, as were the two missiles supplied with the aircraft. However, some frantic work soon repaired the system. That evening, the aircraft was tasked with a sortie into the Amphibious Operating Area (AOA) when the main gearbox started leaking oil and an emergency landing on HMS *Arrow* had to be carried out, this was not helped by various friendly fire control radars locking onto them as they made their approach. The aircraft was soon repaired and retuned to *Cardiff*.

On 13 June, the Flight encountered quite a different problem. The ship had relieved *Exeter* as the Anti-Air Warfare Coordinator and the aircraft had been tasked with a surface search in the area fifty miles south of Falkland Sound. They were on the way back when they were caught by surprise. The first warning the aircrew had was a ripping noise and red streaks flying past the cockpit. A quick check inside the cockpit showed nothing wrong, when the shape of an Argentinian Dagger jet was seen turning towards them. Almost immediately another Dagger shot past to starboard, having just missed the Lynx on a strafing run from behind. Chris Clayton flung the aircraft to port and dived for the sea as the first Dagger turned towards them from dead ahead. Chris kept the turn going to keep the Dagger in sight and deny him a firing solution. However, the Dagger eventually fired whilst still turning and missed by over 100 yards. The second jet now attempted an attack. It was on their starboard side flying straight

106   The Royal Navy Lynx

towards them. Once again the Lynx turned towards the attacker and accelerated. The aircraft were only a hundred yards apart when the Dagger broke off and climbed away. The Lynx crew didn't see it fire and its rounds may have passed overhead. At this point the Daggers broke off and headed for home, probably because they were low on fuel and out of ammunition.

The story of this encounter soon got around the fleet and all the other Lynx crews were full of admiration for a brilliant piece of flying. Having a highly manoeuvrable aircraft probably helped just as little as well.

Despite their scare they were soon airborne again doing a recce of enemy positions for a Special Forces night insertion for which they then provided SAR cover. The next day the Argentinians surrendered and the aircraft took the CO of 40 Commando Brigade to Port Howard to accept the surrender of over 1000 armed enemy troops, which thankfully went smoothly.

On 22 June, XZ 233 was once again swapped with *Brilliant* flight's XZ 721 and the ship remained in San Carlos until relieved by *Exeter* on 30 June. On 7 July, she was relieved on station by HMS *Birmingham* and sailed home.

Author's note: It became a tradition that when ships left the Task Force they would steam past those staying behind to say farewell. The remaining ships would show their 'appreciation' by spraying the leaver with fire hoses and throwing things such as potatoes. On the occasion of *Cardiff's* departure, the Lynx also conducted a very exciting flypast that most would say exceeded the aircraft's cleared flight envelope by three hundred and sixty degrees or so. Presumably, after the encounter with the two Daggers, this was considered quite a straightforward manoeuvre!

Chris Clayton was awarded a Mention in Despatches for his efforts.

HMS *Minerva*

Flight Commander – Lieutenant Commander Graeme 'Jock' Moodie
Flight Pilot – Lieutenant Steve O'Collard
SMR – CPO Des Poulter, Crewman – LS 'Ches' Chesters

Aircraft – XZ 698, nickname 'Ollie' (HMS *Minerva's* badge was an owl.)

Ollie returning home. (*S. O'Collard*)

By Steve O'Collard:

'Where the **** did that come from?' 3 June 1982.

'"Today's mission: go and do a visual recce of the beaches to the east of Stanley, along from Cape Pembroke, looking for an Exocet launcher." Well, as random missions go, that was right up there. There was indeed a launcher, although possibly not there at the time, because HMS *Glamorgan* was hit by an Exocet on 12 June while on the gun line south-east of this area.

108   The Royal Navy Lynx

'To put the day in context, HMS *Minerva* had arrived in the Total Exclusion Zone on 26 May (five days after the landings and the day after *Atlantic Conveyor* was sunk) and had spent a few days operating with the Carrier Battle Group, before escorting a convoy into San Carlos overnight on 30 May (two days after the battle of Goose Green) to relieve HMS *Argonaut* as the air defence frigate. HMS *Argonaut* still had an unexploded bomb in her Seacat magazine and was missing her air defence radar after an air attack on 21 May. Our first mission once there was to locate (we can do that) and stop (not sure how) the *Bahia Paraiso* – the Argentine hospital ship – so we could then return with an interpreter. In the event, they were cooperative and went to flying stations without hesitation. For much of the rest of our time in the area, we were employed on searches using our Orange Crop equipment to look out for incoming enemy aircraft, but they always avoided us.

'We briefed and set off in the dark and in cloud (I see I logged most of the flying as "on instruments") down Falkland Sound, then east past Goose Green and Darwin, along Choiseul Sound and up towards Cape Pembroke. When we arrived the weather was still poor and we couldn't see much even from a few hundred feet above the sea. We certainly couldn't see the coast from just a few miles off. We were watching the ESM equipment closely and could see a few Argentine radars operating. I came back to slow speed and headed towards the coast, just south of Cape Pembroke, watching a fire control radar scanning on the ESM directly ahead of us. The radar then locked on, which produces a very distinctive signal and certainly got our attention.

'I said to Jock: "Oh, he's trying to tell us to bugger off, I suppose we should play the game", turned left through about 140 degrees (to give an opening bearing to the radar, and also to put us on track homewards) and increased speed. After some seconds (possibly around ten, but I wasn't counting and neither of us was in any way concerned), I turned reasonably hard left to give a crossing bearing, thinking to make the fire controller have to work harder. A few seconds after I started the turn, both of us heard and felt a hefty shockwave, which disturbed the aircraft. I looked right, to see a long white missile with four exhaust ports (yes it was that close) just passing abeam heading in the same direction as us. "I guess we'll go home then," I said.

'We set off to retrace our route back to the ship and the fire control radar gave up. After an uneventful flight back to San Carlos and a quick debrief with the captain and PWO and the rest of the Flight, the next thing I did was go to the Wardroom and grab the copy of *Janes Missiles*. I knew it wasn't a Tigercat (HMS

The Falklands War   109

Minerva was fitted with the marine equivalent, the Seacat, so I knew what they looked like). Long, white, with four exhaust ports – it was a Roland II.

'That was the sum total of HMS *Minerva* Flight's "excitement" for the rest of hostilities. We escorted a convoy back out to the Battle Group overnight on 4 June, coming back in on 8 June and remaining in San Carlos until after the end of hostilities on 14 June.

'As a postscript, the following week the ship moved to anchor off Stanley and some of the ship's officers went ashore for a "wander about". They reappeared having located the Roland launcher still in about the same position it must have been when it fired at us.'

HMS *Andromeda*

Flight Commander – Lieutenant Commander Bob Mckellar.
Flight Pilot – Lieutenant Larry Jeram-Croft

SMR – CPO 'Mitch' Mitchell, CPO Tug Wilson, PO 'Spindle' Spindlove, PO Ray McNeil, LAEM 'Danny' Daniels, AEM Viv Potter, AEM 'Stuts' Stuttle.

Aircraft – XZ 722, nickname 'ARFA'.

'ARFA' on deck alert during the war, with two Sea Skua and the Exocet I band jammer on the port side. (*Viv Potter*)

By the author:

Some years ago I dug out my logbook and used my Weblog to post my Falkland's experiences as they happened. Below is an extract:

'HMS *Andromeda* returned to the UK having been in Baltimore when the war broke out. We'd been deployed on our own on the AUTEC ranges in the

The Falklands War   111

Bahamas since early January, so it wasn't really surprising, the ship would need some serious TLC before another major deployment.

'Once back in UK we disembarked to our parent Air Station at Yeovilton while the ship undertook maintenance. We managed a few days leave, but once the weekend was over Bob and I got stuck into various briefings and issues. One that caught us completely by surprise was when we were called to a meeting and handed a strange black box.

'Amongst many of the new systems in *Andromeda* was STWS 2 (Ships Torpedo Weapon System No 2). Homing anti-submarine torpedoes had been around for years and up until then the American made Mark 46 was the device in service. It was pretty old and submariners used to laugh at us about it, as it was easily evaded. They stopped laughing when the Stingray came into service. A far more capable British weapon, it was designed to take out even the most modern of Soviet subs. What's more it actually worked! The STWS system was designed to allow surface ships to launch the torpedo, although the weapons were also carried by most helicopters. STWS 2 was the first version to fire Stingrays. Because of this the ship had magazines and equipment to store the weapon. It was decided that *Andromeda* would take five 'warshot' rounds down south with us. The weapon was not really in operational service at this time, so this was a bit risky, but we were terrified of the submarine threat. The Argies had two German conventional submarines that represented a real problem for us. In fact they never got them working, but we didn't know that at the time and the threat was real. Apparently, quite a large number of whales were torpedoed during the war.

'So the aircraft was to be made Stingray capable as well, hence the briefing. We were literally handed a Stingray pre-setter box and told how to use it, in all of about forty-five minutes. A pre-setter is the control box for the weapon, which in this case was a direct fit and replacement for the existing Mark 46 box. However, the knobs and switches on it were quite different. I can't remember the detail except for one thing – "Don't launch it on the shallow setting if *QE2* is around as it could take her out!" No worries then.

'This was the start of an amazing few days and just the first of several innovations that were going to make our life quite interesting, even before we sailed south.

'The next day, we received another surprising brief. We were to fly ARFA down to the Naval Air Station at Lee-on-Solent and have an emergency piece of kit fitted.

'The Exocet missile was causing serious concerns. Not only was it fitted to many of our ships, including *Andromeda*, but the Argies also had it. What was worse was that they had at least five of the longer range air launched AM39 variants. The weapon's seeker head was very clever, but someone had come up with an idea to turn that cleverness around. One way to defeat a missile's radar is to jam the signal. However, with Exocet, if you tried that it simply said, "thank you very much you must be my target" and homed in on the jamming source. If the jamming source was six hundred feet up in the sky, the missile could do nothing about it as it flew at a pre-set skim height and couldn't climb. So we should be able to pull it away from any surface targets and get it to come for us – we would be safe (wouldn't we?). Great in theory, but would it work? We would start to find out the next day.

'We set off that morning to the airfield at Lee. We were to report to the NATIU (Naval Aircraft Trials Installation Unit) to start work on the jammer. The forecast was not good and the airfield at Lee no longer had any radars to control aircraft in poor visibility. I should know, I flew the last Ground Controlled Approach to the airfield in a Sea King the previous year. The closer we got, the worse the low-level fog became. By the time we were approaching the Solent, there was about four hundred feet of low cloud/fog shrouding the whole area. We weren't going to let that stop us getting in and in the first of quite a few breaches of the "rules" over the months to come, we descended into the gloop with Bob ensuring the area of the Solent was clear using our own radar. The rules of instrument flying state you have to be "clear of cloud and in sight of the surface". Well at thirty feet on the radar altimeter that's exactly what we were. I could see the sea and we weren't in cloud (it was fog!). Using a combination of radar and me recognising certain buoys marking the various channels in the Solent (from my yacht racing days), we 'grobbled' our way in, i.e. slowly and carefully. The airfield is right by the beach and we saw it and the perimeter fence in good time, if you count seeing them in just enough time to avoid flying in to them. We soon landed at the NATIU site.

'The NATIU guys and Flight team worked miracles that day and by mid-afternoon the back of the aircraft was full of electronics and a funny aerial thingy was hanging off the port weapon station. Basically, the system consisted of a jammer taken out of a Canberra bomber and shoehorned into a Lynx. The biggest worry was that the transmit and receive aerials were mounted next to each other, whereas on the bomber they were on either wing. That afternoon we got airborne and turned it on. It all seemed to work. Mounted on a building at the Admiralty Surface Weapon Establishment on the Portsdown hills was an Exocet head. We flew the aircraft towards it and were able to pick up the radar on our Orange Crop ESM equipment. The problem was getting the exact frequency for the jammer. Mounted on the dashboard ahead of Bob was an old fashioned dial which swung around as the receiver swept the frequency band. When it intercepted the frequency of the missile head, a chirping noise could he heard over the intercom and Bob could mark that point on the dial with a chinagraph pencil. He could then turn on the jammer and tune it to the same frequency on the dial by aligning the needle with the dot. Yeah right! In a vibrating helicopter, on a dial needle that moved quite fast, with an old fashioned grease pencil. It worked, sort of, but it was clear to us that it was a bodge too far.

'We were despatched back to Yeovilton that night while the boffins at NATIU thought up more cunning plans. That evening I arrived home late, just as the nine o'clock news came on. The look of shock and tears streaming down my wife's face were a surprise to say the least.

'"HMS *Sheffield* has just been sunk", she told me. "They weren't sure whether it was a torpedo, but now they're saying it was probably some sort of missile."

'What we were going to try over the next few days had suddenly taken on a frightening importance.

'When we got to NATIU the next day, the engineers ripped out the dashboard dial and fitted a very strange device on the floor between Bob's legs. Quite simply it was a "Spectrum Analyser" which you will find on the benches of many laboratories and workshops. This one came overnight from Holland as it was the best specification. Its delivery was a story in its own right. Its job was to analyse the receiver signal and give us an exact picture of it on its small display screen. Ergonomics and safety were clearly not that important, as there were several sharp corners all around Bob's nether regions. He asked me to be gentle when landing.

'As soon as we were airborne on the test flight, it became apparent that it was going to do its job. Although the switches were small and it took several minutes to warm up, once operating, it did what it said on the tin. We could see a nice clear spike which was the missile seeker radar and when we turned on the transmitter we could see both signals and could easily tune one on top of the other.

'Time to try it out for real. To do this we needed a missile range and the one we would use was the one at Aberporth off the Welsh coast. There were already Lynx facilities there as an aircraft was based there doing Sea Skua missile trials.

114   The Royal Navy Lynx

So, at the end of the day we headed off to Aberporth where we would operate for the next two days.

'The next day I learnt a great deal about Exocet. We flew three times with the jammer. The first two trips were to check the system out and get the range procedures sorted for a live firing from *Andromeda* later that afternoon.

'One thing we had been told was that, if it came to it, we could jam two missiles at the same time. This was because once locked on to a jamming source the Exocet would wait two seconds before going back into its own search if the jamming source stopped. We could therefore switch between two missiles and keep them both deceived.

'On the last sortie of the day, we were at six hundred feet hovering off to one side of a barge covered in radar reflectors to make it look like a frigate to any unsuspecting sea skimming missile. The countdown began. *Andromeda* fired her missile. We picked it up on Orange Crop and shortly afterwards on the Spectrum Analyser. Bob turned on the jammer and tuned the transmit spike on top of the biggest signal. And that was the problem, there seemed to be several other spikes and some were quite big. Knowing that we could tune off quickly and not lose the missile we did so and confirmed we were on the biggest signal.

'The missile flew directly over the target.

'Bugger!

'That evening, when we got despondently back to the range offices, the staff seemed surprisingly bullish, especially when we explained what we had done with the jammer. Apparently, the missile turned towards us as soon as we started jamming, but turned back immediately we tuned off, even though it had only been for less than a second. So much for the "two second" idea.

'The next day we got airborne again but had to wait a while for *Andromeda* to clear the range. A couple of bolshie welsh fishing boats didn't want to get out of the way and literally had to be persuaded at the point of a gun. Wartime byelaws were in place.

'We eventually got the go ahead and took up the hover position off to one side of the barge. The countdown started and I'm pretty sure I saw a plume of smoke on the horizon. Then nothing happened until the Orange Crop lit up with the signal from the Exocet radar. Bob was totally focused on the analyser and very soon picked up the radar as well. He turned on the jammer and tuned it to the same frequency and then left it well alone. Can you fly a helicopter with all your fingers and toes crossed? I did. Suddenly, I could see the white pencil shape of the missile ahead of us with a spit of yellow flame coming from the back. Within seconds it had flown past – this time directly below us and nowhere near its target.

'Deep joy all around. I decided a celebratory beat up of the little airfield was in order. We then landed for the debrief. I should mention that for all these flights we had a couple of passengers in the back, one was a commander from C in C Fleet, and as soon as he had recovered from my unplanned aerobatics he was apparently straight on the phone to No 10 Downing Street, so important were these trials considered.

'So, I can honestly claim to be the only pilot in the world who has deliberately seduced a surface-to-surface missile in flight and made it home on my own aircraft rather than its intended target. OK, it couldn't climb at us and we were probably quite safe, but never let the truth spoil a good story. Mind you, some of the civilian range staff objected to the trial, saying it didn't meet safety guidelines. They were ignored.

'I managed a telephone call home to say goodbye to my family and that was it. Time to go to war. That afternoon we embarked in *Andromeda* and headed south in company with other ships as the "second wave". By the time we arrived we were more like replacements than augmentations.

'The trip down was busy as we got the ship ready and flew every sort of sortie we could think of. In particular we looked hard at how to actually use the jammer. It was going to have to be reactive and we made some preparations to allow us to get off the deck quickly – they would come in rather handy sometime later.

'About midnight on the day before we arrived inside the Total Exclusion Zone I was in my normal aircrew position of horizontal in my pit, snoring away, when there was a knock on my door. Bob stuck his head around and told me to, "get dressed, we're flying."

'Someone had a radar contact out to the east and no one knew who it was. We were briefed to load up with 4.5 inch flares and go and find out. To say I was apprehensive about this is a gross understatement. Dropping flares at 1500 feet on a potential enemy is not the most sensible thing to do. The tactic had been developed with the Wasp and called a DIDTAC which we all reckoned stood for "Death In The Dark". Still it was time to earn all that flying pay, so off we went. It didn't help that the weather was looking pretty foul with low cloud and a big Atlantic swell.

'Climbing up into the gloop we soon found the contact and proceeded to get upwind. Orange Crop was silent, which was good. Maybe they didn't know we were there – they soon would. The idea was to drop the flares upwind of the target and then loop round and descend, so that hopefully the silhouette of the ship could be seen against the light of the flares. We used three flares and then turned and descended. I got down to one hundred feet and saw exactly nothing except the distant loom of the flares somewhere in the gloop. Shit! So up we climbed to use the other three. If he was an enemy, he certainly knew we were there now. This time we kept the circuit tighter and I continued down until the radar altimeter was well below fifty feet and we saw her. A black silhouette with a red flashing light. My first thought was that they were shooting at us with tracer, but we immediately recognised the shape of RFA *Appleleaf*, a British replenishment ship. The light was a red tinted Aldis lamp. I used to be pretty good at reading Morse code, but not there and then. I was busy doing other things like trying not to fly into the sea.

'So, all's well and back to *Andromeda*. We got on the glideslope, but with no sign of the light of the Glide Path Indicator. The ship was controlling us and with my instrument rating I was allowed to descend to 125 feet. At that height I could see absolutely nothing and had to overshoot. We tried again with Bob monitoring the approach on our own radar. I asked for the lights to be turned up to max brightness. Still nothing, even though I go way below my minimum height. At this point the controller in HMS *Bristol* chips in. He has clearly been watching what's going on and gives us more vectors. Suddenly, I saw the lights very close and far too bright. Calling for them to be turned down, we plonked down on the deck in very thick fog. The problem with dark nights is that you can't see when the fog rolls in. Had we known, we would have gone into full Poor Visibility Approach mode and done things very differently. The debrief was very interesting for all sorts of reasons! But thank God for the Lynx. There's not another helicopter in the world I would have wanted to be caught out in conditions like that with.

'The next day was our first day with the fleet. After all the hassle and excitement of the trip down we finally get airborne to do a real job. "ESM AEW" was a task all the Orange Crop fitted Lynx were to conduct and we did our share.

'Have you any idea how boring, stooging around at slow speed in a helicopter can be? It doesn't take long before even the most wound up, motivated, steely eyed aviator starts to settle down. However, there was one thing in our favour. The whole fleet was trying to be stealthy and radar silence was universal, so if anything "cropped" up we would hear it instantly. The system gave us a visual indication of frequency, bearing and other parameters on the display, but also an audio sound as well. Every now and then someone briefly transmitted. Often it was one of the Sea Kings on anti-submarine patrol. Heart rate seems to be directly proportional to audio input.

'So, two hours of boredom interspersed with a little excitement. We detected nothing – that day.

'Initially, our general employment was a combination of "Postman", which meant taking mail and packages around the fleet, although with a cabin full of electronics we were more limited than most of the other Lynx and these AEW sorties.

'Two days later things got even more interesting and I can safely say that we broke at least two world records in the process.

'To set the scene – a quick explanation about the Sea Dart system. The missile was an anti-aircraft area defence weapon. It was fitted to all the Type 42s, *Bristol* and *Invincible*. It worked by following a fire control radar (909) and was generally quite successful. This would be a good and bad thing as far as this day goes.

'Once again we were at 6000 feet, way up ahead of the main force. Behind us in a line were three ships. *Andromeda* was to the north, *Exeter* in the middle and *Avenger* to the south. I can remember cruising along eating Peanut Treats and arguing with Bob about the shapes of various clouds. His mind always came up with more obscene ideas than mine, but it kept us laughing and passed the time. On several occasions, a Sea King turned on his radar and gave us palpitations, but all seemed routine.

'Suddenly, with no warning, all hell broke loose. The Orange Crop started beeping with a strange radar which was clearly "Handbrake". We immediately called the controller in *Hermes* and gave the bearing which was to the south of us. At the same time one of the ships also called the radar and confirmed our alert. The Task Force went to action stations at the code word "Zippo One" and started firing chaff and doing everything they could to defend against Exocet attack.

'We had done our job. There was nothing else we could do as we were far too far away to deploy the jammer. We had already decided what to do next – run away! We knew it was possible that the Argies would have escorts for the Etendards and that we could get caught up with them. The only thing an unarmed helicopter could do was hide. I accelerated up to our max speed of 150 knots and headed for a nice big fat cumulus cloud back towards the force. We never got there. Suddenly, a continuous tone screamed out from the Orange Crop. Bob immediately recognised it as a 909 radar lock on. He looked over his left shoulder and uttered those immortal words, "shit they're firing at us." I banked the aircraft hard left and looked. I actually saw the smoke trail of at least one Sea Dart coming up at us. I still have the odd nightmare about it. I knew we were dead. To this day I have no idea if what I did next saved our lives, but in an instinctive reaction, I pushed the cyclic stick fully forward. We dived, and thank God I was in a Lynx, because no other helicopter in the world could have taken the abuse. We pulled out at about two thousand feet, amazed we were still in one piece, just in time to see a long streak of flame on the horizon. I have no idea how fast we went, but I'm certain that I broke the world speed record for a helicopter by some significant margin. Just a little shaken, we realised that it had all suddenly gone quiet on the radio. To the north I could see a ship with smoke pouring out of it and flashes of something. We gingerly went to investigate. It was *Exeter* and it was only smoke from her funnels and the sun glinting on her radars. Slowly, everyone checked in and it was clear no one had been hit. We went down to *Avenger* where a Wessex V had had the presence of mind to hide behind her bulk and then we saw some dye in the water. On investigation we saw the remains of an aircraft and an ejection seat with a body still in it, sinking. The dye was from the survival kit in the seat.

'Later we got the full story. The Etendards had come in from the south, fired one missile and turned for home. It was the last AM 39 in their inventory. They were accompanied by four A4s. Two were then shot down by *Exeter*. The Sea Darts we had got in the way of were in fact aimed at them and the wreckage in the water was the result of one of them. *Avenger* claimed to have shot down one Exocet with her 4.5 inch gun. It seems petty unlikely and maybe they saw the flames of the crashing A4s as I suspect we did. However, one Exocet definitely locked on to *Andromeda*. They had the "Eyewater" radar of the missile on the ship's ESM and were tracking it with the Sea Wolf system. What's more, some of the crew on *Exeter* actually saw it crossing their stern and heading for *Andromeda*. On board, everyone had hit the deck and were praying that our Sea Wolf point defence system would do its job when the missile ran out of fuel and fell into the water just outside Sea Wolf engagement range. Relief was tempered by annoyance that we hadn't proved the system against an Exocet for real. So when we got back there was bugger all sympathy for us! And rightly so I guess. Oh, and in *Exeter* they knew all about us and that we were in the way of their firing solution on the A4s, but quite rightly they fired anyway.

'Some years after the war, I heard that the two surviving A4 pilots claimed to have bombed HMS *Invincible*. There is a plethora of evidence that they actually bombed *Avenger* and missed, but irrespective of all the smoke and mirrors that time throws up, I can absolutely say that I saw a streak of flame in the sky ahead of me as I pulled out of my dive and in the same position a few minutes later

The Falklands War 119

I saw the remains of a downed A4 sinking in the water. This was within two miles of *Avenger*. This provides an absolute datum. The four A4s were together, and having lost two of them to one ship's Sea Darts, the remaining two would have to have flown another twenty miles to reach *Invincible*, which even at five hundred miles an hour, would have taken several minutes. In the main Task Force surrounding the two carriers were a number of warships. Each carrier always had a permanent "goalkeeper", normally a type 22 or *Andromeda*, because we had Sea Wolf. Then there was HMS *Bristol* with her Sea Dart, plus other Type 42's, and of course *Invincible* herself with her own Sea Dart. There were several Leanders and Type 21s with the less effective, but still capable Seacat, as well as at least one DLG. Most of these ships also had 4.5 inch guns as well as small arms. So these two A4s would have to have flown through a barrage of missiles, guns and small arms and bearing in mind that one Type 42 was able to shoot down two of them within minutes, what chance they would have got anyway near one of the carriers? Then they would have to have turned around and run the gauntlet back out. Oh, and there were just a few Sea Harriers around as well. In fact, the alert Harrier on *Invincible* was scrambled, but only got a fleeting glimpse of the retreating A4s miles out to the west, which would definitely not have been the case if they had overflown *Invincible*! They were clearly very brave pilots, but no one could have survived a trip into the Task Force for twenty miles and back out again however brave they were.

'So we got back on board for tea and no medals. Everyone was a little rattled, to the extent that that evening Bob and I broke our no drinking rule. After all, the Argies never attacked at night – did they? I can clearly remember watching the film *Jaws 2* in the wardroom and starting in on my second whiskey when the bloody actions station alarm went off, quickly followed by the command "Scramble the Lynx". We had agreed that the word "Scramble" meant get airborne as fast as possible, no checks, no paperwork, just get off the deck. We always left the aircraft in a very non-standard state for just this eventuality. As I ran down to the flight deck, they fired the chaff rockets on the deck above my head and I thought the world was ending there and then. Then, as I got to the aircraft, I tripped over a lashing and almost knocked myself out on the nose of one of my warshot Sea Skua missiles. However, I scrambled in and started making switches. I knew the No2 engine was a bit difficult to start and so put the engine control lever a bit further forward than normal to help it, before flashing around the cockpit to try and get other systems on line. Just as Bob climbed in, the flight staff started gesticulating wildly at the starboard engine. The normal maximum start up temperature was 720 degrees – it was past 950 and going up.

I retarded the lever back to its normal position. Apparently, the exhaust flames were quite spectacular. I looked at Bob.

'"Shit, I've burnt out the number two."

'"Well, is it still working?"

'I scanned the gauges. "It all looks OK, hang on," and I accelerated it to get the rotors up to full speed. I pushed the lever fully down in negative pitch and the engine responded normally.

'"It looks good Bob and anyway we've got two of the bloody things."

'He nodded and we launched. It was only when we got to two hundred feet and settled a little did we both realise we hadn't even strapped in. After all that, it turned out to be a false alarm. One of the ships officers told us later that it was less than three minutes from the alarm going off to us getting airborne, despite all our little mishaps – isn't adrenalin a wonderful motivator? And our second world record of the day.

'That night, as I tried to get to sleep, I remember thinking that we had come pretty close to not making it and nearly all the problems had been caused by our own side. Despite all we had put it through, the aircraft was back on deck and would be ready the next morning. What the hell was going to happen next? It wasn't a particularly encouraging thought.

'In fact the answer to that was more of the same. We flew every day, a combination of more AEW and load transfers. We helped retrieve a Special Forces team and their equipment from a Hercules drop and took them into San Carlos. HMS *Glamorgan* was hit by the last Exocet of the war fired from ashore and that night we broke yet another rule and took twenty-one underslung loads off her flight deck at night. Night load lifting was specifically banned. We proved it was just another silly rule and got on with it.

'The day after the surrender was a very interesting day that started off with us taking the captain across to the *Canberra* for a meeting and then us leading her into Port Stanley. We were the first British ship to get there.

'The first bit of fun was that the Argies had declared a minefield in the approaches to Stanley and although we were "fairly" sure we had a safe route in, someone had to go first – guess who? The photograph below was actually taken during this transit. We had gone to full action stations because of the mine risk and then realised on the flight deck that this would probably be the last time we would be at action stations for real and so ought to get some photographs. The fact that we should really have been looking over the side in case we saw something in the water seemed secondary. It sort of summed up our feelings at the time.

Grrrr! What we got up to when not flying – not looking for mines! (*Author*)

'We got in okay and anchored with *Canberra* in the outer roads. The reason for us being there was that *Canberra* already had some prisoners of war on board and was going into Stanley to take on more.

'The final part of the day was when we were tasked to go ashore and report to Government House for tasking. It was weird to land there. There were arms and explosives everywhere and there still seemed to be loads of Argie soldiers wandering around, although they were more likely the officers who had been given parole to keep order. Anyway, Bob went into the building and we were tasked to take a passenger cross country to San Carlos, which we duly did. The fun came on the way back as it was getting dark. The weather was closing in and heavy snow showers were setting in, forcing me down between the peaks of the mountains which had seen all the fighting recently. At one point I was in zero visibility, far too low, with nowhere to go in heavy snow and icing conditions. Silly sod! Luckily we broke out of the cloud and made it back. That would have been a good ending to the war – flying into the side of Mount Harriet.

'We stayed down south for quite some time after the surrender and then along with *Penelope* and *Avenger*, were the last ships of the war to get back. We really wanted to come alongside with the ship but had to fly back to Portland. Plymouth Hoe was packed as we entered the Sound. All three Lynx launched and flew past the ships and around the corner of the Hamoaze, past the dockyard where all the families were waiting on the dock. I swear to this day I could hear them cheering from inside the cockpit.

'The more you want something to happen the longer it often seems to take. We sailed for the Bahamas on 4 January, and apart from five days at home had been at sea continuously for the whole year. The ship had done 138 days at sea with no support – a record for a steam frigate. When we got back to Portland – three Lynx in formation, Fiona my wife, said she knew which one was us as we were so far away from the other two Lynx – I never particularly liked flying in close formation with another helicopter and was damned if I was going to make a mistake now. For months I had dreamt of the moment when the rotors would stop for the last time. Then finally it happened.'

'In all we flew 106 hours, twenty at night, and nine hours were in actual Instrument Flying Conditions. We did 165 deck landings and forty-one radar controlled approaches to the ship. On only one occasion did the aircraft become unserviceable when the No 2 engine oil pressure gauge failed. It was fixed within the hour. We are the only helicopter crew in the world who can claim that they

Penelope, *Avenger* and *Andromeda*'s Lynx (closest) landing on at Portland, the last Lynx to return. (*Chris Mervik*)

deliberately seduced a sea-skimming missile to home on them rather than the intended target, and I still claim the world helicopter speed record (vertical).'

Another perspective:

Although these are primarily accounts by aircrew it is also important to get a perspective from the men who maintained the aircraft in often dreadfully difficult conditions. Air Engineering Mechanic Viv Potter was the most junior member of Andromeda Flight. Here, he gives his account of joining his first front line unit and immediately heading to war:

'At sixteen, I had no idea in which direction my further education and career should go. All I had by means of interests (apart from the usual teenage suspects) was a love of anything mechanical. So, it was a chance passing of a Lynx helicopter displayed in a RN careers office window that spurred my interest.

'Six months later and after passing basic Royal Navy training, I found myself at the School of Aircraft Engineering at HMS *Daedalus*.

'Apart from learning "parrot fashion" the endless safety related lists of precautions and acronyms, we spent a great deal of time with seemingly ancient Whirlwind helicopters, practising mechanical repair procedures and to demonstrate our new skills under exam situations. On successful completion of this stage, I was absolutely delighted to have been drafted to RNAS Yeovilton to complete my training, working on the very modern looking Lynx helicopters of 702 Squadron.

'It was a revelation of new technology when compared with the Whirlwind. The rotor head was almost a sculpture of simplicity compared to the complex and cumbersome rotor heads seen previously.

'I completed Part 4 training and became qualified to maintain the Lynx and to sign for work undertaken in the aircraft logbook (MOD form 700).

'I remained at 702 Squadron for a further eighteen months, gaining valuable experience. I remember being super keen to get involved with the more intense repairs rather than the less exciting but necessary flight servicing and inspections based on flying hours or time. I often hovered around the AMCO (Aircraft Maintenance Control Office) waiting for a "downbird team" requirement to fly out to carry out repairs to an unserviceable Lynx. I recall one occasion where a Lynx had suffered an engine failure and had to make a precautionary landing to Portland. The AMCO was buzzing, I definitely wanted this gig! Within minutes, I was with a team flying down to Portland to replace the port engine. It certainly sharpened the focus knowing that you will be flying back in the repaired Lynx.

124   The Royal Navy Lynx

This was my first experience, of many occasions, being outside the comfort zone of Lynx HQ.

'I was notified in August 1981 that I would be joining 815 Squadron as the flights M3 (Air Engineering Mechanic) attached to HMS *Andromeda*. She was a recently refitted Batch 3 Leander class frigate equipped with Exocet and Sea Wolf missile systems.

'Leading up to joining the Flight I required more intensive and specific training. This ranged from a few weeks at the Lynx training cell at HMS *Daedalus*, ships and aircraft firefighting, weapon loading courses and various survival equipment maintenance courses. A particularly painful part of the training was to discover I suffered from seasickness whilst spending two weeks on the flat bottomed RFA *Engadine* in the Bay of Biscay, gaining experience of maintaining and operating a Lynx at sea. (I wasn't on my own.)

'This soon revealed the inherent difficulties with even the most basic routine tasks, like spreading and folding the rotor blades, or fitting a gust lock onto the tail rotor in a Force 8.

'On 2 April 1982, I joined 815 Squadron. This coincided with the Argentinean invasion of the Falkland Islands.

'There was a monumental level of activity at RNAS Yeovilton. The hard standings were dominated by Hercules and several commandeered Belfast heavy lift civilian aircraft to assist with the huge logistic operation of mobilising two Sea Harrier squadrons, three Commando squadrons and the distribution of the 815 Ship's Flights stores and equipment to Ascension Island.

'I joined Andromeda Flight. They had just returned from the States and were granted a few days leave before re-deploying south to join the Task Force.

'So, there I was – on my "Jack Jones", with just myself and Lynx helicopter XZ 722.

'Naval maintainers call their helicopters "cabs" and specifically, this one was named ARFA. (This turned out to be a derogatory name.)

'I was tasked with preparing and carrying out various service operations to "buy" a few extra flying hours by bringing forward service checks. I was also given free rein to paint the "cab" in war colours. The white call sign 472 and bold ROYAL NAVY letters had to be toned down to matt black. On reflection, I have no idea why this had to be done because you could hear a Lynx coming from miles away and radar doesn't discriminate colour when choosing its target. Anyway, it kept me busy, and dare I say it, it gave me an immense sense of pride and a belonging to the Flight already.

The Falklands War   125

'The Flight personnel returned from leave and we were to join HMS *Andromeda* alongside at Devonport dockyard. Our Lynx was to fly to Aberporth in Wales to conduct pioneering tests on the recently fitted and designed Exocet jamming radar.

'I was on the flight deck of HMS *Andromeda* as she fired an Exocet missile at our own helicopter to test the ability to seduce the missile away from its target – Larry Jeram Croft can tell you how that went.

'All I knew was that an Exocet launch was a phenomenal thing to watch and since leaving the breakwater in Plymouth, seasickness was NOT an option.

'We were to recover ARFA just off Aberporth. (It went well) This was my first ever experience of operating and maintaining a Lynx on a warship. The simplicity of having terra firma to operate from can never be overestimated.

'The Lynx recovered to the ship and for the first time I witnessed the immediate security the harpoon gave as it locked into the grid on the flight deck, as well as the ability to literally push the aircraft into the deck using negative pitch.

'As we stowed ARFA into the hangar, the ship changed it's heading to south and the compass direction remained constant for nearly three weeks.

'During our transit south, we conducted various training scenarios for any potential requirement further down the line.

'Being 18-years-old, I didn't have an arsenal of experience. Everything was completely new to me in the ship sense. The Flight's junior rates were billeted in the "stokers" mess. I quickly realised the competitive edge between the general service and the Fleet Air Arm.

'The Lynx Flight worked with the demand required. I'm sure the stokers mess didn't see us battling with the elements on the flight deck with every aspect of naval aviation thrown on a few people called WAFU's.

'As we left the spring of UK, we enjoyed the advancing warmth as we headed south.

'Beyond the comfortable training environment of a Somerset Naval Air Station we were required to be a rapid "sea going" loading team for the Sea Skua missiles and the Stingray torpedo. After a few practise loads we were as slick (if not as quick) as an F1 pit stop crew. Everyone knew their job. The concentration and pure will to ensure the operation ran as smoothly and as accurately as possible was tangible.

'At this point, I fully appreciated how much effort had gone into making the Lynx a viable weapon at sea. From the ingenious device attached to the nose wheel enabling safe movement to and from the hangar, to a dedicated aircraft controller in the ops room deep inside the ship.

126   The Royal Navy Lynx

'All of this "ship" stuff was still quite alien to me – if not incredibly exciting. I remember feeling overwhelmed by the intensity of completely new experiences. Bizarrely, the Lynx was extremely familiar and working on this particular airframe felt like home from home. However, a few of the usual annoyances of the Lynx prevailed.

'Who was responsible for inventing the tri wing screw? The tri wing had three slots in the head. Tightening screws was easy, but when undoing them, the blade of the driver just slipped out.

'When you're hanging off a lashed down stepladder on the back of a pitching flight deck, trying to remove the tail rotor gearbox fairing screws wasn't a joke. Especially when your focus is on the critical component that's hidden by the fairing, that finds itself shy behind the blooming tri wing screw.

'More immediately serious was being part of ARFA's deck landing crew. (We conquered the tri wings.) As we continued south and towards a war environment, the honing of our collective skills was ever more evident.

'The ship had to comply with operational lighting restrictions. Deck landing lights had to be switched off during the recovery of the Lynx. The Lynx often had a radar approach at night and on finals it relied on bright lights across the hangar as a horizon. Operational requirements meant that this was as dim as a "dim thing".

'Suddenly, out of the murk, the Lynx was battling awful weather and visibility. Myself and the flight crew waited with fire-fighting equipment on standby. The horizon bar lighting was switched on briefly to full dimness. The whole Flight crew watched as the Lynx struggled to match the seas unpredictable storm movement. The ship's movement and the Lynx stability made it look impossible to land, but in one tiny lull of sea movement Larry pulled the cyclic to the right and tempered the wind with loads of rudder. ARFA was on the deck and within a split second Larry was applying negative pitch and the harpoon was engaged. Lashings were applied immediately by us and within minutes ARFA's blades were folded and he was safely stowed in the hangar in time for us to carry out essential maintenance procedures.

'I found myself working most of the time with the Flight's M1 Petty Officer Ray McNeil. I felt so "green" and probably under prepared for the variances of operating as part of a very small team on a Lynx Flight, but Ray was a brilliant and patient mentor.

'As we entered the Total Exclusion Zone around the Falkland Islands things quickly began to get very real. We had to wear protective anti-flash gear, fireproof overalls and carry our respirator at all times, with the threat being the very likely attack from Argentinean aircraft.

'During this time the flying became more intense and often required us to man the flight deck whilst other helicopters delivered stores and equipment. Some helicopters required in-flight helicopter refuelling, or carrying out high line transfers of personnel from ASW Sea Kings, Commando Sea Kings, Wessex V's and III's, Wasps or other Lynx.

'The relative calm of performing maintenance operations on ARFA was, to me, a semblance of normality in an uncertain time of war.

'ARFA was incredibly reliable, despite its previous form. We only had a handful of "out of routine" servicing repairs to complete, one being a fault with the lateral hydraulic servo jack. I remember thinking how well designed the aircraft was with maintenance in mind, except for a few deviations, one example being the virtual impossible feat of securing the lower air intake fairings with a pip pin that required a blind fit with only feel as a guide (probably a French design input).

'There were countless routine maintenance operations carried out even with war time servicing hours extended. The excitement of those hours in *Andromeda's* hangar were very long, but quite unforgettable. The moments you remember are enabling a serviceable aircraft to conduct its role. One such being a call to action stations at night. ARFA was scrambled. Minutes after the Lynx was launched the flight deck was illuminated in an instant. The noise so intense that it felt like something was inbound. I threw myself onto the deck to see the whole ship illuminated with chaff rockets being launched all around me. The PWO calmly announced that the threat had dissipated. All I knew was that we had narrowly missed being hit by an Exocet missile earlier in the day and ARFA had launched without the MS5 (five seat liferaft normally stored in the cabin) that was right next to me, and was tangibly in reach for an abandon ship scenario.

'I think the next day we were worrying about tail rotor gearbox changes.

'We returned safe and triumphant from the Falklands and I spent the next five years every day with the Lynx in some form or another, and most of this time at the Aircraft Support Unit (NASU) at Yeovilton.

'XZ 722 found itself at NASU during 1983/4 and I had the privilege to continue with some deeper maintenance and modification programs with that airframe. Strengthening the cabin nomex honeycombed sections in the cabin roof and carrying out undercarriage sponson modifications were but a few.

'It seemed quite surreal that a line of "lame ducks", stripped to the core and balanced on jacks, were, just a few months before, THE Lynx force of Operation Corporate'.

HMS *Avenger*

Flight Commander – Lieutenant Morris Mc Bride
Flight Observer – Lieutenant Neil Sibbit
SMR – CPO AEA Underhill (Maintainers: Forsythe, Harris, Thompson)

Aircraft – XZ 249

The *Avenger* team in party mood, although Neil Sibbit (far left) denies all knowledge of the reason for the whisky bottle. (*Neil Sibbit*)

In March 1982, HMS *Avenger's* original Flight were embarked on HMS *Brilliant* for exercises and that is where they remained for the rest of the war. This meant that *Avenger*, who was undergoing maintenance at the time, had no aircraft. Consequently, a new Flight was formed at short notice and embarked on the 26 April for sea trials. During this period XZ 249 briefly returned to Yeovilton to be made Sea Skua capable. HMS *Avenger* then sailed on 10 May as part of the 'Bristol group'.

Aircraft tasking was similar to others, with ESM sorties interspersed with NGS for the ships gun (*Avenger* fired over 1000 rounds), surface search, troop insertions and more general delivery work. On 30 May, HMS *Avenger* was involved with the last Exocet raid of the war. One air launched Exocet was fired and four A4s conducted a close in attack. Two were shot down and the remaining two, unsuccessfully, bombed the ship. More details of this are in the accounts from HMS *Andromeda* and HMS *Ambuscade*. Unfortunately, *Avenger's* aircraft was unserviceable at this particular time.

Neil Sibbit recalls some of their experiences later in the war:

'We had a number of unserviceability's during the conflict, one of which I think was a sensor which put us out of action from 8–12 June. From my logbook we flew a post-engine change check test flight on 1 June, so assume we had some form of engine failure having also flown a test flight the previous day.

'On 13 to 14 June, we conducted what was to be our final spotting for NGS (and Exocet decoy) with others shelling targets around Fitzroy, Bluff Cove and Stanley, I recall it was like bonfire night with the sky lit by gunfire and illuminants as our forces made their final approaches to Stanley. Our position was just on the edge of the Roland missile system range and we occasionally had to take avoiding action as Orange Crop gave warnings of radar lock on. Unfortunately, prior to that we were on the same gun line as HMS *Glamorgan* when she was hit by a shore based Exocet, killing and injuring many of her ship's Flight and ship's company.

'On the night of the 14/15 June, we were due to conduct more shelling, but were tasked to patrol off Fox Bay. We flew that evening, I think for the first time with live Sea Skua to search, and if necessary, fire upon the *Bahia Buen Suceso*, an Argentine supply vessel which was thought to be fleeing the Falklands. We were unable to locate her at sea and *Avenger* then patrolled off the mouth of Fox Bay to try and confirm whether the ship was still in the bay. In the end, only by flying low and slow over the settlement with the landing light on, were we able to confirm the ship was aground close to the settlement. It was not until we turned to the ship that we heard of the surrender.

'The next morning we flew in to the settlement, with, I think, the gunnery officer, to collect the local garrison commander, an Argentine colonel. The Argentinian forces in Fox Bay had been unaware of the surrender when we overflew the settlement the previous night. The colonel appeared in full dress uniform complete with sword and pistol. We did remove any of these weapons, but popped him in the back of the Lynx and returned to the ship where Captain Hugo White received him and took the formal surrender.

'I do not have vivid memories of the day, except that the villagers were extremely pleased to see us and we flew several sorties to and from the ship with supplies – in particular fresh bread. Our landing party numbered eighteen, to disarm and organise 989 Argentine soldiers! The Argentine officers, though subdued, were unkind to their conscripts and on occasion had to be restrained from kicking and hitting them as *Avenger's* team went through the searches. The conscripts were living in awful conditions, some in the settlement chicken hutches and many were just kids. They seemed relieved it was all over. One of our tasks was to recover items that had been looted from the settlement, generally small things like radios, but again the locals were most grateful.'

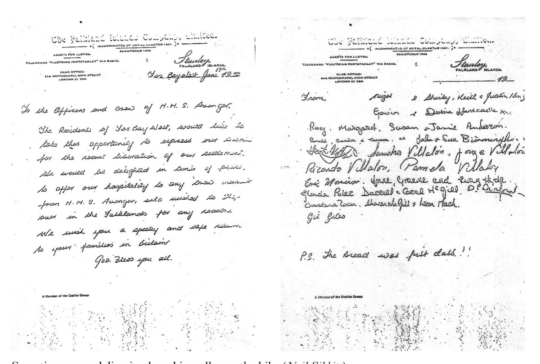

Sometimes even delivering bread is really worthwhile. (*Neil Sibbitt*)

HMS *Penelope*

Flight Commander – Lieutenant Chris Mervik
Flight Observer – Lieutenant Nick Last

SMR – CPO Tony Loveday, CPO Pete Cronshaw, PO Geoff Bridge, PO 'Charlie' Chester; LAEM Geoff Hymas, AEM Phil Abel, AEM Keith Trelfa.

Aircraft – XZ 691 – no nickname, as it was only used for the conflict and then returned.

The *Penelope* team, along with a sense of humour. (*Chris Mervik*)

By Chris Mervik with help from Nick Last:

'It was during a short period of pre-embarkation leave in April 1982, prior to joining HMS *Penelope* for operational sea training at Portland, that "events" forced a change of plans for our Flight.

'Based at that time at RNAS Yeovilton, the Flight had transferred from HMS *Cleopatra* earlier in January and I took over as Flight commander, fresh from my

132   The Royal Navy Lynx

Lynx conversion course at the beginning of March. We had one of the newest and most up to date aircraft (XZ 730) fitted, with amongst other things, the Sea Skua and Orange Crop – XZ 730 was a beautiful aircraft, smooth and vibration free in the air, well cared for and resplendent in the Oxford Blue paint scheme of that time. The Flight maintainers were already a well-integrated and very effective team, and I suspect, may not have been enormously looking forward to the forthcoming work up in a frigate which had emerged from many years as a trials ship and a recent conversion to equip her with the Exocet missile system.

'We had probably just slipped away on leave as the Argentine invasion of the Falkland Islands got underway – which was pure coincidence as neither side knew that to be the case!

'Over the following days, along with many other war fighting spares, vehicles, equipment and personnel, XZ 730 was shipped out to the Falkland Islands with the Task Force. Back at Yeovilton, Penelope Flight was given a much more tired aircraft (XZ 691) in its place. Our ship underwent a very much foreshortened period of sea training, which for X Z691 was a period punctuated by persistent fuel leaks, electronic component failures and radio problems. Nevertheless, the Flight maintainers, led by the hugely experienced Senior Maintenance Rating, CPO Tony Loveday, dug deep to make the aircraft serviceable, enabling us to play our part in the sea training whilst also joining a number of anti-ship missile countermeasure trials of "Chaff H" and with an alarmingly large radar reflector bolted onto the left-hand side of the aircraft. We were then tasked to go to Lee-on-Solent and had an active I band jammer fitted, the same that was fitted to the Lynx of HMS *Andromeda*. We were lucky in that we went home for the weekend, whereas *Andromeda's* crew headed up to Aberporth in Wales to prove the system against a live missile. Together, all these bits of kit reflected the depth of concern about the threat from Argentinian Exocet missiles.

'The Flight embarked on 10 May for the dash south with the "Bristol Group" – a deployment that was going to call on all of the experience that Nick and I, the maintainers, and the ship's company had under our belts. Although I was not to know it at the time, the two distinct phases of my past naval experience were going to be of great help in the coming weeks.

'Before my flying career began, I had specialised as a direction officer, serving in two carriers and an air defence frigate. The job involved a significant amount of radar control of fighters and helicopters working at a radar console in the operations room; and 'blind pilotage' – which entailed navigating the ship solely by radar when entering and leaving harbour or confined waters in poor visibility.

'My flying experience prior to Lynx, was firstly as a 'Junglie' pilot, flying Wessex Vs – specialising in mountain, arctic, and low flying, carrying troops and lifting underslung loads, with embarked periods in HMS *Hermes* and operational flying in Northern Ireland. Secondly, I had spent two years as a flying instructor on the Gazelle helicopter at RNAS Culdrose – an experience that honed my own flying techniques and instrument flying. The need to "believe your instruments" and the ability to fly at very low-level at night, in poor visibility and foul weather with precision, was going to be vital in the coming weeks, not only for the completion of missions, but also for survival in an unfriendly environment!

'Nick Last, on his first tour as an observer, already had an excellent understanding of the aircraft's systems, a firm grip of his role in the crew and most fortunately, given the challenges we were about to face, a strong and flexible intellect and an analytical and mathematical mind. In a Lynx, the observer takes the lead in navigation (particularly at sea), operates communications systems and active and passive sensors from the left-hand seat. There are consoles of weapon and systems controls along the centreline, with shared or allocated responsibility amongst the crew. The pilot flies the aircraft from the right-hand seat. Because of this each can see the ability and performance of the other, and that close proximity also allows effective crew cooperation to take place – built on experience and trust – and Nick was an easy man to like and to trust.

'*Penelope's* departure from Devonport on 10 May took place in a very different context from the exuberant mood surrounding the departure of the main task force some five weeks earlier. The *General Belgrano* and HMS *Sheffield* had both been sunk – and although peace initiatives were still being proposed by third parties, war fighting had begun in earnest. As Nick and I flew from Yeovilton to Devonport that morning to embark in *Penelope*, a delay in the ship's readiness to receive us presented an opportunity to fly over my home on the edge of the Cornish village of Mullion to wave a final farewell to my wife and three young daughters.

'To deny the Argentinians any intelligence about our group, the passage south was a fairly covert affair, conducted under radar and radio silence with ships darkened at night. As we carried out night surface searches ahead of the group this "cloak of silence" around the ships put a premium on Nick's ability to keep an accurate plot of our position with particular reference to *Penelope's* progress down her intended track. The Lynx helicopter's passive ESM and visual searches for surface contacts would allow the group to alter course to avoid contact with neutral shipping, some of whom may have been from nations well-disposed towards Argentina. They might give away details of

134 The Royal Navy Lynx

the composition and location of our ships. Success would be measured by the thoroughness of our sweep ahead of the group – and critically for us, by finding and getting back to a "silent" *Penelope* in order to land safely back on board at the pre-briefed recovery time. This was not a good time to lose important helicopter assets by getting lost in the middle of the Atlantic Ocean, so Nick set to with some very accurate, good old fashioned navigation carried out with plotting chart and pencil in an already very cramped observer's side of the cockpit to get us back to the ship – and then there was the business of getting back on deck!

'Under normal circumstances at night, the helicopter controller in the ship, or the observer in the aircraft, would use radar to position the helicopter at the right range and position in relation to the flight deck, taking account of the ship's course and speed. He would then talk the aircraft down a glide path while the pilot flew on instruments monitoring an illuminated glide path indicator until at a 1/4 mile from the ship. At that point, the pilot would be guided and assisted by the flight deck lighting. But with radio and radar transmissions disallowed, and all the ships darkened, it was up to the aircrew alone to identify their own ship from the others in the group, assess her course, and set themselves up for an approach to the flight deck – as opposed to any other less useful part of the ship – all in the inky darkness of an Atlantic Ocean night. There would be no ship's navigation lights to help to orient ourselves with her course, no glide path indicator light down which to fly the approach and no illuminated horizon bar on the hangar roof to judge the pitch and roll of the ship.

'Flying over the ship with our instrument panel lights dimmed as low as possible, at a height of about 200 feet above the sea (staying sensibly above the tallest mast in the group!) afforded us the best chance to make out a ship "shape" in the blackness of the sea surface.

'To a very limited degree, we were assisted by a rudimentary and blurry hand-held night vision scope that Nick was peering through. However, the light from the scope's screen served mainly to destroy his own night vision!

'As we flew over the ship, the distinctive noise from the tail rotor of the Lynx would be the only signal to the flight deck team that we were about to position for an approach and landing. If those on watch in the ops room and on the bridge stuck to the brief, the ship would be turned onto the pre-planned flying course. Realising the near impossibility of a "blind" approach to an unlit flight deck at night, the flight deck team would raise the hangar door to head height and five of them would prepare to put a "Pusser's Right Angled Torch" against its bottom edge. The torch lenses were heavily daubed with blue permanent felt tip ink so as to give just a faint glimmer of light. In the cockpit, the task was to open out to a position on the port quarter of the ship, using "dead reckoning", flying accurate speeds and timed turns until rolling out on the approach heading – then begin a slow and steady approach to – not very much!

'Accurate heading, steady rate of descent, easing back the closing speed, watching the radar altimeter, then washing off the speed as the passage of time and the unconscious tightening of your grip on the controls told you that the deck was now very close…

'On the flight deck, as the noise of the Lynx grew louder and the flight deck team assessed the aircraft to be very close, their torches were switched on and a rudimentary blue horizontal line appeared, giving some hint as to what the deck was doing. As the aircraft was brought to a hover alongside the deck at some twenty feet above the sea, a warm glow of red "night lighting" just discernible from deep within the partially shuttered hangar gave further clues to the heaving of the deck, allowing a swift and sure landing. As ever, the firm pull of the harpoon engaging with the flight deck grid marked the conclusion of the sortie.

'For the flight, much of the journey south and the first days with the carrier Task Group 100 miles east of the Falklands was spent either at "Alert" (at fifteen or thirty minutes notice to fly), or airborne, moving personnel and stores between ships or recovering stores parachuted into the sea by Hercules aircraft that had flown south from Ascension Island.

'On 30 May, after taking a medical evacuation (MEDEVAC) to the sick bay of HMS *Hermes*, we were sitting with rotors running on her vast flight deck as an approaching air raid was detected. We were told to launch and take up a "Guard" position astern of the carrier. We launched in the midst of a fusillade of Chaff rockets as she carried out countermeasures to defend against possible Exocet attack.

'In the otherwise peaceful setting of the South Atlantic ocean we hovered over the wake of the carrier, pointed our sensors and jammer towards the threat and mused as to whether our box of Chaff H skillets, with the deceptive capability to transform our position into the biggest radar contact around, or whether our electronic countermeasures suite, which would invite an incoming missile to turn towards us rather than the high value ships of the Task Force, might have the desired effect. In the event, the action took place thirty miles to the south of *Hermes*.

'Back on board *Penelope* later that night, the ship went to action stations as another air raid was detected and the Flight personnel optimistically took up defensive positions on the flight deck armed only with SLRs and a sense of humour!

'Keeping a helicopter serviceable and available for tasking in the isolation of a frigate or destroyer requires some extraordinary effort from a team of engineers who need to be at the top of their game to meet all the complex challenges a helicopter can throw at them. And so it was that the following day a signal from the Naval Aircraft Materials Laboratory informed us that the results of routine oil samples taken from our engines required them both to be removed and we were grounded until that was done. Some might wonder why we didn't just press on and accept the risk of an engine failure – after all, there was a war on... However, that was the very point – the Lynx was far too valuable an asset to lose to a predictable engine failure in flight while there was a war still to be fought, but it was also too valuable an asset to have it sitting unserviceable in the hangar for long.

'So, although the weather was cold and wet and the ocean swell was significant, and despite all the difficulties that the ship's movement created, the Flight's engine change team, led by CPO Pete Cronshaw, worked throughout that night and into the next day. Unless you have seen the myriad pipes, cables, nuts and bolts that are involved in the fitting of a gas turbine engine into the confined space of a small helicopter, the scene on the windswept flight deck would be too hard to imagine. The Flight maintainers worked on precarious platforms fifteen feet above the heaving deck in the dark of night, with hugely expensive, rare and vital spare engines suspended from hoists waiting for that quiescent moment in the ship's movement to take the next step in an operation that would not forgive any miscalculation or inattention. Yet, by the afternoon, after less than twenty-four hours, the replacement engines had been successfully fitted and "ground run" on deck. Then typically, in a display of confidence in his team's work (and very likely for the sheer enjoyment of getting off the ship and airborne, if only for half an hour), Pete Cronshaw strapped himself into the back of the aircraft to accompany us on our check test flight. A perfect result, and within hours XZ 691 was once again heaving air-dropped stores out of the South Atlantic. "Bravo Zulu, boys! – very well done!"

'After these first few days with the carrier group, the Flight's tasking began to develop a more war-like feel. A pre-dawn ESM search and barrier patrol in support of a "Black Buck" (RAF Vulcan) anti-radar missile strike; an ESM and visual search along the north coast of Pebble Island, followed by a later visual search around its airfield. These sorties were flown at 3000–5000 feet, probably

The Falklands War   137

not a good place to be if fighters or shoulder-launched surface-to-air missiles were about.

'With that minor concern in mind, it was at about this time that it struck Nick and I that we really didn't know very much about the military situation on the ground and yet we were being tasked to fly close to, as well as over, land that had been in enemy hands. Reassured by *Penelope's* ops officers that we knew all there was to know, we pressed on dutifully, but kept a weather-eye out for the unexpected. Much later, after the fighting was over and once the pace of life allowed some reflective discussion in the wardroom about the war, one of the ops officers told us that, as we were thought to be at risk of capture and interrogation if shot down, or if we had to make a forced landing in the vicinity of Argentine forces, we were only to be told what we "needed to know".

'Nick and I did discuss some "tactical" issues which might have had a bearing on the ops officers' assessment of our vulnerability to capture. We were each armed with a 7.62mm SLR, with one magazine apiece. We concluded that after a forced landing, the rifles would simplify the survival situation considerably as there were plenty of sheep on the Falkland Islands (though not much seasoning), but we never really came to a definitive answer as to what we would do with the weapons if an Argentine platoon was to appear over the horizon. In light of this, their assessment of how much we should be told might appear quite sensible, but as you will see, the lack of information was soon to cause us one or two problems!

'Very often, *Penelope* would be in San Carlos during the day. She would then sail at night to escort merchant "Ships Taken Up From Trade" (STUFT), carrying vital supplies for the force. Their route to the Falkland Islands took them past the potentially hostile shores of Pebble Island, which lay just beyond the northern entrance of Falkland Sound, then south into the Sound and east into San Carlos Water by daybreak. To support the ship in this task, the Lynx was employed to search the coast and coastal waters from where the risk to these vital supplies was at its greatest. Despite the uncertainty as to what Argentine forces were still in that region and what their capabilities might be, the mere possibility that they may be able to launch an attack against STUFT convoys, perhaps with trailer-based Exocet missiles from ashore, was too great a risk to ignore. Not being privy to the staff assessment of that risk, we were left to draw our own conclusions from such information as we might glean from third parties.

'On our very first pre-dawn patrol to the north of Pebble Island, as first light illuminated the area around Pebble settlement, we could see fixed wing aircraft on an obvious airstrip with what looked very much like two helicopters off to

138   The Royal Navy Lynx

one side. These observations were reported by radio to a "controller" who had clearly been in the Falkland Islands ahead of us with the initial Task Force. Our report was dismissed out of hand. We new boys were informed that the aircraft we could see were those that had been destroyed on the ground by Special Forces before our arrival in theatre. Somewhat crestfallen, we continued our sortie and discussed what we had seen on our return to the ship. Not convinced by the put down we had received, we decided to take another look next time we were in the vicinity and, sure enough, this time the helicopters were nowhere to be seen.

'The coast on the north of Pebble Island around Elephant Bay, and near to the settlement, is low lying with beaches and sand dunes, whereas to the south just behind the settlement are cliffs, though I can't remember quite how high they were. Descending to sea level to the east of Pebble Island, we turned back and flew westwards at very low-level beneath the cliffs until just adjacent to the settlement, we pulled up over the cliffs and flew past the few buildings. There was no sign of military activity, indeed no sign of any activity at all as we pressed on towards the airstrip. We circled once, counted the Argentine aircraft for future reference and satisfied ourselves that they were indeed damaged, then headed north and out to sea. So far so good we thought.

'The following day, our tasking specifically required a visual search for trailer-based Exocet along the north coast of Pebble Island, perhaps based on some form of intelligence received, but if so we were not aware. On this occasion, we searched along the north coast from east to west, flying at low-level, with one eye on the broken cover offered by the sand dunes. Approaching Elephant Bay, the view through the overhead Perspex screens of the cockpit was suddenly filled with the intermittent, brilliant trails of tracer fire which arced over us and out to sea.

'Nick later told me that in the instant that he saw the tracer and was processing what he was seeing, the fact that the aircraft, still at thirty feet, was now in a ninety degree angle of bank turn away from the island, reassured him we were carrying out a text book "running away" manoeuvre appropriate for an unarmed helicopter under anti-aircraft fire. Once clear of danger, Nick reported the contact and we returned to the ship to take up the jammer station, showing Chaff H in case the Argentine follow-up was to launch a missile at *Penelope* or the convoy. Eventually, we landed back on board relieved to see that there were no holes in the aircraft.

'I have no idea what use, if any, was made of the information that there were enemy troops on the ground in Pebble Island, but had I not allowed our earlier report to have been so swiftly discounted as a mistake by newcomers to the theatre, the risk to ships and aircraft around Pebble Island might have been better understood. An amusing footnote to those events at Pebble Island came to light after the war was over when talking to a small group of islanders out in "the camp". One man recounted the surprise we gave both him and the Argentine occupiers in his home as our Lynx flew over the Pebble Island settlement on the first occasion on our way towards the airstrip. He went on to say that the Argentine troops soon recovered from their surprise and fired their rifles and machine guns at us as we flew away. We were totally unaware of this at the time. Who said ignorance is bliss?

'Whilst many of the more operational sorties were pre-planned and launched before dawn or at dusk, some of the most demanding were those in response to short notice tasking by operational staff in other ships, or from our own ops room reacting to a threat or concern. It seemed that these calls invariably happened at around one o'clock in the morning – a time that became my "witching hour"!

'Unless the aircraft was already tasked to fly, or was "down" for maintenance, we would almost always be at Alert 30 overnight (thirty minutes notice to be in the air). We slept dressed in full flying clothing with "Goon Suit" (a waterproof immersion coverall) close to hand. Our cabins were just above the ops room and we would be in there just moments after being called. We needed to quickly orient ourselves in relation to land, other ships, the enemy or threat, and absorb a brief from the captain or the ops officer on watch. Nick would remain behind in the ops room to compile as much information as possible to make the sortie happen. I would "move purposefully" through the darkened ship to the hangar, sign for the aircraft and do a walk-round and start the aircraft. Well within the given thirty minutes, the aircraft would be "turning and burning" on deck with Nick strapping into his seat, firing up his radar and sensors – then off into the gloom.

'It was on such an occasion that we were launched in the dead of night to an area south-west of Port Stanley, near the entrance to Port Fitzroy to search for two landing craft missing, I believe, from HMS *Intrepid*. What they were doing and why they were missing, we were not told in great detail, but as this took place in the early hours of 7 June, I can only guess with hindsight that they were part of the plan to move the Welsh Guards ashore near Fitzroy that ended in such tragedy at Bluff Cove.

'We were going to be operating sufficiently close to Port Stanley for us to take note that an Argentine surface-to-air missile site was situated to the north, on top of a 235 foot high hill overlooking the area. It was a Roland 2 SAM system which we needed to learn more about. A petty officer in the ops room dug out the latest

Jane's book of missile systems which gave us what we needed to know, including the size of the warhead, which just at that minute I really didn't need to know! A brief discussion as to whether the system could "look down" and "fire down" at a small target (us) over the sea was inconclusive.

'During a two hour search, our radar sweep of the area found no sign of the landing craft which it later transpired had remained in more sheltered waters for the night. Our radar transmissions did, however, alert the Argentine Roland 2 SAM site on shore to our presence. The first indication we had was a "Band 3" radar warning on our Orange Crop – a warning light illuminating on your instrument panel in an otherwise dark cockpit is an unwelcome event at the best of times, but accompanied by Nick identifying it as a SAM site's search radar required action. In the case of Roland 2 and being surrounded by open sea, the "running away" manoeuvre was not going to get us out of this pickle.

'Years before, as a "Junglie" pilot, I had thoroughly enjoyed my fighter evasion training, which seemed to me to be an opportunity to throw the aircraft about with great enthusiasm in order to counter the fighter pilot's attack "solution". Though this training sometimes took place in mountainous or difficult terrain and at low-level, it was invariably practiced in daylight. Now, in the dead of night, I sent the aircraft diving towards the surface in the hope that we might drop below the enemy radar's horizon – no such luck! "Band 2, Fire Control lock on!" from Nick, was not good news. Rapid changes of heading at very low-level over the sea were called for and frequently broke lock, only for us to be locked on to again as soon as we steadied up.

'We had been briefed to conduct the task under radio silence to avoid giving the Argentinian forces in Stanley too many indications that something was afoot. We kept silent, racking the aircraft around to break the SAM firing solution. In *Penelope's* ops room, the radar trace of our frenetic movement must have been perplexing, as it was enough to cause the ship to break silence to order us to "go closer inshore!" Working hard in the cockpit, this was not the time to break radio silence to make a reply, particularly as it would simply have transmitted Nick's verbal commentary on Roland's attempt to get us, punctuated by my expletives!

'Not too far away were two Type 21 frigates who I think were on a "gun line" for shore bombardment. It seemed sensible in the absence of any cover to consider using the ships to interrupt the radar's repeated efforts to lock on to us. As we closed towards one of the ships, they in turn locked onto us with their fire control radar and we were told to clear off. Of course they were right to do so, but as we had started out in the war acting as decoys to defend ships from missile attack, it seemed not unreasonable to hope they might return the favour. However, at the same time Nick chimed, "Band 4 Missile Launch!"

'I honestly don't know how the story ended, other than I carried on vigorously flying evasive manoeuvres. We saw no missile (though my attention was firmly on avoiding flying into the sea). The Orange Crop fell silent and with no sign of the landing craft, we returned to the ship.

'On a number of occasions, we launched in fog that was forecast to persist throughout the sortie, including the recovery. This was not so much of a problem out at sea where the well-practiced procedures for a poor visibility approach would be put in place for our return to the ship. However, on one particular occasion, having launched at sea in fog, the brief was to return at the end of the task to San Carlos Water, where *Penelope* would be at anchor in fog – an altogether different challenge.

'San Carlos Water's strength as a defensible anchorage was provided by the natural fortification of the surrounding hills and its narrow entrance from Falkland Sound. But, for a helicopter trying to return to its ship at night in dense fog, all of these presented obstacles to any previously practiced form of recovery to a ship. The situation required something novel.

'Flying as slowly as the accuracy of our instruments would allow, we managed to reduce our speed over the water to some 30 knots and descended to about 30–50 feet with the radar altimeter "warning bug" set to warn us if I dropped below 30 feet. Nick drew a series of index lines on the radar screen just as I once had many years before when carrying out "blind pilotage" on board ships entering harbour in fog. In this way we "fast taxied" down Falkland Sound, turning into the entrance to San Carlos Water, keeping a safe distance from the steeply rising shoreline until we identified *Penelope's* anchorage on the radar and taxied up to the flight deck. Peacetime weather minima, along with many other flying restrictions, were understandably set aside, yet it was the beauty of the Lynx cockpit layout that allowed such novel procedures to work and the extraordinary trust and crew cooperation that had developed between us helped us through the most challenging of circumstances. Returning in the pitch black goldfish bowl of a foggy night, with the radar screen brilliance turned down and the hood removed, I was able to glance across and take confidence from the greater situational awareness the radar image provided. Nick, in turn, was able to see from the flight instruments that the flying was safe and accurate and going to plan.

'During the daytime, when *Penelope* was at anchor in San Carlos Water, we were often at alert or conducting routine tasks moving personnel and stores. Although

142   The Royal Navy Lynx

the "action" had moved inland as our forces pressed on towards Port Stanley, the ships were still responding to each report of Argentine aircraft approaching the Falkland Islands as a potential air raid on San Carlos. Our pre-planned response was to get airborne and land the aircraft on the shores of San Carlos Water. We would sit there ready for SAR or Casevac should any ship, including our own, be damaged, or any personnel be injured in an attack.

'Leaving the aircraft turning and burning indefinitely whilst waiting for the air raid warning state to reduce was not a good idea and thinking that a helicopter on the shores of San Carlos might make too tempting an opportunity target if a Skyhawk was deterred from pressing home its attack on the ships, I would stop the rotors, leaving one engine running for a quick start. Then we would move away from the aircraft! In the event, during our time there, Argentinian aircraft did not make any further attacks on the ships in San Carlos and I am left with the slightly comical image of Nick and I sitting with rifles across our laps on mess deck chairs that had washed ashore, possibly after the sinking of HMS *Antelope*, listening to the distant air raid reports on the aircraft radio via long-leads – more Jed and Jethro Clampett than anything resembling Britain's finest!

'During this time, it was not only fog that was to play a part in our tasking, but also the "fog of war". On 13 June, I was called to take a brief in the ops room on a secure radio net from the duty staff officer in HMS *Fearless*. A Harrier returning from a mission had sighted an Argentine patrol craft in Choiseul Sound – one of possibly two patrol craft (because a similar report had been made by a Hercules some time earlier). It was reported as being tied up at an island. I was given the coordinates and the task was to load "maximum Sea Skua", which was four missiles, carry out a search of Choiseul Sound and find and destroy the patrol craft.

'PO Geoff Bridge, the Flight armourer, went about his task with great glee and soon he and the others in the Flight had XZ 691 loaded with four Sea Skua, with the system tested and ready to go. We had no clue as to what enemy forces might lie between us and Choiseul Sound, nor any confidence that anyone else might know. So I decided we should remove the cabin windows and with a very enthusiastic volunteer in the back of the aircraft in the form of CPO Pete Cronshaw, armed with a Light Machine Gun (LMG), we set off fast and at very low-level, hugging the contours along our route. I remain uncertain as to who would have been more alarmed by Pete Cronshaw and his LMG if we had encountered any hostile fire on our way - the enemy on the ground, Nick and I in the front, or Pete himself in the back!'

Max warload. (*Chris Mervik*)

'In the event, we arrived at Choiseul Sound in good visibility and began a radar and visual search for contacts. There was no longer a patrol craft tied up at the island reported by the Harrier and no sign of any craft underway in the sound. Flying at low-level, tucked in against the shore, we spotted a patrol craft in the far distance tied up to the shoreline. Our conclusion was that the craft had left the island in the period since it was sighted and had repositioned further down the sound. The brief was to attack and destroy, but we had no certainty that the Sea Skua system could, or would, discriminate between the patrol craft and the shore. There was only one way to find out.

'We turned away from the patrol craft and opened the range between us and the target until we were beyond the system's minimum range to fire. We climbed swiftly to the minimum launch height and Nick set about locking onto the radar echo that was clearly discernible against the radar picture of the shoreline. Surprisingly quickly, and without hesitation, the system locked on to the target and was ready to fire. Our only pause for thought was over who would press the button. It was something we seem not to have discussed previously! Nick chivalrously said the job should be mine and with one small stab of my finger the aircraft lifted slightly as the missile fell away, shortly reappearing ahead of the aircraft with a thin trail of white rocket efflux as it

144   The Royal Navy Lynx

stepped down in stages on its way to the target. Then, a small, explosive plume of white smoke signalled that the missile had hit. Descending to low-level, we closed the target sufficiently to make a damage assessment. The patrol craft appeared to be heeled over to starboard and slightly down by the stern and certainly out of action. With no further sightings of Argentinian patrol craft, we headed back to San Carlos.

'Having been out of radio contact with the ships at San Carlos throughout the task, the first indication of what had transpired was our arrival alongside the flight deck with only three missiles on the aircraft. Anticipating a warm reception, we reported to the captain who seemed pleased. The warm bubble burst when news of our action was reported back to *Fearless*. I suspect a watch change amongst the staff had resulted in the realisation that the Harrier had misreported the position of the patrol craft and that it was, in fact, one that had already been attacked and disabled by a Sea Harrier on 25 May. It might even have been repairable and put to use by British forces had we not done further irreparable damage with our missile. So tea and sympathy, but no medals!

'Those who might dismiss this event as little more than a waste of a very good missile, might now want to consider that at the very least the "experience" was not wasted. Almost a decade later, when I was first lieutenant of HMS *Manchester* during the Gulf War, I was pleased to serve alongside Nick once more. He was now *Manchester's* Flight commander. In that war, Nick was credited with destroying one fast patrol boat and two minelayers, all with Sea Skua. He was mentioned in despatches and subsequently awarded the Air Force Cross "for services to the Lynx in Peacetime and War".'

Authors Note: Accounts of this action appear later in the section relating to the Gulf Wars.

'Though I have chosen to illustrate some of the effects of the fog of war, the vast majority of sorties were accomplished without such hindrance. Some were supported by unusual amounts of intelligence effort and planning. For example, a night insertion of a small team from the Special Boat Squadron onto Carcass Island in the far west of the Falklands, demonstrated the sort of resources that could be committed to an operation by Special Forces. A Harrier reconnaissance mission produced detailed photographs of the island and they were then flown to *Penelope* by Sea King helicopter. The SBS team studied the images and maps spread across the dining table of our wardroom and a suitable landing site was selected on the coast where we would drop the team. They would then make their way to a vantage point overlooking the settlement where it was suspected Argentine Forces might be located.

'As a "Junglie", I had operated with SBS on several occasions, but would never claim to have had any special insight into their methods or thinking. They were secretive, highly professional and impressively skilled, and seemed to me to balance their delight in their role with an intense seriousness about their purpose. Though today, a great deal of their story has been exposed in paperback and the media, back then they were shadowy figures. But for all that, they were only flesh and blood and it was that vulnerability that brought home the weight of responsibility on Nick and I to get them onto Carcass Island without compromising their operation or their safety. We discussed their chosen landing site on the south coast some distance from their objective – as I recall, it was right at the water's edge, with sand dunes or rising ground ahead that would shield us from sight and be a barrier to the sound of our arrival and we were readily drawn into their determination to achieve the task.

'An hour after midnight, with both the ship and the Lynx darkened, we lifted from the flight deck and made the short hop to the landing site. That night, with the four man SBS team in the back we were either the best protected aircrew in the Falklands or the most at risk. Despite the planning, or because of it, the insertion took place during the astrological event of the month – a full moon! It was our job to make the run in towards the island without being silhouetted by its brilliant loom. As we came to a very low hover on the shore – all lights off – I was immediately grateful for the light of the moon as it picked out the most suitable patch for Nick to disembark the heavily laden troops onto the otherwise treacherously uneven, rock-strewn surface. So swift was their exit that Nick's commentary from the back went along the lines of, "one out... all out!" The whole sortie took just five minutes, to this day the shortest "Duty Carried Out" flight recorded in either of our flying logbooks. Our small part in their mission complete, they made their way to their chosen vantage point where, I understand, they watched the settlement for a day and a half; and seeing no sign of enemy forces, made their way into the settlement and made contact with the islanders there.

'After the Argentine surrender our flying consisted mainly of patrolling the waters around the Falkland Islands and helicopter delivery service tasks that are the bread and butter of ships' flights. But even the HDS tasks had a degree of danger. On one occasion, having dropped the captain at Stanley

146   The Royal Navy Lynx

for a meeting, we parked the aircraft at the racecourse and went to collect mail from the post office. Nick and I begged a lift back to the aircraft with a couple of soldiers driving a captured Argentine jeep. Sitting in the back, perched uncomfortably on a large stack of blue plastic "cubes", we asked what they were, and were told that they were Argentinian land mines! They may well have been pulling our legs, but if so, it had the desired effect as the rest of the journey was infinitely less comfortable than it had been before. Later, the rumour mill had it that some Argentine vehicles had been booby-trapped by pulling the pin on a grenade, wrapping it in masking tape and placing it in the petrol tank, with the expectation that the petrol would dissolve the glue, release the firing mechanism on the grenade, and… Bang!

'Having a bit of a ramble around Stanley racecourse, I discovered the Cable & Wireless office almost deserted. The solitary operator was very welcoming, and when I asked if I could phone home, unbelievably, he said, "sure!" Lucky! Soon I was listening to the familiar sound of our phone ringing almost 8000 miles away in our small bungalow in Mullion and it kept ringing until the realisation dawned on me – there was nobody home! Unlucky! But at that moment, I realised that for too many families there would be no calls home from their loved ones, and for all that Nick and I had been through together in just thirty-five days, we were very fortunate indeed.

'From 27 May – 15 June we flew 36.10 hours by day, 11.15 hours by night, 6.10 hours on instruments and conducted fifty-one deck landings by day and eleven by night.

The Aftermath

The Falklands war was a wake-up call to the British military and politicians alike. Prior to the war, HMS *Invincible* was going to be sold to the Australians and severe force reductions put in place. Some would say that this is a mistake that politicians have a habit of repeating, particularly when a political party regains power. However, for the Royal Navy it was a welcome stay of execution. Over the next few years, many lessons learnt from the war were put into place. No warship since has been designed without a gun for instance. Close in weapon systems to defeat sea skimming missiles were also a priority.

It seems strange now that all the Lynx Flights that took part in the war were not called together to compare notes immediately after they were all back in the country. The window to do this was actually quite small, as many of the Flights were almost immediately redeployed, either to other parts of the world, or even straight back down

The Falklands War   147

to the Falklands. This book has brought nearly all the stories of those Flights together for the first time, arguably over thirty-five years too late.

However, as is often the case, military need accelerates military development. Several of the systems procured and developed in a hurry carried on further in service. (It should be noted that this does not include the use of office swivel chairs as machine-gun mountings). One item in particular, the jammer fitted to several of the Lynx, which subsequently became known as 'Hampton Mayfair', was developed a great deal further to become the 'Yellow Veil' system that was used during the various Gulf conflicts, more of which will be covered later in the book.

Although already identified as an issue, it was clear that the Mark 2 aircraft was limited in the weight it could carry. During the war, a blanket one thousand pound increase in all-up weight was authorised. This allowed the aircraft to carry a full fuel load and full weapon load. However, this would not be sustainable in peacetime and there was a need to improve the aircraft's basic performance. The next chapter will look at the upgrades that the aircraft received to turn it into a Mark 3.

Chapter 5

The Lynx HAS Mark 3 – Beefing Things Up

It was clear that the Mark 2 needed more grunt. (*Steve George*)

As previously explained, the Falklands War identified the need for the Lynx to operate at a higher all-up weight in order to be able to carry full fuel and full weapons. To do this it would need more engine power and consequently a stronger gearbox to take that power. In addition, the piecemeal installation of Orange Crop and Sea Skua needed to be standardised across the fleet of aircraft. A weakness in the aircraft's flotation system had also been identified. In addition, during its life, some of the modifications that were introduced to produce the Mark 8 were fielded in the earlier Mark 3.

Over the next few years all the Mark 2 aircraft would be upgraded to the new Mark 3 standard.

The GEM 42 Engine

The original Gem 100 engine produced 900hp. The Gem 42 was rated at 1000hp with a contingency rating of 1120hp. It certainly had enough power to meet the requirements of the new aircraft. However, in the early days it still suffered from problems similar to that of the 100 series, i.e. degradation of the high-temperature part of the engine as well as leaking oil, particularly on shutdown. When initially introduced into service, it had a further problem of engine surge.

In order to get more power out of a gas turbine, the engine has to be capable of tolerating higher airflows. With the initial Gem 42 design, this caused problems of surge. Surge is a condition similar to a backfire in a car engine. It happens when the pressure in the combustion chamber of the engine exceeds that of the pressure being produced by the compressor. The net result is a reversal of airflow through the front of the engine. This can be caused by several factors. Damage to the compressor caused by ingesting a foreign object is a common cause. However, allowing too much fuel into the engine – especially at low speed – can have the same effect. Depending on the design, the effects can vary from a minor inconvenience to catastrophic failure. In order to control surge, engine fuel control systems have to be carefully designed. In the case of the Gem 42, the initial design solution was to fit bleed control valves to the side of the compressor. At low speed these would be open to allow air to bleed away. However, at high speed, they would close to allow full airflow through the engine. The solution worked, but with one problem. When accelerating the engine they would close at one power condition, but when then slowing down they would reopen at a lower power setting. This often put the engine into a surge condition for a few seconds. It was not damaging, but caused a loud bang and shudder in the airframe which is exactly the sort of thing aircrew don't like. In particular, many aircrew misdiagnosed it as a bird strike. The number of aircraft returning to the air station at Portland, thinking they had an emergency situation, significantly increased.

In the end, the solution came in two parts. Initially, grooves were cut radially into the intake of the compressor, which had the effect of altering the airflow so that the bleed valves could be removed. Subsequent engine builds, modified the compressor casing even further to increase the margin of safety.

This period in the development of the engine was the start of a major programme by Rolls-Royce to address all the engine's issues. Over the years, what had started out as an unreliable and rather underpowered engine, slowly became significantly more reliable.

The Three Pinion Gearbox

In order to be able to take the increased power levels of the new engines, the aircraft's main transmission also had to be upgraded. The key element that needed improvement was the main gearbox. As previously described, the Lynx gearbox was deliberately designed to keep the overall height of the aircraft to a minimum and utilised conformal gears. The design was relatively simple with one large gear wheel driven by two pinions. The solution was to add a third pinion to spread the load throughout the gearbox. This design remains in service to this day.

The Lynx Monobloc rotor head on top of the main drive gear and pinions. The improved gearbox incorporated a third pinion. (*WHL*)

Improved floatation gear

The first verse of the first song in the Fleet Air Arm songbook sums up the problem:

> *They say in the Air Force landing's okay,*
> *If the pilot gets out and can still walk away,*
> *But in the Fleet Air Arm the prospects are grim,*
> *If the landing's p**s poor and the pilot can't swim.*

Keeping an aircraft afloat after a controlled emergency landing in the sea has been a perennial problem for all navies. Probably the worst solution was the large clamshell flotation bags fitted to the Lynx's predecessor, the Wasp. In flight these devices caused enormous drag and severely affected the performance of the aircraft, as well as resulting in the cockpit being underwater once they deployed after a ditching.

The Mark 2 Lynx solution wasn't that much better. It had two flotation bags fitted to either wheel sponson. It didn't take a rocket scientist to work out that if they deployed, the cockpit would then rotate downwards, leaving the aircrew several feet underwater. Consequently, with the Mark 3, two more flotation bags were fitted either side of the nose. This configuration has been retained ever since. Although, because of the relative weakness of being able to mount large inflated bags in these positions, more often than not they rip off at impact.

The Lynx HAS Mark 3 – Beefing Things Up   151

A pre-production Mk 2 with the sponson flotation gear deployed. With most of the aircraft's weight ahead of the bags, its easy to see what would happen once in the water. (*WHL*)

A Mk 3 with the 4 bag system - the green covers can clearly be seen on the sponsons and below the pilot's lower window at the nose. Often this was the only way to visually tell the difference between the two marks of aircraft. (*WHL*)

How it was meant to work – and all too often didn't. (*RNFSC*)

152   The Royal Navy Lynx

Further Mark 3 Variants

During its service career the Mark 3 operated in a number of sub variants. Specific modifications to allow it to operate in the Gulf will be covered in the section dedicated to Gulf operations. The same will be done for the aircraft that operated in the Arctic.

However, the aircraft was used as a progressive test bed for many of the items that subsequently appeared in the later Mark 8 variant. Some of these are discussed here.

BERP rotor blades

This slightly unfortunate acronym stands for British Experimental Rotor Programme. This was a joint programme between Westland Helicopters and the Royal Aircraft Establishment (RAE). It was designed to produce a helicopter rotor blade more suitable to high-speed flight.

When a helicopter is sitting in the hover in still air, the rotor blades are all travelling through the air at the same speed. As soon as the aircraft transitions into forward flight, the blade that is moving with the aircraft (the advancing blade) now experiences the additional airspeed of the aircraft. However, the blade on the opposite side (the retreating blade) has the aircraft's airspeed subtracted from that which it had been experiencing in the hover.

The consequences of these effects is that there are two problems to solve to make a helicopter go fast. The first is that airflow at the tip of the advancing blade soon reaches transonic speeds and problems with shock waves and vortices become significant. The second is that the retreating blade needs more and more angle of attack to maintain the necessary lift and eventually starts to stall from the root outwards.

In addition, rotor blades, because of the nature of their shape, i.e. long and thin, do not have much strength in terms of twist. Therefore, it is important to ensure that the position where the lift is generated does not move significantly as blade angle increases. Historically, this has meant that blades have a symmetrical aerofoil shape. Although this solves this particular problem, a symmetrical aerofoil section is not the most efficient, particularly when dealing with a large range of speeds.

The BERP programme sought to overcome these issues. The first obvious difference to a conventional rotor blade is the large paddle at the end of the blade. This has a swept back tip and other aerodynamic devices built into it to ameliorate the onset of high Mach number vortices and shock waves at transonic speeds. However, much of the efficiency of the rotor blade actually comes from design factors that are not so obvious. By using modern composite materials it was possible to produce a very stiff rotor blade. This meant it was possible to move away from a symmetrical aerofoil section. In fact, with these blades, the aerofoil section changes along the length of the blade to cope with the different speeds experienced at different positions along its length.

At high speed in the early Lynx, with its conventional aluminium rotor blades, vibration levels increased significantly above 120 knots. This was primarily due to the rotor blade on the retreating side starting to stall as more and more angle of attack was required to maintain the necessary lift. When the blade started to stall from the root outwards, the stall would be almost instantaneous across the width of the blade, hence causing the vibration levels to increase very quickly. The aerofoil section of the BERP blade and the end paddle was specifically designed to make it stall progressively from the trailing to the leading edge and so smooth out the ride. The large paddle tip was then also able to cope with the issues of high Mach number on the advancing side.

The BERP rotor blade fitted to a Lynx. (*WHL*)

In 1972, a prototype Lynx broke the world helicopter speed record by achieving 199.9 knots. However, in 1986, Westland fitted the new BERP blades to their demonstrator aircraft, along with specially modified and uprated GEM 60 engines. Piloted by their Chief Test Pilot, Trevor Eggington, it achieved a speed of 249.06 knots. This record still stands today. The speed of the tips of the advancing rotor blades were almost supersonic, at a Mach number of 0.97.

The record-breaking Westland demonstrator G-LYNX that took the world helicopter speed record on 11 August 1986. (*WHL*)

Soon afterwards, a program to replace the metal blades with the new composite BERP blades was established for the naval Mark 3 fleet. The author was lucky enough to fly one of the first naval aircraft fitted with these blades. First impressions were that vibration levels at the normal cruising speed of 120 knots were not significantly different. However, when speed was increased to the maximum of 150 knots, it was quite clear how much smoother the aircraft was. In fact there seemed to be very little difference, whereas with the old blades at that speed it was sometimes difficult to even read the dashboard instruments.

Reverse direction tail rotor

As mentioned previously, the tail rotor had been designed to ensure that it was clear of the tail assembly when the aircraft was at high speed. However, the problems this imposed on the operating limits of the aircraft when at sea were seen as a major limitation as the aircraft could not accept any significant winds from the starboard beam. Consequently, in the mid-80s Westland modified an aircraft with a tail rotor rotating in the opposite direction. Unfortunately, this aircraft barely made it out of the hover before the intermediate gearbox failed and it crashed. The cause was a very small oil feed in the intermediate gearbox that should have been repositioned. However, once an engineering fix was incorporated and a new aircraft was fitted, it became clear that not only was the high speed issue not a problem, but the performance of the system was much improved and the issue of 'running out of pedal' had been solved. Although not an original part of the Mark 3 upgrade, all Lynx were fitted with the reverse direction rotor over the next few years.

Centralised Tactical System and secure speech

One of the issues with the display of the Sea Spray radar was that it was completely analogue. In order to track a target the observer had to place a clear plastic overlay onto the radar display and literally put a grease pencil dot onto the overlay and note the aircraft position from the navigation system. He would then wait either three or six minutes and then join the dots up. This would then give an approximate speed and direction of the target. Surprisingly, it was reasonably effective, but in reality could only cope with a limited number of targets. There was a clear need for a more modern system. This came in the form of a Centralised Tactical System, which was fitted in the centre console of the aircraft. Initially, the observer manually transferred data to it, but as will be discussed later, it was subject to several rounds of improvement. Although primarily aimed at the new Mark 8 aircraft, a number of Mark 3s were fitted with it, both to gain experience of its technical performance as well as developing its tactical use. More detail on this system and how it was developed is in the later chapter on the Mark 8 aircraft.

In addition, the radios fitted to the aircraft could only transmit clear speech. This meant that when the need arose to use tactical information, laborious manual encryption techniques had to be used to ensure that anyone overhearing the conversation could not make use of the information. For the Gulf, a number of Mark 3 aircraft were fitted with secure radio systems (AD3400 Lamberton). The main downside to this was that only the observer could talk on the secure channel, and the pilot could not listen in. So, again, in advance of the Mark 8 programme a full secure speech system was used in some Mark 3 aircraft, giving them the designation Mark 3(S).

M3M Machine Gun

As will be seen in the next chapter, the Mark 3 underwent a number of specific modifications that were necessary for hot weather operations and to counter specific threats in the Gulf. One of these was a forward firing, half inch calibre machine gun (HMP). In the eventuality, it proved of limited success. In addition, the door mounted GPMG used in the Falklands and after, was also of limited use (even when not mounted on an old office chair). In 2002, both the HMP and GPMG were replaced by the much more capable M3M half inch calibre door mounted machine gun. This weapon has been developed from the Second World War M2 and is in use around the world in various versions; in fixed wing aircraft, ground vehicles and door mounted on helicopters. In the Lynx, a 600 round magazine feeds the weapon with either solid or high explosive rounds. It is effectively recoilless, and since introduction it has proved remarkably reliable and far more effective than its predecessors.

The M3M recoilless 0.5 inch machine gun, far more effective than its GPMG predecessor. (*Alex Sims*)

Chapter 6

The Gulf – 1980 to the Present Day

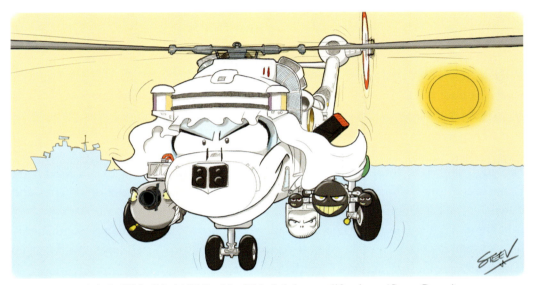

The Lynx Mark 3 Gulf Modified (GM) with all his fighting modifications. (*Steve George*)

If the Falklands War was a short sharp shock for the Royal Navy, then involvement in the Gulf was a long slow burn, lasting thirty-five years and still ongoing. That is except for the First Gulf War, which was a phenomenal success for the Lynx. In just two days, two aircraft effectively neutralised the Iraqi Navy in what became known as the 'Battle of Bubiyan'. Several accounts of this and other actions are included later in this chapter.

In 1980, the Shah of Iran had been deposed and the government of Iran was in a state of flux. Iraq saw this as an opportunity to reclaim disputed territory, and with the tacit approval of the west, invaded Iran. The subsequent war would be the biggest to occur on the planet with the exception of the two world wars. It didn't end until 1988, making it the twentieth century's longest conventional war. In order to protect British shipping, a Royal Navy warship and supporting Fleet Auxiliary were despatched, and there has been a continual naval presence in the area ever since. This was known as Operation Armilla, or more commonly the Armilla Patrol. Initially covering the Gulf

158   The Royal Navy Lynx

of Oman, by 1988 operations had moved into the Gulf itself and particularly the Strait of Hormuz, the narrow and dangerous passage into the waters around Iran and Iraq. The period prior to the invasion of Kuwait was known as the 'Tanker War' and the threat literally came from both sides of the Gulf.

There were then the two Gulf Wars. For British forces these were known as Operation 'GRANBY', commencing in Aug 1990 and Operation 'TELIC', starting in March 2003. In the mid-2000s operation KIPION was started, primarily to deal with piracy in the Indian Ocean and now the two have been merged, with KIPION covering both areas.

Irrespective of these various operations, they have all involved ships with Lynx Flights embarked. Operating in the Gulf immediately brought its own problems for the Lynx both in the threat that was faced and also the extremes of the environment. A Mark 2 Lynx had significant trouble operating in the high ambient temperatures that could be experienced in summer months, as well as being particularly vulnerable to various weapon systems it could encounter in the region. Within a few years, a specific variant of the Mark 3 was developed, known as the Mark 3 (GM) i.e. 'Gulf Modified'. Later on, all the performance improvements and a rationalised suite of avionics and defensive aids were incorporated into the Mark 8. This meant that all Mark 8s were capable of Gulf operations. The downside was that as the aircraft was significantly heavier than its Mark 3 predecessor, it was not so capable in the summer months when temperatures of 40–45 degrees C could be experienced.

The unique and often changing nature of the military threat also produced some interesting role equipment modifications, some of which are still in use today.

The environment

The following extract from *Cockpit* Magazine, written by Lieutenant Damian Belgeonne of HMS *Manchester* Flight in the late eighties, sums up the problems of operating in such extreme conditions:

> *'The following is an insight to hot and sunny operations in the Gulf. Royal Navy helicopters have been operating in the Gulf since 1980. At first, operations were confined to the central areas of the Gulf of Oman. Recently, operations have included the Gulf itself, to support and protect UK shipping interests. This change to the modus operandi has also led to Lynx role enhancements to enable it to carry out its tasks more effectively.*
>
> *'The high ambient temperatures, particularly in the summer months, were already a cause for concern to all aviators in the Gulf. Typical temperatures in July are 38*

The Gulf – 1980 to the Present Day   159

degrees in the shade and up to 48 on deck in direct sunlight. The associated problems with this over the years have included cracked windscreens, degraded avionics, lack of sufficient cooling and reduction in power margins, the latter having been particularly acute in the Lynx Mark 2 and early Mark 3s with Gem 100 engines.

'Weapons and sensor enhancements mean that the aircraft's all-up weight is increased beyond the capabilities of the Gem 100 to operate in high ambient temperatures with any reasonable endurance. The answer to this problem was the more powerful Lynx Mark 3 with the Gem 42 engines, but the problem of cooling remained. This was resolved with the introduction of the Lynx Armilla cooling package.

'This package was designed to improve the cooling in four main areas: MGB oil, hydraulic fluid, the engine bays and the intermediate gearbox. The following have been fitted: a more powerful MGB oil cooler with a thermostatically controlled air shuttle valve, an electrically operated fan with ducting to each of the hydraulic reservoirs, modified intake and exhaust ducts on the engine cowling to form an eductor system for each engine, and finally, a fan fitted to the intermediate gearbox input shaft.

'These improvements required some major rework by the aircraft repair yard at Fleetlands and the new aircraft was designated the Lynx Mark 3 (GM) and it has proved to be very successful, greatly increasing the flexibility of the aircraft.

'Despite the extra power available from the forty-two series engines, the aircraft, when fully fitted with role equipment, still operates at its maximum weight, which when corrected for the ambient conditions places the ship in its most restrictive set of limitations. Additionally, careful consideration has to be given to the safe single engine speed (which at the time of writing is normally between 30 and 34 knots). Certain role equipment is wire locked to the carriers and therefore cannot be jettisoned in an emergency to reduce weight. Another penalty of high weight is the aircraft's inability to hover for long periods. This is also affected by overheating which is partly addressed by the cooling package. Operating "hot and high" heavy conditions places considerable loads on the rotor blades and it has been found that the blade track has to be adjusted more frequently.

'Increased airframe vibration levels owing to the hot temperatures and high weights are significant and levels have to be monitored very carefully. Manchester Flight have reduced the aircraft's normal cruise speed in an attempt to keep levels down. The problem is further increased by the physical nature of the role equipment. Also, the effects of increased vibration may well have an adverse effect on the airframe and equipment life over a longer period.

'The problems of high temperatures are perhaps more acutely felt whilst the aircraft is on deck ranged at alert. The flight deck temperature recorded in direct sunlight exceeds the maximum laid down for the Lynx avionics systems. To help get round this a white canvas cover has been provided. More affectionately known as "the condom" this does reduce the temperature within the aircraft on average to between 34 and 36 degrees. It also protects the windscreen, which is prone to cracking at these high temperatures.'

HMS *Beaver* flight in the summer of '88, with the aircraft wearing its 'condom'. (*Peter Spens-Black*)

'Prevention of corrosion is a constant battle in the Gulf in view of the warm and very humid conditions. Sand also gets everywhere and on occasions after a flight, the aircraft has a positively reddish tinge. However, the engine compressor blades are nice and shiny! As a result, throughout any day, the Flight can be found conducting continual seek and destroy missions against corrosion.

'Personnel are another major consideration in these hot conditions. Whilst we are duty ship, the Lynx remains at alert from sunrise to sunset and on average conducts four to five hours flying per day. These duty periods last up to six days. The hangar and flight deck are outside the ship's air-conditioning boundary, so there is little respite *from the heat of the day. I feel sure that the Flight will one day evaporate away, not to mention suffer from sunstroke, heat exhaustion and skin cancer.*

'In terms of physical and mental pressure, a flight of one hour equates to a two or three hour flight in temperate climates, which is quite demanding over an average day's flying when on duty. After each sortie, the Flight have to decant the soaked aircrew out of the aircraft and supply them with copious amounts of liquid to replace the large amount that has been lost through perspiration. The knock-on effect of this is the rather unsavoury smell that tends to hang around the aircrew. The Task Group operations officer has been heard to say that the Flight commander's overalls could be the first line of defence against any attack. Indeed, once removed there is no doubt that they could find their own way to the laundry.

'People could be forgiven for thinking that hot and sunny weather presents no problem to the aviator, as we get so little of it in the UK. In the Gulf it is normal and at an extreme, with no respite. Operating in these conditions day in day out brings extra problems to the aviators and maintainers.'

Weapons and sensors

Towards the end of the 80s, the 'Tanker War' was taking place in the Gulf and Strait of Hormuz region. In order to keep up with the various threats that evolved, more equipment was fitted to the aircraft. In 1986, 829 Squadron, that had previously operated the Wasp, took on the Lynx Flights of all type 22 Frigates, towed array Leander class Frigates and HMS *Endurance*. The squadron had the lead in the trials of these various modifications and the additional aircrew training required to operate the special equipment fits. The following is an article that appeared in the navy's *Flight Deck* magazine, written by Lieutenant Commander Legg, the then commanding officer of 829 Squadron:

'In 1986, attacks on merchant shipping in the Arabian Gulf increased as the Iran-Iraq war escalated and many ships fell victim to their air launched M39 Exocet, as well as Chinese made Silkworm missiles fired by Iran from the Faw Peninsula. During the Falklands War the Hampton Mayfair anti-Exocet jamming equipment was fitted to the Lynx and briefly deployed, but for Armilla it was decided to introduce a much improved, properly funded and trialled system to protect UK shipping in the Gulf. The Yellow Veil jamming pod was procured and is now a standard fit on all Lynx in theatre. The system is reliable and not only can it be used to protect shipping, but can be used against a wide range of radars and missiles in all spheres of anti-surface warfare.'

A very rare photo of an early Mark 3 with the Hampton Mayfair jammer fitted. This had been improved over the version used in the Falklands War as can be seen by the extra aerials on top of the weapon carrier. (*Malcolm Legg*)

'As the Iranian Revolutionary Guard (IRG) gained more experience with infrared missiles it was clear that the Lynx required a much improved infrared countermeasure capability. The "throw the chaff out of the window, fly towards the missile and pray" tactic was not good enough. A combined chaff and IR dispenser was trialled and deployed with HMS Boxer on a flight in January 1988. This has proved to be a reliable system with the capability to release a predetermined number of chaff skillets and infrared decoys for self-protection. Chaff, of course, can be used in all spheres of above water warfare, and the new dispenser is an improvement on the manual method of "hand launch from the window", where, on occasions, more chaff ended up inside the aircraft than out. To combat the more sophisticated infrared missile menace (the Soviet made SA7 in particular), HMS London Flight deployed in the summer of 1988 with a fixed infrared jammer mounted on the port and starboard – on the weapon carriers. (Note this was not too successful as it severely restricted access to the cabin and so was not often fitted.) By 1990 the system will be repositioned on top of the cabin roof, where it will become a permanent fit.'

The Gulf – 1980 to the Present Day

HMS *London*'s Lynx being loaded with a drill Sea Skua during their work up for the Gulf; the Challenger IR Jammers can clearly be seen mounted on the cabin roof either side of the aircrew. (*Ian Farmer*)

> 'To counter the threat of the small but well-armed 'Boghammer' boats, the cabin mounted machine gun was replaced by a podded, half inch cannon, known as the HMP (Heavy Machine-gun Pod). This relatively cheap and very cheerful, fixed, forward firing weapon has been most successful and gives the Lynx a potent close-range air-to-surface (and air-to-air!) capability.'

The Helicopter Machine-Gun Pod fitted to both weapon carriers, plus the Yellow Veil pod outboard. The HMP could be fitted both sides, but often only one was flown. The white panel on the nose was there in an attempt to keep the UHF radios inside cool and improve their reliability. (*Richard Scott*)

The results of the HMP against a splash target towed by the ship. (*Peter Spens-Black*)

> *'As these and previous modifications have been fitted, the aircraft's basic weight has grown over the years and its appearance has changed from slender beauty to that of a "snarling warthog". The latter will not change, but by improving the power output of the Gem engine and the load strength of the main rotor gearbox (with the introduction of the Mark 3), the aircraft can still fly with full fuel in the extreme heat of the Arabian summer. Additional modifications are in the pipeline and are linked to the Mark 8 programme, but for the Arabian Lynx, the most important current modification is the introduction of new radios which will enable the aircraft to talk, not only to the merchant vessels, but to the warships using a secure speech facility. So there it is, the Lynx modified to the hilt, capable of many more tasks than it was originally designed to perform, all aimed at improving its performance in the anti-surface role. Despite these unscheduled developments the aircraft has not suffered from any limitations following modification, but has been greatly improved to become a credible weapon system capable of operating in all extremes of weather anywhere in the world.'*

As an article for public consumption this was accurate but arguably slightly optimistic. As can be seen from the previous article, operating in the heat of summer months still caused significant problems, but none of them were showstoppers.

The problem of 'Bog Hammers' was very real. The term 'Bog Hammer' originates from the name of a Swedish company who produced small fast boats, the company being called Boghammar Marin AB. These vessels were – in all senses – force multipliers in that their effect was significantly more than their capability. Often with a crew of as little as three, they operated in packs and could cause significant damage to an unprotected merchantman and even warships. The USS *Vincennes* has been criticised for her role in shooting down an unarmed Iranian passenger aircraft. What is not often mentioned is that at the time, she was fighting off eight 'Bog Hammers' – so

The Gulf – 1980 to the Present Day   165

was understandably rather busy. The HMP was brought in as an urgent requirement to counter this threat. Its range was known to be less than the likely missiles being fired from the 'Bog Hammers'. However, its purpose was to keep the enemy's head down and spoil his aim. In this, it fulfilled its requirement. That is not to say that it did not have its problems. Until the muzzle of the gun was modified, it had a habit of destroying the aircraft's navigation lights and damaging the panels which were situated just ahead of it. It also took the Royal Navy some time to learn how to tune and maintain it. In fact, by the time the First Gulf War started, it was rarely used.

Yellow Veil was a quantum leap from the earlier Hampton Mayfair jammer. However, once again its utility in the Lynx was not as great as originally hoped and once again, as in the Falklands, it was Sea Skua that proved its worth when Iraq invaded Kuwait.

Subsequent to the above article, another piece of equipment that was procured quickly for the First Gulf War was Sandpiper. This was a forward looking infrared device that was mounted on the port inboard weapon station and proved invaluable when identifying enemy targets as hostile before they were engaged. This capability proved so important that when the Mark 8 Lynx was being developed, a much more capable system called Sea Owl, otherwise known as the PID (Passive Identification Device), was mounted on the nose of the aircraft.

One final, unusual, piece of equipment was tried out in the Lynx in the Gulf in a very different role. One of the major threats to shipping from Iran and Iraq was the laying of mines. Due to the clear waters of the Gulf, a system called the Demon Camera was fitted to some aircraft. This actually looked down and could identify mines visually from above. In the end it proved of limited capability, but who would have thought the Lynx would have had a mine hunting role at some point in its career?

In fact, it can be argued that there was never a final definitive 'Gulf Modified Mark 3', because the modification package changed regularly as the operational scenario and threat changed, as well as when new equipment became available. However, by the time of the First Gulf War, the GM package included:

The cooling modifications.

Secure speech radios – an interim fit called 'Lamberton', which gave the observer the ability to discuss classified tactical information in the clear, but not the pilot. In fact the observer had to disconnect the lead from his helmet and reconnect it to the secure speech system. This was not so much an issue if the captain of the aircraft was the observer, but often the pilot was the senior man and so he was out of the command loop at a critical time. That said, the radio was a vast improvement over the previous system that used authentication tables and complicated verbal challenge and response to pass classified material over unencrypted radios.

ALQ 157 Challenger IR Jammer – now fitted to the cabin roof. However, it was heavy (over 100kg) and often unreliable. Because of its weight and position it could significantly increase the vibration levels in the aircraft. In the First Gulf War at least two Flights removed it because of these reasons.

Mode 4 IFF – an additional IFF system needed for international operability.

Sandpiper Thermal Imager – mounted on the inner port sponson and viewed on the same screen as the Sea Spray radar. It proved invaluable identifying targets in the poor visibility of the Gulf for some Flights, others found it unreliable and preferred the well tested 'Mark One Eyeball'.

Helicopter Machine-Gun pod – proved useful during the 'Tanker War' against 'Boghammers', but of very limited value in a full maritime conflict.

Yellow Veil – there was a significant threat from both Silkworm and Exocet missiles and the jammer was capable of seducing both. However, once again it was of limited use once the sea battle of the First Gulf War started. (In part, because the Lynx sank most of the missile carrying ships!)

M130 Chaff and Flare – fitted on the rear of the aircraft this is a combined launcher for chaff and IR decoy flares and was considered extremely valuable.

Trimble GPS – an early system mounted on top of the Sea Spray radar display. Modern readers will now realise how significant this was to the aircrews who found it invaluable.

A 'snarling warthog'. HMS *London*'s Lynx. Mounted inboard on the port weapon station is the white dome of the Sandpiper IR sensor and the long pod outboard is the Yellow Veil radar jammer. The black boxes mounted at the rear below the exhausts are the M130- chaff and IR decoy flare launchers, with the IR jammers on the cockpit roof. Depending on fuel load, Sea Skua or an HMP could be carried on the opposite weapon stations. (*Ian Farmer*)

The Tanker War

Spot the Lynx. (*Mark Graham*)

As mentioned earlier, as the Iran Iraq War hotted up in the late eighties, so did the task of protecting UK shipping. In September 1988, whilst on Armilla patrol, HMS *Southampton* collided with the Motor Vessel *Tor Bay* while transiting the Straits of Hormuz. This necessitated an emergency replacement. Below is an account from Sub Lieutenant Mark Graham of HMS *Boxer* Flight, who were given the job:

Jake and Ellwood each with an HMP. On the deck are 4.5 inch flares, a Stingray torpedo in a storage cradle, and in the foreground General Purpose Machine Guns plus ammunition. (*Mark Graham*)

Flight Commander – Lieutenant Jerry Stanford
Flight Pilot – Sub Lieutenant Nick Clarke
Flight Observer – Lieutenant Ralph Dodds
Flight Observer 2 – Sub Lieutenant Mark Graham

Aircraft: XZ 724, XZ 239, Nicknames: Jake and Ellwood

'*Boxer* had returned from a full gulf deployment to the UK, had some leave and was participating in Exercise Teamwork 88 in the Greenland-Iceland-UK gap. When the captain announced over the main broadcast that we were to make a fast passage out to the Gulf for the remainder of the year, a huge cheer went throughout the ship. It's always better to be operational than be practising. In all we spent ten months on, or going to or from, Armilla in 1988.

'The primary mission of the Royal Navy's presence was to "accompany" entitled shipping through the Straits of Hormuz. Entitled merchant ships were those that were British flagged or had a British master. We would regularly cross pollinate personnel between the British flagged ships and *Boxer* to increase

The Gulf – 1980 to the Present Day   169

working knowledge and practices. As this part of the sea was entirely within Iranian and or Omani territorial waters, we could not 'escort' the merchant ships, as this was a 'military act' and contrary to the Freedom of Navigation agreements. The entire area was also in range of Iranians Silkworm missile batteries. Invariably we were at Mine Warning Red for these transits as the Iranians were caught several times deploying mines. So the biggest ship was put at the front as a "kinetic minesweeper" as they were large enough to withstand the blast. As the tankers were high in the water and empty, this would be a crocodile (the nickname for the line of ships that wasn't a convoy that we weren't escorting!) inbound to the Gulf. Invariably, as the crocodiles formed, non-entitled ships would also tag on the end, increasing their chances of a safe passage. The sole time that *Boxer* "escorted" anything was when we were accompanying the barge carrying the salt water damaged Sea Dart missiles from HMS *Southampton*, to be sunk in the explosive dumping area of Dubai.

'We had to take care when operating with the Americans. They allegedly hit an oil platform off Dubai and also allegedly sank the navigation buoy marking the corner of Omani territorial waters (they claimed twelve nautical miles and the neighbouring emirate only three nautical miles, creating a 90 degree corner in territorial water); the Americans made us very nervous! The only way for ships to effectively find the height of air contacts was to lock up to them with fire control radars. If deemed a threat, a challenge on Guard (the international emergency frequency) was issued. The Lynx at this time did not have secure speech V/UHF, so were unable to participate in the NATO Navy chat frequency. Due to strong atmospheric temperature inversions and ducting, quite often you would not get the call on Guard and a few times our own ship would have to intervene on navy chat as the US escalated through their Rules of Engagement (ROE) calls with us blissfully unaware. It was not uncommon to be locked up to ten or twelve times in a one hour sortie by NATO or Soviet warships.'

The burning remains of an oil platform allegedly hit by mistake by the Americans. (*Mark Graham*)

'The normal configuration for the Alert 15 aircraft on deck was for it to be fitted with both HMP and yellow Veil, and also carrying four, 4.5 inch reconnaissance flares. We maintained Alert 15 from half an hour before dawn to half an hour after sunset. A tactic had been developed to drop a circle of flares around attacking boats that enabled enough light to carry out a visual night attack. The ISIS reflector gunsight for the HMP that hung from the frame above the pilot was identical to the one used in a Spitfire! The second aircraft in the hangar could then be ranged spread and folded in fifteen minutes after the first one was launched. Flying could be difficult because of the "goldfish bowl" low contrast caused by a very strong temperature inversion at 400 feet, which trapped dust, reduced contrast and visibility and made the horizon quite ill-defined if the sea was totally calm.'

Ellwood at Alert 15 with HMP and Yellow Veil plus 4.5 inch flares. The horizon is very indistinct due to the atmospheric temperature inversion. (*Mark Graham*)

'We would sometimes climb up through the inversion to cool down, but this rendered radios and the radar useless as they could not penetrate back through the inversion. I do recall one day, when we were twenty miles off Oman, getting the coast of Gujarat on the radar screen (600 miles away) due to skipping.'

'Elwood', landing on the motor vessel *Karama Maersk* after she was attacked by Iranian Revolutionary Guard boats. She had suffered penetration of her cargo hold and the burning oil was leaving a trail in the water for about a mile and a half. This photo was taken by the ship's medical officer who we had landed earlier, having responded to the Mayday call. It is thought our appearance caused the Iranians to move back into their own territorial waters. The *Karama Maersk* was well prepared for the gun and rocket propelled grenade attack and no further assistance was required. Amusingly, the doctor rushed to the bridge (quite a distance from where the aircraft had landed) with his first-aid bag, to be told 'everyone is quite all right, would you like a cup of tea?' The press helicopters from Dubai had arrived by the time Elwood landed on to recover the out of breath doctor and footage was shown on the BBC news that evening. (*Mark Graham*)

'I started out as the second observer on a two aircraft Flight, and then took over as the Flight observer when we returned to the UK in June and returned to a normally manned Flight. As a young 20-year-old on his first flight, I was going straight on operations with all the latest kit, it was very exciting and I remember feeling quite privileged. We worked hard, in extreme weather conditions – we had three sets of flying overalls each on the go, as you sweated so much, you had one for flying, one for living inside the ship (if you were in the silkworm envelope you slept clothed in your action working dress) and one in dhobey for the next day. We were there as a deterrent, to prevent casual attacks on British merchant ships. Our stance was totally overt, and it worked. In both deployments we only saw an Iranian military ship once and intercepted an F-4 Phantom radar once on Orange Crop. We tried to keep out of their way and I got the impression that they were doing the same. We were always on the lookout for mines, although never saw any. The Soviet Navy were doing something similar and had an at sea logistic base we called the SCFMLB (Soviet Contingency Force Mobile Logistics Base). It consisted of a Don and an Ugra (both support ships) which supported the two Udaloy and one Sovremenny warship they were using to accompany their merchantmen. We would often go and photograph them, and they would do likewise. It was all very cordial. The Americans had several incidents during our deployments. The USS *Stark* was hit by Iraqi Exocet missiles. We had a similar incident when we sailed from Jubail, Saudi Arabia with lots of Saudi officer cadets aboard. As we were in territorial waters, the Seawolf anti-aircraft missiles were not loaded, nor the chaff dispensers. An Iraqi Badger (bomber) started an attack profile on us and the last and only line of defence we had was a Royal Artillery Javelin Detachment that we were able to get ready in time and deployed on the flight deck. It was interesting that in a very British way we pretended that we always meant to go to action stations and there was no need for our guests to concern themselves. It was all part of the show! The USS *Samuel B. Roberts* hit a mine while we were there, but we were not involved and all hell broke loose when we were en route to Mombasa and the Americans sank an Iranian frigate and severely damaged another. Rumour has it that one was hit by twenty-five Harpoon missiles. The *Vincennes* incident happened while we were back in the UK, and by the time we arrived back in the Gulf all was quiet again. I remember the cigarette boats smuggling between Iran and UAE, but they were none of our concern.'

The First Gulf War – Operation GRANBY

'Bruiser loose'*

A painting by Anthony Lawrence of HMS *Gloucester*'s Lynx attacking an Iraqi surface unit. (*David Livingstone*)

By the time that Iraq invaded Kuwait, the Royal Navy and Lynx crews were well versed in Gulf operations. Unlike the Second Gulf War, where it was primarily a land operation and so the Royal Navy Lynx had little chance of success, the First Gulf War had a significant maritime element. Kuwait had been invaded and the Iraqi Navy was still intact, in fact, many of the warships used by the Iraqis were actually captured from the Kuwaiti navy. Phil Needham, the flight commander of HMS *Cardiff*, actually met the Kuwaiti captain of one and had to confess to sinking it! In total there were fifteen confirmed Sea Skua strikes. Three Distinguished Service Crosses and four Mentions in Despatches were awarded to Lynx aircrew.

It should be noted that the threat to the environment and the tactical situation in the Gulf at this time was exactly what the Lynx had been designed to counter when the decision had been made to arm it with Sea Skua after the sinking of the Israeli Destroyer *Eilat* in 1967. The Iraqi navy had a large number of small and fast vessels armed with missiles such as the Exocet, which made them a serious tactical threat despite their size.

It should be understood that this book does not seek to give an exact, day-to-day analysis of the war. Late January and early February of 1991 (what became known as the Battle

---

* 'Bruiser Loose' is the rather appropriate radio call made by a Lynx when firing a Sea Skua.

of Bubiyan) was an incredibly busy and demanding time for the Lynx crews. They were often operating miles away from their parent ships in an extremely hostile environment. The weather was hot, with very limited visibility, and the Lynx were often subjected to shore anti-aircraft fire and attacks by surface-to-air missiles. Identifying targets was difficult and it was often not possible to conduct damage assessments. Consequently, it was not always possible to confirm sinkings, or even identify the type of target with total confidence. The 'Fog of War' was very prevalent in the northern Gulf in 1991.

In addition, the presence of the large fleet of ships and aircraft that were assembled to retake the country increased the challenge significantly. Tactics had to be worked up, particularly with the US Navy, most of which were from their Pacific Fleet and had different operating procedures from those the Royal Navy were familiar with. The following is an extract from an article written by Lieutenant Commander Alan Rycroft and reproduced here by permission of *Defence Helicopter Magazine*:

'On paper, the Iraqi maritime force appeared an ideal target for the Lynx; lightly armed fast attack craft with no organic air defence capability other than shoulder fired surface-to-air missiles. In reality, when threat analysis and "tabletop tactics" had taken place, the capability of the Lynx against these targets was irrelevant until the final stages of the conflict. There were many more important tasks for the aircraft. The prospect of fast, manoeuvrable, anti-ship missile armed craft operating within a cluttered surface environment was sobering. Reaction times to missiles would be extremely short and the identification problem with conflicting fixed wing traffic enormous. This was further complicated by the need for a comprehensive and accurate cover of all surface contacts moving within these waters, in what were proving to be demanding flying conditions.

'The ability of the Iraqi Navy to lay mines was already proven and there was increasing concern that a minefield could do more to delay offensive operations than any fast attack craft. It was also an unknown threat that had to be incorporated into any war planning.

'Finally, the Iraqi air force had demonstrated its anti-ship capability in the past and was a very real threat to the Allied forces until their superiority had been established. Whilst anti-air warfare (AAW) does not immediately spring to mind as a constraint upon the Lynx anti-surface operations, two of the Royal Navy platforms in the area were two Type 42 destroyers with dedicated AAW assets (Sea Dart). When they deployed forward, their Lynx went with them.'

'Until air superiority had been established, the gap between the forward AAW screen and the majority of the surface forces would be extensive. Lynx would have to

176   The Royal Navy Lynx

deploy forward and operate in their immediate vicinity for their safety. It was at this stage that airframe hours began to escalate quickly.

'The Persian Gulf is an area of high surface contact density. Routine merchant shipping, combined with the smaller dhow traffic and many offshore platforms, wellheads and other structures, made the surface picture compilation task demanding. Locating and isolating this routine traffic, attempting to establish patterns of flow and becoming familiar with all the natural man-made radar conspicuous objects in the area was vital.

'The first product of these discussions was the introduction of US Navy Seahawk/ Lynx consolidated operations (CONOPS). The Seahawk, with its excellent radar, processing power and data link, was an ideal platform from which to generate an area surface picture. The Lynx could work hand-in-hand in its probing role to identify contacts, allowing the Seahawk to remain in direct communication with the ASUW Commander. The Lynx could, in turn, respond to changing scenarios by shifting from the recce role to the attack role with Sea Skua. As ever, the only restrictions on operations were the range of the aircraft from supporting platforms with fuel and flying hours.

'Throughout December and January, a succession of Lynx staged through the northern Persian Gulf, operating with US Navy counterparts, refining procedures and becoming familiar with each other's way of operating. Although some of the units had operated together in their NATO role, many of the US Navy ships were from the Pacific Fleet and had not worked with the Lynx before. That the procedure was so successful was due to the flexibility of both sides.

'The Lynx/Seahawk combination was a small part of the overall picture compilation system. The availability of US Navy carrier borne fixed wing aircraft within the four carrier battle groups meant that in addition to the normal combat air patrol flights working in close cooperation with the forward AAW screen, there was also the luxury of dedicated surface reconnaissance aircraft and surface combat air patrol aircraft (SUCAP).

'The availability of so many assets was, in fact, a two edged sword. Whilst there was the capability to respond very quickly to a threat, de-conflicting the fixed wing and rotary wing aircraft at extreme range, and in difficult radio propagation conditions, caused problems.

'The answer was relatively simple. The ASUW Commander would generate the tasking for the whole of the northern Persian Gulf. This included all air assets. If a radar contact needed identifying, the ASUW Commander would select which asset was to be used. If a Lynx or Seahawk was available within an acceptable timescale, it

would be directly tasked. If not, or if the contact was threatening surface units, a fixed wing asset would be used.

'The radar target would then progress from being a Contact of Interest to a Critical Contact of Interest, until identified. This would inevitably involve either the Lynx closing until within Sandpiper range, or a direct overflight by SUCAP. If the target was subsequently identified as hostile, the ASUW Commander could use the same procedure to allocate an attack platform.

'The onset of war saw the Royal Navy units dispersed over a large area. HMS Gloucester and Cardiff, as AAW destroyers, were fully integrated into the AAW barrier to the north, with what became known as "the shooters". The flagship, HMS London was halfway between Qatar and Kuwait in close company with RFA Argus, the Primary Casualty Reception Ship (PCRS), whilst HMS Brazen, with its twin Lynx flight, was acting as guard dog to the massive Allied support shipping south of Qatar.

'The Iraqi Navy was, to a large extent, still around its main naval base at Umm Qasr, although some units, notably the OSA class missile patrol boats, were either operating from Kuwait or at sea. The units coming down from Umm Qasr had to transit down past Bubiyan Island and out to the east and south to get to the Allied units. The units operating from Kuwait appeared to concentrate their activities to the south and east of Faylakah, although they were constrained by their own mine laying activities, by now at a peak.'

An aerial photo of the naval jetty at Umm Qasr with bomb damage clearly visible. The white arrow is pointing to an ex-Kuwaiti TNC 45 corvette that was sunk the next day by HMS *Gloucester*'s Lynx. (*David Livingstone*)

'Transiting up to one and a half hours from their parents, **Cardiff** and **Gloucester** flights operated largely to the north-west around Bubiyan. Using the most northerly American naval platforms as fuelling points, both Flights were flying in excess of seven hours a day.

'*HMS* London's *Flight was largely tasked in support of the flagship, flying the Yellow Veil Jammer to counter the threatened air-to-surface missile launch.* Brazen *Flight forward-operated one of their two Lynx through* London *up to the north and supported* Cardiff *and* Gloucester.

'*The Lynx would launch from the AAW screen during the first hours of daylight, armed with two or three missiles. This gave the extra range necessary operating right in the north-western corner of the Gulf.*

'*Once on task, the Lynx would declare its presence to the ASUW Commander and be allocated its primary task of identification of Contacts of Interest. This would normally entail working in close company with a Seahawk when available. If the contact had been identified as hostile, or needed positive identification, the Lynx would be tasked. Flying at fifty feet and below, at speeds in excess of one hundred and twenty knots, the Lynx would close to establish identification.*

'*With visibility often less than a mile, identification was determined by several methods. Intelligence support would indicate that no known friendly Saudi or Kuwaiti boats were in the vicinity; it was therefore up to the Lynx to establish, by any means possible, that the contact was indeed military. The forward-looking infrared (Sandpiper) was an obvious asset, although the Orange Crop ESM was the major aid.*

'*Once the contact was identified as hostile, the ASUW Commander would order it to be engaged. The Lynx would then update the target position with its navigational equipment and open to set up for a Skua attack.*

'*Even against the most advanced shoulder fired weapons, the Lynx was effectively safe outside three nautical miles from the target, even in ideal visibility. This allowed the Lynx to close more than it would do against a more capable target and optimise the missile attack.*

'*The radar would be locked against the target, the missile selected, fused and armed, then released. The aircraft could then turn away from the threat, if necessary, although all attacks were conducted well outside counter fire range. On completion of the attack, the Lynx would then try to achieve some visual confirmation of damage inflicted. This turned out to be simpler than first thought, as most Skua hits were spectacular and were often followed by secondary explosions, easily heard and seen by the crew, particularly at night.*

'*As the Lynx were establishing their credibility to the north, the Allied maritime forces began their move toward Kuwait, the priority being to establish safe water for the battleships to conduct naval gunfire support on both Faylakah Island and the Kuwaiti coast. The primary threat shifted to the mine.*

'*As the ships progressed north, the Lynx and Sea King helicopters flew surface surveillance sorties looking for floating mines, a cheap but highly effective maritime*

The Gulf – 1980 to the Present Day 179

weapon. Intelligence had indicated where the most likely areas the mines were and the surface units moved to a position just north of the Doora oilfield.

'*The UK and US mine countermeasures vessels then progressively worked their way towards the Kuwaiti coast, carving out a path for the battleships and their attendant destroyers. The latter had a crucial role to play in providing air defence to the minehunters.*

'*The group finally established an operating area extending from the southernmost borders of Kuwait to Bubiyan Island area with minehunters working seven miles from the coast. The entire area was initially established as an amphibious operating area (AOA) and became a microcosm of the larger surface battle. Approximately twenty by fifty miles, the AOA needed constant surveillance to guarantee the safety of the mine hunting assets.*

'*This surveillance was in addition to the already high tasking to the north-west. The plan was to use the Lynx by day with its Skua missiles and the Seahawk by night, calling on Cobra attack helicopters and Lynx if required. A further head-to-head with US Navy aircrew led to a second procedure being developed using the Cobra gunship in support of the Lynx. Designed on 14 February, it was christened 'Valentine'. The Cobra had an awesome weapon load capability, but lacked a radar or sophisticated navigation system. The Lynx had a radar and navaids, but was finding that, for some of the targets, Sea Skua was too big a stick to use. The smaller Iraqi launches were difficult to lock radar to and of such low freeboard that it would have been questionable despatching a Skua.*

'*The solution was the combination of the two aircraft. The Lynx would find and identify the target, report, and then either vector the Cobra, or lead to a pre-planned position from the enemy, allowing the Lynx to break away and let the Cobra create havoc. Although used only once in anger, it proved to be an effective combat tactic for both aircraft. It also did little for the morale of the small boat's crews.*

'*It was as the Allies were establishing themselves comfortably off Kuwait that the ground offensive began. The naval gunfire capability of the battleships was unleashed with devastating effect and suddenly everything was over.*

'*Many lessons were learned during the campaign. Some were a surprise and some were well documented shortcomings. The Lynx did between six and seven months flying in six weeks and they achieved outstanding serviceability rates. The Sea Skua missiles scored fifteen confirmed hits against all types of enemy units, the majority of hits inflicting terminal damage.*

'*Lynx aircrew performed extremely well, flying at four times the normal peacetime rates, under considerable stress and in highly demanding weather conditions. The maintainers, a small highly professional body, kept the aircraft availability at unprecedented levels. Even with non-NATO units of the US Navy, cooperation and interoperability was remarkable. It reflects very well on standards of operating and training.*

'The Lynx yet again proved to be an unqualified success. As the only long-range air-to-surface missile-carrying helicopter in the theatre, it played a key role.

'Operation Granby was an example of the importance of a flexible, potent and highly manoeuvrable maritime helicopter in the modern warfare scenario.'

Whilst this article clearly outlines the overall tactical situation and effectiveness of the Lynx there now follows some actual accounts of those who flew the sorties.

The Gulf – 1980 to the Present Day

HMS *Cardiff*

Flight Commander – Lieutenant Phil Needham
Flight Pilot – Lieutenant Guy Haywood

Aircraft – XZ 230 (known as 'Rudolph' for at least one day – see below)

Cardiff Flight- Phil Needham far right, Guy Haywood third right. (*Phil Needham*)

In July 1990, HMS *Cardiff* returned from the Gulf after nine months on Armilla patrol. On 2 August, Iraq invaded Kuwait. Shortly afterwards the ship's captain cleared lower deck on the flight deck to assure his crew they would not be required to sail back to the Gulf. On 3 October, XZ 230 re-embarked as the ship sailed for Operation Granby!

To be fair there were good reasons for this; the ship was worked up for Gulf operations and both the ship and aircraft were fitted with the necessary special modifications for operating in the area. On 24 October, *Cardiff* took over from HMS *York* on station and remained there until 12 February the following year. It wasn't until 17 January that hostilities with the coalition forces commenced and the Flight was in action the next day.

It wasn't always hard work though. The ship was alongside in Dubai before Christmas and managed to have a cocktail party. During a conversation with a local business man at the party, the Flight commander 'had an idea'. As a result, a few days later, two five litre cans of water soluble red paint were delivered to the ship. The ship subsequently sailed, but on the evening of Christmas Eve all the Flight got out their paint brushes and converted the Lynx into Santa's sleigh, the idea being to deliver some goodwill around the fleet the next day. Phil Needham recalls:

'It seemed like such a good idea, but maybe I should have agreed it with my captain first, before we applied the paint. So the next morning, with a great deal of trepidation, I went to the bridge to tell him what we had done. As I arrived, I saw the officer of the watch fiddling with the colour contrast on the flight deck cameras as the aircraft was being ranged. He looked very confused. Luckily, the captain saw the funny side – much to my relief. We then spent much of the day flying around the various ships, delivering Christmas cake. It took a while for the Americans to catch on, but in the end it all went very well. We then spent that evening washing the paint off. Thankfully it did come off well, although we did have slight pink tinges on the aircraft throughout the subsequent war.'

Rudolph, delivering cake via the winchman. (*Phil Needham*)

The Gulf – 1980 to the Present Day   183

However, it was soon time to take life very seriously. The Flight was one of the most successful of all those operating in the area, sinking a total of five ships in twenty-six days.

On 18 January, in conjunction with a USN SH-60 Seahawk, they searched for two Zhuk class patrol boats, but they weren't found. On 24 January, during a surface search, two small Iraqi landing craft were identified, which were later sunk by American A6 jets.

On 29 January, the Lynx from HMS *Brazen* and *Gloucester* had already attacked small craft in the vicinity of Mina Saud. *Cardiff's* aircraft then arrived, along with an SH-60 and carried on with a surface search. The end result was the first Royal Navy sinking of the war when the Lynx fired a Sea Skua and sank an Iraqi Spasilac minelayer.

The 30 January was again busy and again working with an SH-60, the Lynx located an Iraqi T43 minelayer which was hit with one Sea Skua. After refuelling, the aircraft returned and fired a further three missiles against two TNC 45 missile-armed warships.

Things were quiet for a few days and it was assessed that the Allied successes the previous week were keeping the Iraqi Navy in port. However, on 8 February, an SH-60 vectored the Lynx towards another target which was sunk with one Sea Skua and turned out to be a Zhuk class patrol boat.

The final attack was on 11 February, in the early morning near Faylakah Island. A moving target was identified as a Zhuk patrol boat and eventually sunk with a Skua. However, there was some confusion over the targeting as will be described later.

Those are the bald facts; below, Phil Needham provides a little more personal detail to two of the incidents:

'The evening of the 29 January saw us conducting a surface search along the Kuwaiti border starting at dusk. Lynx from *Brazen* and *Gloucester* had already been in the area and fired missiles, but had had inconclusive results [See Note 1 at end of chapter]. We were tasked to search the area along the coast together with an American SH-60, call sign "Lone Wolf 41" (well it was an American). We had practiced low flying a great deal in previous weeks and Guy Haywood was doing his usual excellent piloting, keeping us at only twenty-five feet on the radar altimeter. In the vicinity of Ras Al Qulayah, we came under fire from shore batteries. There is only one thing to do in a helicopter when this happens – run away. Guy turned, banked hard, and commenced a weaving manoeuvre away from the coast. As I peered left and right over my shoulder, I saw what looked like a missile's plume of smoke coming towards us and instinctively fired the M130 chaff and flare dispenser. For the next few seconds things became "interesting".

The surface of the sea was covered in oil (deliberately released on the orders of Saddam Hussein). The flares fire outwards and downwards and for obvious reasons are quite bright. As the ambient light had almost faded and we were very low, the glare from the flares against the oily surface illuminated the cabin in a sudden bright glow. I suppose we should have expected it, but when you are under fire, a sudden bright light could mean several things. Guy didn't let it affect his flying and we quickly realised what it was, even if it took a while for heart rates to reduce.

'With adrenalin levels reducing, we decided it was time to return to *Cardiff*, but being low on fuel elected to go to the duty petrol station, our American buddy ship the USS *Nicholas*, an Oliver Hazard Perry Class frigate. Once on deck, I was "invited" to go to the ops room whilst Guy got on with the refuelling. Lone Wolf 41 was still airborne and was reporting a moving hostile target and we were being asked to get airborne and attack it. I was not entirely enthralled to learn that the hostile position was exactly where we had been fired on previously. I returned to the aircraft to pass on the "good news" to Guy, who not only had gotten the aircraft refuelled, but had also received copious amounts of pastrami sandwiches from the Americans. We got airborne for this next mission, but since I had never eaten pastrami before, we elected to fly a couple of orbits and have an early supper before getting on with the war! We eventually returned to the reported position; the target was identified on radar and we were given weapons free. However, because of communication problems, we had to conduct three attack runs before we acquired a good firing solution at four and a half miles. Once ready, we fired one Skua and were rewarded with a large explosion. The SH 60 reported the target fading from radar. Because of the closeness of the coast and the likelihood that we would come under fire again, we weren't able to close and do a full damage assessment, but it was later confirmed that we had sunk a Spasilac minelayer and had achieved the first Royal Navy sinking of the war.'

Guy Haywood looks on as the Flight team load two more Sea Skua. (*Phil Needham*)

'On 11 February, at 0300 hours, I was in the normal place for a naval aviator – fast asleep in my bunk – when I was woken with a call "Action Lynx". An RAF Nimrod patrol aircraft had reported numerous targets off the Kuwaiti coast. Although on Alert 45, we managed to get in the air in 16 minutes. Proceeding to the reported position, I was already becoming concerned, and once there, I asked our light blue friends what it was they were looking at on their expensive ground stabilised radar. The contacts they reported were all known barges that had been anchored in the same place for years. I asked if there had been any movement around them, assuming that maybe small craft were hiding in the vicinity, but was surprised to be told that they had detected no movement for over two hours.

'Not impressed, we started to look on our own radar and immediately spotted a moving target at Faylakah Island. Even less impressed that the Nimrod hadn't spotted anything, we moved towards it to make an identification. The problem was that, marked on the chart, in the exact position, was a large navigation buoy and the contact was staying in close proximity such that it was hard to tell which target to lock up to with the radar. Sandpiper came into its own now as we closed to within visual range, although this was not without its problems as we then came under fire from anti-aircraft batteries on the island. However, we were able to identify the target as another Zhuk patrol boat. In the end we needed to make about six approaches to reconcile the target from the buoy. We finally fired a Sea Skua. Which produced little in the way of an explosion, which either meant the weapon hadn't armed correctly or that we had indeed hit the buoy. We then fired a second missile and were rewarded with a substantial explosion and fire and we were credited with out fifth and last kill. None of this stopped the Flight claiming the buoy as well!'

The nose of XZ 230 and its kills. Five confirmed ship sinkings and one 'oops' or a navigation buoy!

All Lynx Flights are given an identifying number. In the case of Cardiff this was 214.

For their efforts Phil Needham was awarded a Distinguished Service Cross and Guy Haywood a Mention in Despatches.

The Gulf – 1980 to the Present Day

HMS *Gloucester*

Flight Commander – Lieutenant Commander David Livingstone
Observer – Sub Lieutenant Martin (Florry) Ford

The Battle of Bubiyan – 30 January 1991

Aircraft involved:

410 – HMS *Gloucester*: Lynx XZ 720
335 – HMS *Cardiff*: Lynx XZ 230
331 – HMS *Brazen*: Lynx XZ 724 and ZD256. Lieutenant Commander Mike Peary (Observer) and Lieutenant Simon Janes (Pilot)

HMS *Gloucester*'s Lynx showing their kills on the cabin door. (*David Livingstone*)

188   The Royal Navy Lynx

Below is HMS *Gloucester's* operations room narrative, with additional contemporaneous debriefing record by the *Gloucester* aircrew (in shaded italic). This was originally handwritten in the ship's operations room at the time and as the day progressed, so gives a fascinating insight into the action as it developed.

Time	Narrative	Notes
0842	2ND FPB FOUND IN SIMILAR AREA. LYNX / SH-60 POSSIBLE ATTACK TEAM	FPB – Fast Patrol Boat SH-60 – US maritime helicopter
0843	ACTION LYNX	Command order for launch of 410
0847	CANCELLED ACTION LYNX	
0840	2 x POLNOCNY FOUND POSITION 29.45N 048.46E HIT BY SUCAP. LARGE EXPLOSION OBSERVED. BURNING FULL LENGTH. 1 STILL IN AREA – A6 SUCAP TO INVESTIGATE. POLNOCNYS IN SAME POSITION AS LAST STRIKE. 2 POLNOCNYS MAYBE 1 HIT TWICE OR EACH HIT ONCE (!). *CARDIFF LYNX AND SH-60 EN ROUTE FOR STRIKE ON SECOND POLNOCNY (but target turned out be Spasilac)*	Polnocny – Class of Landing Ship Tank SUCAP – On task Surface Combat Air Patrol strike aircraft A6 – US Navy's Intruder fixed wing aircraft
0920	1 POL STRUCK AND SMOKING STILL UNDERWAY. 2 SUCAP CLOSING FOR BACK-UP AND FURTHER STRIKE IF REQUIRED	
0921	CONTACT OF INTEREST POSITION 29.08N 048.42E. *CARDIFF LYNX & SH-60 EN ROUTE*	
0945	CONTACT OF INTEREST (TRACK 7772) POS 29.42N 048.50E REPORTED BY LONE WOLF 41	LONE WOLF 41 (LW41) – An SH-60 from the USS *PAUL F FOSTER* TRACK – A numerical identity for a contact in the force's combat plotting system
1022	410 AIRBORNE. 2 POB ENDURANCE 1222 ENROUTE TO AREA WITH 2 LL SKUA. 410/SH-60 TO INVESTIGATE 29.45N 048.40E	POB – persons on board Endurance – the time at which fuel reaches minimum level SKUA – Sea Skua missile LL SKUA – a variant of Sea Skua designed to fly at Low-level (down to approximately four feet skim height)
	TAKE OFF GLOUCESTER ENDURANCE 2 HRS 10 MINS	

The Gulf – 1980 to the Present Day   189

Time	Narrative	Notes
1031	*LONE WOLF 41 NOMINATED AS CONSORT*	
1033	*335 REPORTS 21 POSSIBLE CONTACTS 323 SAUSAGE 44 MILES*	*SAUSAGE – one of a number of known geographical report points allowing a certain level of security from enemy interception of radio traffic. On that day SAUSAGE was position 28.56N 048.53E*
1045	*GOOD TWO WAY [COMMUNICATIONS] WITH LW41*	
1050	*ON TASK 10 NAUTICAL MILES SOUTH EAST OF BUBIYAN ISLAND. OVERT RADAR POLICY IDENTIFYING BUOYS / WRECKS. OVERT TO AVOID STUMBLING INTO MEZ*	*MEZ – Missile Engagement Zone, a danger area based on the range of surface-to-air missiles on the enemy craft*
1106	INVESTIGATE 7746 & 7745	Track numbers
1112	*1 TNC-45 IDENTIFIED POSN 29.45.5N 048.35.0E AT RANGE 3.5 MILES. 410 EGRESSED TO SOUTH-EAST TURNED IN AT 7.0 MILES. WEAPONS FREE REQUESTED AND GRANTED (1118 HOURS)*	*WEAPONS FREE – permission to engage*
1115	29.44.9N 048.36E 410 LOCKED UP AND READY TO ENGAGE A TARGET AT ABOVE POSITION. 410 REQUESTS APPROVAL TO ENGAGE OR HE WILL LOSE TRACK 7762-7766	LOCKED UP – 410's radar in firing mode pointing at a target
1118	WEAPONS FREE FROM NS	November Sierra – The Anti-Surface Warfare Commander (ASUWC)
1118	410 ACKNOWLEDGE	
1120	BRUISER LOOSE	BRUISER – generic name for air to surface anti-ship missile, in this case a Sea Skua LOOSE – weapon fired
1120	*1 SKUA RELEASED 6.0 MILES 300 FEET 100 KNOTS FOR 45 SECONDS. MISSILE OBSERVED TO RUN NORMALLY BEFORE LOST TO SIGHT. DURING FLIGHT SECOND TARGET VISUAL IDENTIFIED APPROXIMATELY 0.5 MILES ASTERN (TO WEST) OF FIRST TARGET. SKUA HIT FIRST TARGET – SKUA HIT BRIDGE AREA. ENGAGEMENT COMPLETE – RE-OPENED TO SOUTH-EAST*	
1121	CONFIRMATION WEAPON HIT. 2ND CONTACT IN 410'S AREA TO WEST. DIRECTED TO INVESTIGATE	

Time	Narrative	Notes
1124	ACTION LYNX 331	331 – HMS *BRAZEN'S* Lynx which was then using HMS *GLOUCESTER* as a forward operating base
1124	BRUISER LOOSE FROM 410. CONTACT / TARGET ASSESSED T43	T43 – An Iraqi minesweeper / layer
1124	*SECOND BRUISER RELEASED AT SECOND (WESTERLY) TARGET. IDENTIFIED AS T43. RELEASE PARAMETERS 6 MILES RANGE 300 FEET ALTITUDE 100 KNOTS AIRSPEED*	
1125	*MISSILE HITS ABAFT [BEHIND] THE BRIDGE*	
1125	2ND BRUISER HIT T43 AWAITING DAMAGE ASSESSMENT. FIRST TARGET WAS TNC45. LONE WOLF 41 TO CARRY OUT DAMAGE ASSESSMENT. 410 LOW FUEL & AWAY TO *CURTS* FOR TOP UP. SUCAP ENGAGES POLNOCNY POSN 28.58N 048.45E	USS *CURTS* – A US frigate stationed in northern areas of the Gulf on Combat Search and Rescue duties. The CSAR frigates were very handy fuelling sites
1126	*COMMENCE EGRESS RTB [RETURN TO BASE] VIA USS* CURTS	
1134	TNC45 HIT BELOW BRIDGE DEAD IN WATER DISABLED. T43 HIT MIDSHIPS AND DISABLED. BOTH TARGETS DEAD IN WATER. BOTH REPORTS CERTAIN	DEAD IN WATER – this refers to the target ship being stopped and non-functional, rather than human bodies in the sea
1139	331 AIRBORNE WITH 2 SKUA	
1146	WEAPONS FREE ALL COMBATANTS VICINITY BUBIYAN FROM NS	The ASUWC decides to allow aircraft to engage enemy ships without further clearances
1154	SUCAP AT POSN 29.59N 048.43E. SIX CONTACTS SUNK OR SINKING. MULTIPLE SMALL CRAFT HEADING TOWARDS UMM QASAR INLET (KHAWR ABD ALLAH BUOYED CHANNEL)	
1159	*CARDIFF* CALLED IN VIEW OF RECENT ACTION DO YOU REQUIRE ME TO LAUNCH A/C EARLY. REPLY FROM GLO "YES PLEASE" (DECISION TO RIPPLE LYNX TO MAINTAIN WEAPON CARRIER ON TASK)	GLO – HMS *GLOUCESTER* RIPPLE – to sequence the launch and recovery of the three Lynx to even out the aircraft presence at the scene of action over 100 miles from the *CARDIFF* and *GLOUCESTER*

The Gulf – 1980 to the Present Day   191

Time	Narrative	Notes
1202	*LAND ON USS* CURTS *DEBRIEF COMMANDING OFFICER CURTS*	
1203	FROM *ARK ROYAL*: WELL DONE BOYS. GO GET EM	HMS *ARK ROYAL* was stationed in Eastern Mediterranean and was obviously monitoring the tactical radio circuits
1203	*TAKE OFF* CURTS *RTB* GLOUCESTER	
1221	410 LIFTED FROM *CURTS*	Having refuelled, the *GLOUCESTER* Lynx how starts its 100 mile transit back to its parent ship to re-arm
1227	PICKING UP PLB TRANSMISSIONS IN VICINITY OF POLNOCNY STRIKE	PLB – Personal Locator Beacon, and emergency radio installed on life rafts
1227	331 ONE MINUTE FROM BRUISER LOOSE ON HIGH PRIORITY CONTACT	
1230	331 BRUISER LOOSE – 1ST MISSILE DITCHED OPENING UP FOR FURTHER SHOT	
1233	*LEFTWICH* LAUNCHED LONE WOLF	USS *LEFTWICH* was another CSAR frigate stationed in the northern Gulf
1234	USS *ROOSEVELT* LAUNCHING TWELVE SURFACE STRIKE CRAFT	USS *ROOSEVELT* – A US aircraft carrier
1235	RAID TAKING PLACE AGAINST REPUBLICAN GUARD	
1238	331 RETURNING – BOTH BRUISERS DITCHED (331 APPEARS TO HAVE A SYSTEM FAILURE BOTH MISSILES FAILED. ASSESS PROBABLE RADAR [DEFECT] AS SAME PROBLEM ON 29 JAN)	
1245	*LAND ON* GLOUCESTER	
1249	TWELVE AIRCRAFT FROM *ROOSEVELT* EN ROUTE TO ENGAGE CONTACTS	
1255	335 UNDER CONTROL OF *CARDIFF* WITH TWO BRUISERS	
1255	ACTION LYNX 410	
1256	CYRANO WARNING BEARING 205. FALSE ALARM – TANKER	Cyrano was a radar type carried by Iraqi Exocet-capable Mirage F1

Time	Narrative	Notes
1258	TEN JAGUARS BACK FROM BASRAH	RAF Jaguar light bomber aircraft
1305	410 AIRBORNE 2 POB	
1305	*LAUNCH FROM* GLOUCESTER *ENDURANCE 2 HOURS 10 MINUTES*	
1311	335 BRUISER LOOSE	
1314	DEEP SEA REPORT 3 TNC-45'S IN POSN 29.53N 048.41E (THIS TIES IN WITH POS OF TWO TNC-45'S ONE OF WHICH IS BEING ENGAGED BY CAR 335)	DEEP SEA – Maritime Patrol aircraft, either a US P-3 Orion or an RAF Nimrod aircraft
1315	335 ENGAGED, HIT STERN OF TNC-45 SECOND EXPLODED IN FLIGHT. 2ND TNC-45 UNDAMAGED. 410 TO ENGAGE.	
1317	331 ON DECK *CURTS* FOR REFUEL	
1315	*RECEIVED FROM 335 THAT HE HAD FIRED AT ONE CONTACT POSITION 334 DEGREES SAUSAGE 60 MILES. HIT STERN SECOND MISSILE PREMATURE DETONATION*	
1320	2 TNC-45 [RANGE AND BEARING] SAUSAGE 1 STOPPED IN WATER ON FIRE. 1 NO DAMAGE	
1324	POS SAUSAGE 28.56N 048.53E	
1325	318 [DEGREES] 122 MILES – 2 TNCS FROM GLO	
1330	*ACHIEVED GOOD TWO WAY COMMUNICATIONS WITH LONE WOLF 41 (USS FOSTER SH-60). LW 41 VECTORS 410 TO TARGET. IDENTIFIED AS TNC-45, POSITION 29.50N 048.35E*	
1332	CAR INTEND RE-ARM AND HOLD OFF 335	
1333	*CARDIFF* OFFERS FLT DECK FOR FUEL AND RE-ARM 410 (331 ON RETURN [TO *GLOUCESTER*] TO CONDUCT INVESTIGATION OF HER RADAR TO ASCERTAIN REASON FOR UNIT FAILURE)	
1334	*CARDIFF* REPOSITION 20 MILES TO NORTH TO REDUCE HELO TRANSIT DISTANCE	
1336	HEIGHT FIND TRACK 7642 2000FT SUSPECT WEATHER BALLOON. AIRCRAFT CALLSIGN SHARK INVESTIGATING	
1337	CONFIRMED WEATHER BALLOON	
1340	SHARK BASE MINUS POINT 2	

The Gulf – 1980 to the Present Day   193

Time	Narrative	Notes
1341	CAP TURNING HOT ON THE UP LEG OF RANGE	CAP – air-to-air fighter Combat Air Patrol HOT – firing against hostile units intended
1342	331 AIRBORNE *CURTS*, FOR GLO 25 MINS	
1344	SUNSET [CALCULATED AS] 1814 HOURS	
1348	HEIGHT FOUND TRACK 4407 – 21,000 FEET	
1351	THUNDERFLASHES THROWN OFF STERN TO GET RID OF SEAGULLS	This was to help prevent possible damage to a recovering helicopter by hitting the persistent flocks of gulls that used to follow the ship
1352	6 SEA SKUA REMAIN INCLUSIVE OF TWO ON HELO	
1353	DEEP SEA REPORTS 1 OSA 30.05N 049.15E	OSA – an Iraqi fast patrol boat type
1355	*FIRED FIRST BRUISER HIT BELOW BRIDGE*	
1358	*FIRED SECOND BRUISER HIT MIDSHIPS AT JUST BELOW 1-DECK LEVEL. 2ND TNC 2 NM TO NORTH-EAST NOT ENGAGED – ON FIRE*	*1-DECK – the deck that runs from point of bow to the stern*
1401	410 TO TRANSIT TO *CARDIFF* FOR RESUPPLY. POSN SAME AS LAST 410 ATTACK 29.50N 048.35E. 410 HAS LOCATED 2 X TNC-45 – PUTS 2 X SKUA INTO UNDAMAGED UNIT. BOTH NOW DEAD IN WATER	
1405	*JOINED UP WITH LONE WOLF 41*	
1408	331 LAND ON SHUT DOWN FULL CHECK OF RADAR	
1410	*DIVERTED TO* CARDIFF	
1419	*CARDIFF* RE-ARM 335, ONLY HAS 5 SKUA LEFT. 410 LAND ON RE-ARM FROM *CARDIFF*	
1422	CYRANO BEARING 273 DEGREES – FALSE ALARM FRIENDLY TANKER	
1424	331 BEING STOWED FOR FUNCTIONAL CHECKS OF RADAR. INTENTIONS CHANGED REMAIN ON DECK FOR CHECKS	
1428	CYRANO BEARING 250 – FALSE ALARM TANKER	

Time	Narrative	Notes
1455	*LAND ON* CARDIFF	
1458	335 LOCKED UP BY FEELER (PROB SA-2 BATTERY IN BUBIYAN / AL FAW)	LOCKED UP – a fire control radar is being shone at its target FEELER – a surface-to-air missile fire control radar SA-2 – a long-range surface-to-air missile of Soviet origin
1502	IN POSITION 29.16N 048.38E BODY FOUND IN WATER COMPLETE WITH LIFE JACKET	
1515	DEAD MAN IN POSN 29.16N 048.38E *CURTS* HELO TO PICK UP	
1518	*CARDIFF* LAUNCHING 410 AT 1615 HOURS FOR ANOTHER POSSIBLE ATTACK (LOOKS AS THOUGH 335 HAS RE-ENGAGED T43 / TNC-45 WITH 1 X SEA SKUA BELIEVE SHE HAS THE GROUP OF 2 TNC-45 AGAIN – BOTH DEAD IN WATER	
1520	BRUISER LOOSE FROM 335	
1521	EXOCET WARNER BEARING 176 DEGREES	
1522	RESET ALARM	
1522	EXOCET WARNER BEARING 167 DEGREES	
1524	RESET ALARM	
1532	TNC-45 REPORTED STOPPED IN WATER, NOT ON FIRE. 335 CLOSING TO INVESTIGATE AND ENGAGE	
1535	331 RADAR [FOUND AS] UNSERVICEABLE. PARTS NOT HELD ON BOARD	
1546	T43 STATIONARY IN WATER HELO REQUESTED INTENTIONS	
1538	FROM *CARDIFF*: REQUEST *GLOUCESTER* CONTACT 'NS' TO SEND FIXED WING ASSETS FOR BATTLE DAMAGE ASSESSMENT	
1541	NS HAS SENT 3 AIRCRAFT FOR BDA OVER THE CONTACTS	
1544	FM *CARDIFF* – SITREP TO NS CONFIRMED VIA USS *MOBILE BAY* OVERALL ASSESSMENT ON ASMA FROM *CARDIFF*	ASMA – Air Staff Management Aid communications systems

The Gulf – 1980 to the Present Day   195

Time	Narrative	Notes
1554	RESOLVE TRACK 7667 BEARING 307 – 60 [MILES RANGE] NO MODE 4 MODE 1 ONLY	RESOLVE – an investigation of an unknown contact, involving calculations of height, course, speed, and Identification Friend or Foe (IFF). MODE 4 – an encrypted IFF system
1555	FROM EWD FRIENDLY F-14 CAP AIRCRAFT ON BEARING	EWD – Electronic Warfare Director in the ship's operations room. F-14 – a US Navy 'Tomcat' fighter aircraft
1614	ACTION LYNX 331. TRANSIT TO HMS *LONDON* REMAIN OVERNIGHT	
1618	331 AIRBORNE	
1620	*LAUNCH FROM* CARDIFF *ENDURANCE 2 HOURS 10 MIUNUTES. GLOUCESTER INFORMS 410 THAT OSA IN LOCATION 338 DEGRESS 118 MILES FROM POINT BACON*	*BACON – another reporting point, similar to SAUSAGE*
1621	410 AIRBORNE FROM *CARDIFF* ENDURANCE 1840	
1624	410 TO INVESTIGATE POSSIBLE OSA IN POS 29.48N 049.20E. MAYBE TERRITORIAL WATERS (POS TAKEN OFF LAST HIT BROADCAST)	HIT BROADCAST – an intelligence summary transmitted to all friendly units
1636	410 TO REMAIN ON TASK UNTIL SUNSET 1830 HOURS REFUEL LAND ON GLOUCESTER	
1642	OVERNIGHT INTENTIONS FOLLOW WORDEN, DUE TO OPDEF EOSS AND THE MINE THREAT	USS *WORDEN* – a US Navy anti-air destroyer OPDEF – Operational Defect, a critical defect in a ship's capability. EOSS – Electro Optic Surveillance System, a useful system for visually detecting floating mines.
1644	335 EN ROUTE BACK TO *GLOUCESTER*, AFTER FIRING ONE SKUA	
1648	410 REFUEL ON *CURTS* EN ROUTE BACK TO *GLOUCESTER*	
1649	410 ETA *CURTS* 1810 HOURS	

Time	Narrative	Notes
1650	*ON TASK. NO COMMS WITH ON-STATION SH-60 (SABREHAWK)*	
1656	331 UNDER CONTROL OF HMS *LONDON*, 410 UNDER CONTROL OF *CARDIFF*	
1658	CYRANO BEARING 250 DEGREES – ASSESSED FRIENDLY TANKER, RESET	
1704	USS *JARRETT* HAS OFFERED HER HELO FOR MINESEARCH TONIGHT	
1707	410 LOCKED UP BY FIRE CONTROL RADAR. EVADING	
1712	SECOND UNKNOWN SURFACE TRACK TO NORTH ON FIRE NOW IDENTIFIED AS POLNOCNY	
1719	*LOCKED UP BY SA-2 BANDS 2 AND 3*	*BANDS 2 AND 3 – denotes the frequency of the enemy fire control radar as analysed by the Lynx 'Orange Crop' electronic support measures warning equipment .*
1722	410 LOCKED UP BY FRIENDLY CAP IN POS GRID RED 135-103 (POS 29.36N 048.30E)	GRID – a reporting matrix superimposed on geographical information systems.
1723	*OFF TASK RTB VIA* CURTS *FOR DEBRIEF*	
1739	410 SHUTS DOWN USS *CURTS* FOR DEBRIEF	
1750	LAND ON CURTS. FUEL / DEBRIEF *CURTS* COMMANDING OFFICER	Slight discrepancy in recorded timings.
1743	CYRANO WARNING BEARING 250 ASSESSED FRIENDLY SOS55 [unknown terminology] (BDA REPORT ON POLNOCNY, ALL ENGAGED BY SUCAP. 1 DEAD IN WATER 29.40N 048.27E. 1 DEAD IN WATER BURNING 29.59N 048.44E.)	
1747	USS *MOBILE BAY* 42 IN SURFACE SEARCH IN OUR AREA	
1758	SUN KING REPORTS VESSEL SUNK POSITION 29.53N 048.35E (1 DEAD IN WATER 29.50N 049.20E AFT SUPERSTRUCTURE HEAVILY DAMAGED)	SUN KING – a maritime patrol aircraft.
1815	*RELAUNCH FROM* CURTS	
1815	410 REPORTS NO FUTHER OIL SLICKS OTHER THAN THOSE ALREADY REPORTED	

Time	Narrative	Notes
1850	*LAND ON* GLOUCESTER	
1855	410 RECOVERED (REVERT TO ALERT 15 RELOAD UNTIL 2359 HOURS 2 SEA SKUA IN HANGAR ONE IN MAGAZINE)	ALERT 15 – aircraft to be ready for take-off in 15 minutes.
1821	2 x TANKERS NPG PUMPING OUT OIL. SUCAP TASKED TO ENGAGE AIMING FOR ENGINE ROOMS (NO SUCAP AVAILABLE)	NPG – North Persian Gulf.
2039	1 UNKNOWN IDENTIFIED 29N 049.60E FROM JFNL (ANALYSIS OF THE POSITIONS 335 REPORTED FOR HER 2ND AND 3RD ATTACK SHOW IT TO BE 25 MILES TO THE SOUTH OF THE TWO TNC-45S ATTACKED BY 410)	

One of *Gloucester*'s TNC 45s – a capable warship but no match for a Skua armed Lynx. (*David Livingstone*)

198   The Royal Navy Lynx

David Livingstone's diary entry for that day, and also the day after, read:

30 January.
'I supposed I killed someone today; some wife is a widow, some child fatherless. But I feel no emotion, they are the enemy and they would kill me if they had a chance. They would make a widow of my wife, and my children would not have a father.

'After a frustrating morning, *Cardiff* already having hit two contacts overnight, we launched at 0920 and flew to the north of the Mina Al Bakr terminal. There we ID'd one TNC-45 at 3.5 miles and turned away to engage at 6 miles. As we fired I saw the missile fly to the right, looked to the right and it was going for another target. The first hit the target just below the bridge. We turned and re-attacked the second, a T43. That was hit midships.

'Returned to Gloucester and refuelled and rearmed, went north again and found another TNC-45. Attacked with two missiles on look-shoot-look-shoot. Two hits, one below the bridge and one midships. Contact on fire.

'Revisited the area ninety minutes later, and one contact had sunk and one was well on fire. Considered another bruiser attack but decided that the war was over for that contact. After a brief encounter with an SA-2 radar went home.

'I am very tired, but the adrenalin will not go away.'

31 January.
'Another day, another patrol boat, though fatigue is making me jittery and jumpy.

The mission today started off fine, had a little trouble at Faylaka Island with an SA-2 and AAA radar. Evaded, but expended all my chaff. Diverted to USS *Leftwich* and then went off on Combat Search and Rescue ops to rescue survivors from yesterday's kills. Accompanied by 1 x SH-60 (Magnum 446) and 2 x Sea King (Jaguar 614 and Speargun 611). When on patrol detected another TNC-45, but not convinced that it wasn't one from yesterday. We got too close; I will admit, got locked up by their Bands 3&4 and then evaded.

'Turned to fire after weapons free granted. First Skua seemed to go ok, but no explosion seen. AAA back we believe. Turned back for a second attack, launched at six miles and it hit just aft of the bridge.

'Confirmation that this was a fresh target was received from SUCAP A6 who finished the job with three Rockeye cluster bombs.

'In all it was an unsatisfactory attack that worked, but we ran it too close.

'Saw masts of one FPB I sank yesterday, and photos from USS *Bunker Hill* of the others. T43 beached (see photo) and 1 x TNC-45 written off. Tally for two days for Gloucester Flight: 1 x T43 aground on fire. 1 x TNC-45 sunk. 1 x TNC-45 beached. 1 x TNC-45 damaged, finished off by cluster bombs.'

The beached Type 43 seen over the gun sights of US Navy SH 60. (*David Livingstone*)

For their efforts, David Livingstone was awarded a Distinguished Service Cross and Martin Ford a Mentioned in Despatches.

HMS *Manchester*

Flight Commander – Lieutenant Nick Last.
Flight Pilot – Lieutenant Dickie Boswell.

Aircraft – XZ 694

By Nick Last:

'We embarked off the Nab Tower in XZ 694 on 7 January 1991, then proceeded to the Mediterranean. We spent around two weeks there in the vicinity of Cyprus before being sent to the Gulf on our own. We arrived in the Gulf at the end of January and spent a week and a half near Qatar with the main group. Only *Cardiff* and *Gloucester* were operating in the far north. We relieved *Cardiff* on 10 February, and during the course of the handover, I flew in the back of their aircraft for a familiarisation of the northern Gulf and saw a number of damaged patrol boats and other shipping. It looked like everything was over with regards to the sea war.

'That night our tasking for the following day came through. We were operating as part of an American Pacific fleet and their procedures are completely different to their Atlantic fleet, which we were familiar with. I couldn't work out the tasking as I had no information on the "WW" grid system they used to order the search area for us. Eventually, the ops officer managed to translate the signal and we worked out that the search area we had been allocated was too far away to get to. We arranged to refuel on an American Ticonderoga Class cruiser, USS *Princeton*, so that we could get to where we needed to be. The following day we transited to *Princeton*, and whilst Dickie was sorting out the refuel, their first lieutenant greeted me and commented on the fact we had two missiles fitted and could we sink a coastal patrol boat that was firing on his Seahawk helicopter in the vicinity of Faylakah Island? It was a Kuwaiti patrol boat captured by the Iraqis. Their ops room was something out of Star Trek and designed for the big air picture and their surface plot was a small radar screen, but I got the information I wanted, which was the position of their helicopter.

'I spent most of the transit north trying to get clearance to fire a Skua on someone else's information as that was outside my rules of engagement. The secure speech system we had in the aircraft allowed me to communicate with our ship, but Dickie couldn't hear what was being said. We eventually got clearance, although it apparently went to ministerial level. We met up with the Sea Sprite

The Gulf – 1980 to the Present Day   201

about ten miles from the enemy patrol boat, and as the visibility was only about three miles, I never actually saw it. I turned my radar on and the patrol boat was exactly where the Sea Sprite said it would be and at eight miles I launched one missile. The Sea Sprite's radar was sophisticated enough to track the missile to the target. They carried out the damage assessment and reported the patrol boat completed destroyed with survivors in the water. As they were throwing life rafts to the survivors they were engaged by anti-aircraft fire from Kuwait and had to haul off. On return to *Manchester* our captain met us on the flight deck with a glass of champagne each.

'Four days later, I identified an Iraqi Spasilac class salvage vessel off the coast of Bubiyan Island and, as it had been used as a minelayer, I launched one Skua which disabled the ship. Unfortunately, it did not sink and continued drifting south-west between Kuwait and Faylakah Island and was reported as a different vessel. After *Gloucester's* Lyn carried out an unsuccessful attack, [See Note 2 at end of chapter] we launched in the early hours of 16 February and flew low-level over the sea at a diagonal angle between Kuwait and Faylakah Island. We were given the updated position of the Spasilac by a Canadian Aurora Maritime Patrol Aircraft (MPA). Intent on destroying the vessel this time, I planned on launching two missiles and at ten miles we popped up. Dickie slowed the aircraft down to about 30 knots and I launched the first missile at eight miles. I couldn't initially launch the second missile, and whilst I was trying to sort the problem out the first missile hit the target. Eventually, I launched the second missile and as it was in flight there was an enormous explosion from the Spasilac, which we think may have been a mine exploding. After the second missile hit we returned to *Manchester* at low-level. After about ten minutes the Canadian Aurora informed us the contact had disappeared from its radar screen and they presumed it had sunk.

'I was credited with sinking three vessels, but I am convinced it was only two as the attacks we carried out on 15 and 16 February were against the same ship.

'On one occasion we had a hand-held heat-seeking missile fired at us from Faylakah Island, but as we were outside its range I was happy, but Dickie was relieved when he saw it plunge into the sea when it ran out of fuel about two miles short of us.'

For their efforts, Nick Last and Dick Boswell were both awarded a Mention in Despatches.

202 The Royal Navy Lynx

Notes – The Fog of War

Operating as single units most of the time it wasn't always possible to know exactly what the other flights were doing.

1. Phil Needham only reports an 'inconclusive' attack by *Gloucester* and *Brazen's* aircraft on the evening of the 29 January; this was not quite the case. The aircraft had identified a large number of enemy contacts and moved in to attack. Unfortunately, the Skuas fired by *Brazen's* aircraft malfunctioned. *Gloucester's* Lynx then fired a missile at one of the targets and an explosion was seen, but very slightly short of the target. It is surmised that, as it was fired at a very low skim height, it may well have hit the wake of the ship it was approaching. It is highly likely the explosion would have damaged the vessel in some way. After that, the whole formation scattered. However, sometime later RAF Jaguars conducted a further attack and caused more damage.

2. Nick is actually wrong in his assessment that *Gloucester's* Lynx had previously attacked the same ship that he subsequently sank. Earlier that evening, David Livingstone had been vectored to the area by an RAF Nimrod patrol plane who had found a target moving between Faylakah Island and Kuwait City. For some reason it took several attempts to gain a radar lock. However, eventually they managed to fire two Sea Skuas at the target. As the second was still in flight they saw what they thought were flares being fired over the land. The 'flares' were actually the rocket motors of two Soviet made SA2 SAMs coming their way. The shore batteries on Faylakah Island then also joined in, firing Anti-Aircraft Artillery (Triple A), so David turned away, breaking lock on their Skua and leaving it to fly on its last heading so that they could clear the area. In doing so, he lost the visual references that the shore lights gave him, as he was now flying out into the darkness. Luckily, he saw the radar altimeter warning light come on as they descended through fifty feet. The SAMs flew overhead as the Lynx 'scooped out' at thirty feet above the surface of the sea. Ten minutes later, the Nimrod reported that their target was on fire and identified it as a Polnocny – a large Soviet built landing craft.

Endpiece

At the end of the war, when the crews returned to UK, there was considerable press interest in all the Lynx crew's performance. However, it is probably best summed up in three signals that were sent during the war:

The Gulf – 1980 to the Present Day   203

From: ASUWC Commodore Tom Forbes USN to Commodore Chris Craig (DTG: 251345ZFEB91)

The fun and zest of the ASUW efforts were more pronounced by the contribution made by your Lynx helos. I especially appreciate your efforts to forward base an extra helo for our combined effort.* They were there when we needed them most. One lesson made perfectly clear to us was that an armed helo is a deadly weapon that the US Navy needs desperately.

To the best of my knowledge, the name given was the battle of Bubiyan. Score another for the Brits.

From: Joint Headquarters High Wycombe.
Personal for British Forces Commander Middle East, from Joint Command

I have watched with interest the involvement of RN forces under your command since hostilities began. While all have contributed in their own way, the exploits of HM ships *Gloucester* and *Cardiff* and their Lynx helicopters have contributed greatly to the establishment of Allied control of the Northern Persian Gulf. This has been a very well executed example of sea denial and we have played a notable part in achieving such good results and in paving the way for further operations in the Gulf. I would ask you to pass on my congratulations to SNOME (Senior Naval Officer Middle East) on the performance of our naval forces so far. I am confident that they will keep it up.

From HQBFME Riyadh (Headquarters British Forces Middle East)
To: Task Group 321.1 (RN Forces in the Gulf)

1. The performance of the Royal Navy over recent days has been in the finest traditions of the service. In close cooperation with the US Navy and other allies your forces have made a marked contribution towards the destruction of the Iraqi Navy and the gaining of sea control in the northern Gulf. I have watched with admiration as your people have gone about their business.
2. Well done to all concerned. Keep up the good work.

WITHOUT DOUBT THE LYNX'S FINEST HOUR

---

* *Despite being designed for only one aircraft, HMS* Gloucester *regularly operated two Lynx for extended periods, with the extra asset flying up from the UK ships based in the southern areas of the Gulf nearer to the area of operations, which was yet one hundred miles further north from the two UK anti-air destroyers,* Gloucester *and* Cardiff. *In operating two aircraft, deck movements were exacting, and workload on the single aircraft maintenance team was extremely heavy, with flying rates up to four times that of peacetime.*

204 The Royal Navy Lynx

And then the next twenty-five years...

This was not the end of the Lynx in the Gulf as has already been stated. There has been an RN warship on patrol in the area ever since. The threat was never as high again, even in the Second Gulf War, but even so, the challenges of operating the aircraft in the summer months never went away. In due course, the Mark 3 (GM) was replaced by the Mark 8, which, whilst incorporating many of the capabilities of the earlier aircraft, many of which were greatly improved, was considerably heavier. Whilst the weight of the aircraft had gone up, the engines and transmission remained substantially the same as the Mark 3. Thus there was a trade off in increased capability against operating limitations. Below is an article from *Flight Deck* magazine, written in 2005, when HMS *Argyll* took a Mark 8 into the heat of a Gulf summer which describes it extremely well:

'As HMS Argyll *arrived in Bahrain in March to assume the responsibility of Operation Telic guard ship, the flight were all too aware of the well-documented considerations for hot weather flying operations in the area. Our Telic predecessors in HMS* Marlborough *had covered the winter period and had been pleasantly surprised at conditions more akin to the south coast exercise areas. However, our pre-deployment met brief at Northwood suggested that we would endure altogether more arduous conditions... And so it proved. It became quickly apparent that the operating environment would put considerable strain on the aircraft and individuals, with the potential to affect the Flights operational capability.*

The individual

'With average daytime temperatures at 40 to 45°C and 80 to 90% humidity, conditions on the upper deck were a little unpleasant to say the least. Whilst the usual 5 knot breeze served to make conditions on the upper deck slightly more bearable, the atmosphere in the hangar was insufferable. However, because of the problems associated with hot soaking the aircraft, leaving it spotted to conduct maintenance was not a viable option. Not helped by two months of poor serviceability, the engineering team had to endure long hours in the hangar conducting maintenance with only the sweetener of extra pay for work in unpleasant conditions to ease the burden. The risk of dehydration was very real and every member of the Flight was issued with a Camelback water carrier to help combat this problem. Drinking little and often was the order of the day, with regular breaks within the ships air-conditioning boundary. Careful monitoring of individual performance by the SMR was needed to offset the perils of lethargy, poor decision-making and technical mistakes. On average each job was given a time budget of two to three times the duration one would expect in the UK.

'Additionally, being the first maritime Lynx deployed to the Gulf with a Defensive Aids Suite, extra precautions had to be taken owing to the aircraft's flare fit. When flares were fitted to the aircraft everyone on the flight deck had to wear anti-flash hoods and gloves with their overalls, further increasing the risk of dehydration. In the aircraft the aircrew benefited from a Service Deviation allowing desert pattern CS 95 to be worn in lieu of flying overalls. Although these garments are considerably less fire retardant than flying overalls, they are much more comfortable to wear. Nevertheless, the risk of dehydration was very real, particularly during secondary roles sorties, making Camelback's of water an essential item every sortie.

Aircraft performance

'The Flight had already experienced the limitations of engine performance during training sorties en route to the Gulf in high temperatures. In very light wind conditions and with the ship's maximum available speed further constrained by the reduced performance of its own gas turbines, sufficient wind could rarely be generated for a single engine recovery. As a result, a single engine failure with no viable diversion or spare deck would have necessitated either ditching or a somewhat sporty recovery to the flight deck. Take-offs were even more fun, making full use of the non-power rudder pedal. The expression on one American passengers face when we were obliged to 'dive on' speed shortly after leaving his ship's deck will remain with the aircrew for some time! Although the heat was one of the issues, there was also the problem of airborne particles, at times reducing the visibility to one mile or less and without the benefit of particle separators or dust filters, the effect on engine performance was a worrying and almost unknown factor. That said, the only occasion when an engine suffered FOD (Foreign Object Damage) was over the tarmac dispersal of Kuwait International Airport! Perhaps our concern was misdirected. However, the greatest operating constraint was the restrictive nature of the Ship Helicopter Operating Limits (SHOL). With the ship constrained to a very small operating area (one mile x one mile), Argyll was unable to generate sufficient wind to allow the aircraft to lift the highest all up mass (AUM). Inevitably, each sortie was therefore a compromise between the maximum aircraft mass consistent with tasking and the maximum wind that could be generated by the ship on any given day. To help manage this problem, the aircraft was operated without the weighty ESM processor, life raft, inflatable troop seat and winch. Even so, with the aircraft in the air gunning role, endurance was reduced considerably when flying during the hottest parts of the day. Fortunately, the aircraft was blessed with two very good engines, providing power in hand, above and beyond published performance criteria in the Operating Data Manual. With frequent

delivery tasks to Kuwait, this extra power proved essential in landing and taking off from small landing sites. Inevitably, our passengers appeared with considerably more luggage than briefed and with the arrival of unexpected, yet operationally essential stores and mail, that performance proved indispensable and at times every last ounce of power was squeezed from the engines. In the back of one's mind was always the need to routinely handle the engines with kid gloves so that when called upon to produce maximum power we knew it would be available.

'The aircraft avionics suffered equally from the harsh conditions, particularly from the dust that found its way into every crevice, causing a selection of miscellaneous switching faults in the avionics. At the start of the deployment the tactical system processers and radar components failed far too often, necessitating their careful and judicious use on operational sorties. However, on receipt of our "mid deployment gift" from 815 Squadron – a dehumidifying rig – almost all the avionics problems were cured. It appeared that faults owed more to the high humidity and temperature alone.

Flying routines

'The difficulties described above were exacerbated by flying during the hottest part of the day, from 1100 to 1600 hours and to that end strenuous efforts were made to appraise the tasking authority of the situation. Where operationally feasible, the flight conducted a large part of the programmed flying outside these times, thus allowing a significant improvement in the performance of the aircraft and individuals. Where this was not the case, the employment of the modified alert states in particular the use of alert thirty, keeping the aircraft stowed and out of the sun's glare, continued to provide the command with a realistic alert state while minimising the hot soaking of the aircraft.

Summary

'Whilst originally designed to operate in cooler climates and with a much lower weight, careful management has allowed the much heavier Lynx Mark 8 to operate in hot conditions whilst continuing to provide satisfactory operational capability. On balance, the benefits of a Mark 8 aircraft with improved sensors and situational awareness far outweigh the better performance of the Mark 3 Lynx. The challenge of a Gulf summer has been to continue to provide the highest level of operational capability whilst not compromising the safety of all involved.'

Chapter 7

The Lynx HMA Mark 8 – the Final Version

The definitive version of the Lynx and extremely well equipped, but definitely having put on just a little weight. (*Steve George*)

As previously mentioned, the gestation of the Mark 8 Lynx started with the Mark 3. Indeed it would be fair to say that in its whole life and throughout all its variants, the Lynx has never had a static configuration for long. The Mark 2 was developed quickly and very soon turned into the basic Mark 3. This aircraft was then continually modified, particularly for the Gulf as previously described, as well as for the Antarctic and other operations. In advance of the Mark 8, several of the basic equipments were tested, evaluated and even fielded in Mark 3 airframes.

But first, why was there a need to upgrade the Mark 3? There were two primary issues with the aircraft:

Target compilation

The basic Sea Spray radar was an analogue device and not ground stabilised. This meant that the observer could only directly know the range and bearing of any contact

208   The Royal Navy Lynx

from his aircraft. The radar picture was centred on the aircraft's centre line and therefore the picture moved as the aircraft moved and manoeuvred. This was fine if all he wanted to do was attack a target with his own missiles. However, much of the tasking of the Lynx was to report targets back to the main force to allow them to extend the picture of what was going on around them. To do this, the aircraft needed more than just the range and bearing of the contact from itself. In order to locate its position geographically and then know its course and speed, significant calculation was required. With this early system the observer would place a simple sheet of plastic over the radar display and make a mark on the plastic where the target was using a grease pencil. He would then note the aircraft's position from the TANS and wait a set amount of time before re-plotting the target. With a little mental agility he could then establish an approximation of the contact's course and speed. The original concept was that he should be able to do this for up to ten contacts and report them continually back to the ship. In practice, most observers would have trouble tracking more than six contacts simultaneously and even then would be working like the 'proverbial one armed paper hanger'. Adding to his plotting duties, he would also be looking at the Orange Crop and if necessary, tying in ESM data with his contacts as well as being responsible for navigating the aircraft and making sure they returned safely to their ship. In a word, an early Lynx observer was a very busy man. Consequently, a requirement arose to put a system in place that could allow multiple target tracking and reporting.

Target identification

The Lynx had an autonomous capability to attack surface targets with its Sea Skua missiles at a maximum range of nine miles. In addition, it could fly well ahead of its force and conduct surface search and find targets for the missiles of the force to engage (Exocet and Harpoon). It could also call on fixed wing assets or other helicopters to attack targets it had discovered. The only problem with this procedure was that the aircrew had great difficulty actually identifying the targets without getting so close as to be at risk from their point defence anti-aircraft systems if they turned out to be hostile. On some occasions Orange Crop information could be good enough to identify a target. However, particularly as modern radars became more sophisticated, the limited data that Orange Crop supplied became less and less useful. The best way to identify a target is to see it. Consequently, the requirement for some form of optical device with good discrimination and range was raised. Experience with the Sandpiper system during the First Gulf War only reinforced this need.

The solutions to these two problems formed the core of the new Mark 8:

The Centralised Tactical System

The system has undergone several upgrades over the years, but the core concept was to give the observer a large screen called the Tactical Situation Display (Graphics) (TSDG) on which he could plot radar contacts and ESM bearings to give him a proper situational display. The original system was fitted to certain Mark 3 aircraft. In its early form, the Sea Spray radar remained a stand-alone system and navigation still relied on the Doppler radar fed TANS. Contacts identified by the radar could be transferred directly to the CTS, though this still required a reasonable effort in button pressing and subsequent correlation. The next upgrade was to provide a Digital Signal Processor (DSP) for the Sea Spray radar so that it could interface more efficiently with the CTS. GPS was integrated into the system as well. The net effect did not necessarily reduce the workload on the observer, but significantly increased his capability to track and identify targets. In the final system, up to twenty targets can be tracked in house, but as reports back to the ship have to be over the radio, in practice the aircraft will report up to a maximum of twelve.

The original system, as well as the one that used the DSP, was originally controlled by two Control Data Units (CDUs). In the rear of the aircraft was a large rack of electronics to process everything and manage the data. One disadvantage of this was that the equipment was so bulky that the rear three man seat could not be fitted. In the final version, this was all removed and the processing was done within two Control Data Navigation Units (CDNUs). At the same time the TSDG was upgraded to an LCD screen the input keyboards were simplified.

In addition to the plotting and tracking functionality provided by the system, the functionality of the weapon pre-setters was incorporated into the CTS as well as the ability to manage the radios.

The cockpit of a Mark 8 (SRU). The large central screen is the TSDG and below it are the two CDNUs. The Sea Spray radar is the smaller TV screen with shroud to the left of the TSDG. (*Author*)

The Sea Owl Passive Identification Device (PID)

The large electro–optical sensor on the nose of the Mark 8 Lynx is the optical device selected for target identification. Built by GEC, it uses infrared to discriminate differences in temperature of targets at significant ranges. It is controlled by a joystick in the cockpit and the picture can be displayed on the TSDG or radar screen. It can look up to 140° either side of the aircraft's nose. This device gives the aircraft the capability of identifying surface targets well outside their ability to shoot down the Lynx.

The Sea Owl PID on the nose of the aircraft in its stowed position. In flight it is rotated forward. Such a large mass of metal so far forward has caused vibration problems even though it is mounted on a flexible platform. The repositioned radome for the Sea Spray radar scanner can be seen underneath the nose. (*Author*)

The end of the Cold War

At the time the Mark 8 was being developed, the political situation in the world was rapidly changing. In particular, in 1989, the Berlin Wall fell, and then at the end of 1991, the Soviet Union was dissolved after the unsuccessful coup attempt against

Mikael Gorbachev, the last and only President of the USSR. In an atmosphere of reduced threat, all military spending came under increased scrutiny. The Mark 8 programme did not escape.

One of the other limitations of the Lynx Mark 3 was the fact that the radar, being mounted in the nose of the aircraft, could only scan ahead through 180 degrees. The original design of the Mark 8 called for a repositioning of the radar scanner so that it could rotate through a full 360 degrees. This would have meant that a Sea Skua could have been fired whilst the aircraft was able to fly away from its target. It would also have allowed the aircraft to compile a far larger and more accurate radar picture. As can be seen from pictures, the scanner was moved, not the least to give a mounting position for the PID, but as a cost savings measure, the radar was never modified to take advantage of its new position and so still only scans in the ahead sector. Another sacrifice was MAD. Early trials on the Mark 2 had been successful as previously mentioned and there was even a short trial to use a MAD sensor along the tail of a Mark 2 rather than having to trail a 'bird' on a wire. This had also given promising results. With the Stingray torpedo now in general use, MAD could have given the aircraft a viable submarine localisation and attack capability. However, it was not to be, and the original idea to put a MAD boom inside the tail cone was dropped. Finally, there was much discussion whether there should be a data link in the aircraft to automatically send the tactical plot back to the force. Data links between surface ships have been in use for many years, as have some between aircraft and ships. However, not only would this have increased the cost of the Mark 8 programme, it would also have required the various ship project teams to find money to put the relevant system into the ships, so once again the idea was shelved.

However, lessons from the Gulf had not been forgotten and the Mark 8 also benefited from:

Defensive Aids Suite (DAS)

This consists of:

ALQ 144 infrared missile jammer similar to those used in the Mark 3 (GM), but now in a position below and behind the cabin, giving 360 degree coverage from a single aerial.

Infrared Missile Approach Warning system (MAWS).

Integrated M130 chaff and flare dispenser which is now fitted below the main wheel sponsons. The system can be set to trigger the M130 automatically or manually.

The ALQ 144 IR missile jammer mounted below the tail. The small circular lens just ahead of it is one of four MAWS sensors, two at the rear and two on the nose. The two M130 Chaff and flare dispensers are mounted just forward, below the wheel sponsons. (*Author*)

Secure Speech Radios

In the First Gulf War, the Lamberton interim secure speech system was difficult to use and precluded the pilot from being able to operate it. However, it proved its worth. Secure speech was becoming absolutely essential, not the least to allow the aircraft to report back the details of the plot it was able to generate.

In the nineties, new AD 3400 radios were introduced to replace the older unreliable PTR377 and they included a full secure speech facility. Initially fitted into some Mark 3 aircraft, they changed the designation of the aircraft to Mark 3(S). This system was then fitted to all the Mark 8s. The encryption system used a large preprogrammed 'brick' which had to be fitted before each flight and in the Mark 8 this was incorporated in the equipment rack at the back of the aircraft.

The final change came about at the same time as the upgrade to CDNU processors and led to the final designation of the aircraft as Mark 8 (SRU), SRU stands for SATURN RADIO UNIT. This system uses newer, highly encrypted, TALON radios

The Lynx HMA Mark 8 – the Final Version   213

which incorporate an anti-jamming system known as HAVE QUICK. Consequently, the acronym SATURN stands for Second generation, Anti-jam Tactical, UHF Radio for NATO. It might be suggested that this is a rather contrived acronym, but does sound good!

None of this increased functionality comes without some cost, and the weight of the aircraft has grown by 450kg (a thousand pounds) over the Mark 3. It still flies with the same Gem 42 engines and three pinion gearbox, although the power rating of the transmission was uprated. As can be seen from the preceding chapter, which describes operating a Mark 8 in the Gulf, this increased weight has imposed some operating limitations. The maximum speed of 150 knots has been reduced, to 144 knots, as have some of the manoeuvring limits, with a maximum angle of bank of 60 degrees. Probably more importantly, the aircraft has never been able to hover on one engine in still air at any weight and has always needed some forward speed or relative wind to help compensate. This is because with all helicopters, it takes more power to hover than is needed in forward flight up to about 70 knots. Consequently, the heavier Mark 8 has more limitations when taking off in case of an engine failure or recovering to a ship on one engine.

Variants

As described, the Lynx Mark 8 grew out of several variants of Mark 3 and itself had undergone several major modification programmes. For completeness these are listed in the table below:

HAS 3	Original version of upgrade Mark 2 with Gem 42 engines and three pinion gearbox
HAS 3 GM) or HAS 3S (GM)	Gulf modified aircraft with Challenger IR jammer, Sandpiper IR sensor, Yellow Veil Jammer, M130 chaff and flare, HMP. Mode 4 IFF. The 'S' designation was added if Lamberton secure speech was fitted
HAS 3 (S)	Fitted with AD3400 secure speech
HAS 3 (ICE)	Modified for Antarctic operations. Cooling mods removed and all lower aerials removed or moved to higher positions. Red Nose and other panels the most obvious change.
HAS 3 (CTS)	Upgraded Mark 3 with the original Centralised Tactical System fitted
HMA 8	Original Mark 8 with PID, relocated radar scanner and CTS
HMA 8 (DSP)	Updated Mark 8 with DSP for the radar
HMA 8 (DAS)	Updated Mark 8 (DSP) with Defensive Aid Suite
HMA 8 (SRU)	Updated Mark 8 with Saturn Radio and SIFF (improved IFF)

On the airframe side, all Mark 8s were fitted with the new BERP rotor blades (BERP became CMRB – Composite Main Rotor Blades – in time as they left the experimental umbrella) and an improved reverse direction tail rotor. In addition, some strengthening was made to the main lift frame area, as well as redesigning the nose of the PID and relocated radar scanner.

One interesting point is that the Mark 2s and 3s were both designated as 'HAS' i.e. Helicopter Anti-Submarine, which is slightly odd, as it actually had two primary roles, not just ASW. When the Mark 8 was introduced this was changed to the more accurate 'HMA', which stands for Helicopter Maritime Attack, which is arguably far more appropriate. Apparently, this was seen as very political, especially in the post-Cold War era and took considerable debate amongst senior staff before it was approved.

Introduction in to service

As described, the Mark 8 grew out of several variants of the Mark 3 and then went to a long period of gestation to arrive at the last version. In 1990, 700(L) was reformed at Portland as the Mark 3 CTS trials squadron. The unit operated for two years and started developing the use and tactics of the CTS even to the extent of fielding operational Flights to sea in Type 21 Frigates.

However, in 1992, politics once again raised their head. With the need to reduce force levels post the Cold War, it was deemed useful to reduce the number of FAA squadrons. Consequently, 700(L) was 'disbanded' and became part of 815 Squadron and renamed the Lynx Mark 8 Operation Evaluation Unit (OEU). This political sleight of hand had little effect at the front line and the unit continued to evaluate and develop the Mark 8 in all its guises right up until 2009. Initially, the unit also had the task of training Mark 8 crews until that was handed over to 702 Squadron.

The Mark 8 (SRU) will be the last naval Lynx variant, as after over forty years in service it will be retired in 2017. Its successor, the Westland Wildcat, is already in service and rather, as the Lynx developed from the Wasp, so the Wildcat has developed from the Lynx. However, in this case it goes one step further. In order to keep costs down, many of the Wildcat components are common with its earlier brother and as Lynx airframes are being retired hundreds of items are being removed to be refitted to the new airframes. So in one way the Lynx legacy not only progresses, but also, literally, flies on.

Chapter 8

There But For the Grace of God Go I …

One description of a helicopter is: '*10,000 totally unrelated, fatigue critical, moving parts, bent on self-destruction, flying in relatively close formation*'. Some would argue that there is some truth in that definition. By the nature of a helicopter's design there are many single load path items that are critical to the safety of the machine. That the Lynx has performed so well for so many years, with relatively few material failures, is a real tribute to its basic design integrity.

The author was the maintenance test pilot at the Royal Naval Air Station at Portland for four years after returning from the Falklands War. This grand sounding job description slightly disguises the nature of the task, which is to conduct annual test flights on all aircraft at the air station and provide detailed analysis of aircraft with technical faults – in other words, fly the problem aircraft that no one else can fix. He was also lucky enough to fly the Wasp at the same time. In those four years, the Lynx provided less heart stopping moments than either the Wasp or the Sea King that he flew previously. That said, no machine is perfect and on one occasion, when flying in Lyme Bay, the cabin floor suddenly became covered in oil from a leaking main gearbox. The aircraft was landed on the coast in a field next to a hotel and immediately shut down, only for the aircrew to realise they had not told Portland that they had landed safely. They then had the embarrassment of having to borrow ten pence to use the hotel's payphone to ring in. There were other incidents in the same period, one of which resulted in a precautionary landing on a nudist beach, but as it was January it wasn't as exciting as some people thought.

However, over the life of the aircraft there has been more than one lucky escape, either due to the strength of the aircraft, the skill of the aircrew, or both. This chapter includes some stories in all those categories. It should also be noted that there are few photographs in this chapter, mainly because the authors were rather too busy at the time to take any!

The following is an extract from an article published in *Cockpit Magazine*, written by Lieutenant Commander Phil Sheldon, and illustrates just how robust an aircraft the Lynx could be:

216   The Royal Navy Lynx

Norwegian wire strike

'HMS Boxer *and my Flight were participants in an annual NATO sponsored exercise (Bold Game) conducted in the northern European command waters. The exercise is designed to familiarise participating units with various tactical concepts by conducting extended Fast Patrol Boat (FPB), operations. Typical tasking is generally surfaced reconnaissance and anti-FPB strike, a role well suited to the Lynx.*

'At 0725, we took off from Aalborg on an Anti-Surface Vessel (ASV) mission in the coastal sea areas north-west of Bergen Norway. Considerable pre-flight planning had preceded the launch. Maps were up-to-date, a comprehensive tactical briefing given and a wire briefing had been received face-to-face with the Norwegian SAR unit at Sola. Norwegian flying techniques had been discussed and the importance of wires and masts in the operating area stressed over and over again. Indeed, several aircraft, including ours, had previously been operating other Norwegian coastal waters earlier in the exercise and had witnessed first-hand the profusion of wires and masts that existed.*

'After a 1 ½ hour transit across the Skagerrak, the aircraft arrived at Sola to refuel. After refuelling, two of us departed low-level in the deteriorating weather to the Bergen operating area for rendezvous. Following completion of initial tasking, both helicopters were further tasked to independently reconnoitre the coastal areas around Bergen in order to sanitise the area. My aircraft's assigned area was in a large north-south fjord. Having established ourselves in the area, the weather settled down somewhat. I estimated the cloud cover at 400 feet with visibility at 4 kilometres. A slight drizzle was falling and the wind was southwest at 15 knots. Almost immediately, we located and identified a type 143 FPB near the centre of the fjord. A successful Sea Skua attack followed, during which we encountered only sporadic simulated gunfire. Two more FPB's were spotted to the north-west of our position departing from shelter. To classify them as friend or foe prior to engagement, we decided to make a low-level probe. Rather than proceed from our exposed position to seaward, we elected to make ground to the west and cross the fjord. From 50 feet above sea level we climbed at 120 knots across the southern tip of Rong Island with the intention to transit northwards up the west coast of the island. Our goal was to arrive at a position to the north-west of the targets hoping to remain concealed during the transit.*

'In pursuance of this plan, we arrived at the western end of the channel from which point we had seen the two FPB's departing earlier. The channel provided an obvious feature down which to fly. At this point we were well above the terrain, level of the predominantly low lying islands and indeed could not have transited at a lower level due to a road bridge that connected the two islands.*

'To our consternation the two FPB's were not visible to seaward as expected when we approach the eastern end of the channel. We had been unable to monitor their position due to the visibility and the partial obstruction of the land as we had crossed the southern tip of Rong Island.

'Slowing the aircraft to 60 knots to discuss our next move, and a quick scan with the radar, offered no further clues to their whereabouts. We began to suspect that they had returned to the cover of the channel when suddenly they came into view. They had seen us too and had probably heard us coming for some time. Immediately, we were engaged by simulated gunfire. Evasion was the obvious response. We quickly considered several options. Climb into the clouds going IMC; reverse course and descend, possibly heading into an area of known wires; or descend straight ahead into the channel to regain our cover and still be able to launch an attack. We chose the latter.

'We made a rapid visual check of the channel opening and checked our map for any wires or pylons, none were found. The mouth of the channel opening still looked clear. I commenced a gentle descent to get down ultimately to 50 feet. The observer was about to transmit an enemy contact report while crosschecking his map. Just as we approach the mouth of the channel flying at 120 feet, we heard the most awful "BANG". The aircraft immediately pitched nose up and rolled violently to the right. My immediate response was that we had suffered a control malfunction. The shot of adrenaline was almost overwhelming. "Wires!" Screamed the observer. I hadn't even seen them.

'Whilst wrestling with the cyclic, I noticed the airspeed drop from 60 knots. The most appalling graunching and high-pitched whining noise was audible. I sensed that in the cockpit there was a feeling of complete disbelief that this was actually happening to both of us. The relative comfort and excitement of what had been a cat and mouse tussle with two FPB's had become a real-life drama of terrible proportions. I managed to arrest the initial pitching and rolling such that I was able to initiate a Mayday call. Instinctively, I lowered the collective, fearing that a control surface failure would follow at any moment as I did so. Flailing wires (I did not know how many) chattered up the windscreen towards the rotor disc. Fearful that they would obliterate the main rotors or pitch control rods, I pulled up the collective. The wires thankfully returned to the base of the windscreen and became tautly stretched across the nose of the aircraft. In addition to those, another wire appeared to be below the aircraft, but it was not possible to ascertain whether or not it was actually snagged on the airframe.

'I had neither the foresight nor the confidence in my ability to retain control to attempt to reverse the aircraft out of the dilemma. I don't know how fast the aircraft was flying at this stage, but certainly the sensation was one of virtually being in a precarious hover with rapidly deteriorating yaw control and marginal cyclic control.

218   The Royal Navy Lynx

Only a few seconds had passed since we had first struck the wires and yet the whole event seemed to be taking place in slow motion.

'Suddenly another almighty "BANG" and both windscreens cracked; mine much worse than the observers, so much so that my forward visibility now became obscured. Almost immediately the lower Perspex window adjacent to the rudder pedals shattered, filling the cockpit with fragments of plastic. It seemed that the aircraft was on the point of breaking up. "I think we are going to die, Phil!" retorted my observer. I think I believed him. As I hung onto the controls, it seemed that we were completely powerless to do anything and a feeling of hopelessness weighed heavily upon us. The grating and whining noise was becoming intolerable. For no logical reason other than the desire to do something in an effort to escape from what seemed like a catastrophe, I pulled up the collective. The aircraft pitched nose down and suddenly there was yet another loud "BANG", accompanied this time with a flash of light. Another "BANG" followed and the aircraft lurched upwards. At this stage I convinced myself that we had suffered a tail rotor failure, since yaw control was becoming more and more difficult. Apparently clear of wires I now dumped the collective. I communicated my intentions to the observer with a second Mayday call, "376 ditching, ditching".

'The observer rapidly conducted the crash checks down to the step "engine condition levers off". At this point, it became apparent to both of us that we would not make the water, but rather a rocky foreshore backed by cliffs, precluding any kind of engine-off landing. With no time to discuss the problem, I snapped, "pulling power" and gingerly raised the collective. To our great surprise and immense relief the aircraft responded and a gentle climb was initiated with an equally cautious turn away from the cliffs. Following a brief control check, we located a football pitch on the outskirts of Rong village. With a careful search of the area, an uneventful landing was completed despite marginal forward visibility through my shattered windscreen.

'Once safely on the ground our sense of sheer relief was overwhelming to the point of tears. What had seemed an eternity had lasted only about thirty seconds from hitting the wires to the moment we had broken free. The evidence of our encounter was only too obvious from the damage to the aircraft.

'One might now ask why didn't the aircrew see the pylons even if the wires were virtually invisible? The answer lies in those few ill-fated seconds prior to the incident. We had located and been engaged by the enemy. During our evasive action our attention being drawn to the tactical situation and not the real threat, the wires! As we looked through the windscreen in the poor grey light, we did not see any wires or even the pylons. I wonder how much of our attention was really centred on the battle rather than a thorough and comprehensive lookout. I had fallen into the trap of thinking that

it was safe to become more aggressive. Had we not been so preoccupied with the battle, then we would have had no cause to descend so readily into the channel opening in the first place. A 180° turn and a safe retreat at the same altitude at which we had first transited the channel would certainly have been more in accord with the prevailing conditions.

'*This incident occurred during a NATO exercise in simulated conditions. Had the engagement been in wartime under hostile fire conditions with the FPB's firing real bullets, then the desire to seek shelter in the channel entrance, I suggest, would have been even more pressing. The question of how safe it is to evade such an engagement, and by what means, in the wire strewn areas of Norway, remains a very real problem for the military aviator.*

Sometimes the aircraft did totally unexpected things:

The Final Flight of XZ249

By the Flight Commander of HMS *Avenger* Flight: Lieutenant Commander Barry Bryant:

Pilot: Lt David Midgley
Aircrewman: LAEM Gary Stewart,
Passenger: Commanding Officer HMS *Avenger*, Captain Peter Woodhead.

'Sunday, 4 May 1983, was just another Armilla day in the Gulf; hot, calm, with local warring nations not being particularly warlike as our tankers sailed through the Straits of Hormuz. It was time for HMS *Avenger* to take a day's stand-down off some godforsaken stretch of desert and the boys were looking forward to a banyan in Bandar Jissa. Except that the captain, an ex-Junglie pilot of some note, and now some seniority, had received a lunch invitation from some old muckers in Oman. Thus the Flight, with their usual good grace at such a time, prepared to give up their day of rest to take the boss into what passed for civilisation. I idly reminded myself that at least we were more relaxed than exactly a year previously when we had been airborne in the vicinity of HMS *Sheffield* when she was hit by the first Exocet of the Falklands conflict.

'A routine taxi trip into Seeb, where we refuelled and cancelled a stores VERTREP as being too hot and heavy. Back to the ship for a quick meal before returning to pick up our sociable boss from the Junglie lunch club. Having installed the amiable captain in the back with LAEM Gary Stewart, the aircrewman, we headed back to *Avenger* looking forward to at least a couple of banyan beers before sunset, but it would be a good few days before we tasted alcohol again. Some fifteen minutes into the flight, the pilot, Dave Midgley, said fairly calmly, "There's something wrong with the pedals". Just to keep us going in a straight line, he was having to apply more and more boot on one side – can't remember which side now, but this was clearly not good and we hadn't got a clue what the problem was. Having made the Pan call we decided to try to close the ship, although it was becoming increasingly apparent that although we could maintain some direction going forward, a deck landing was probably not going to work and still the pedal mismatch kept getting worse. About two miles out and just as we were planning for a controlled ditching alongside, there was a loud bang from the general direction of the tail rotor and life became very exciting for the next twenty seconds or so. It was probably about twenty seconds, but it felt rather longer.

'I called, "Mayday, tail rotor failure" etc. and although I don't remember doing so, I apparently kept transmitting updates fairly calmly throughout the descent. The aircraft pitched violently and began a spin into the sea which was probably at an angle of only about thirty degrees, but it felt vertical. There was certainly a lot of sea coming towards the windscreen! Survival seemed unlikely, not that there was much time to consider it, but it seemed slightly ironic having survived bombs, bullets and icebergs the previous year. We hit the sea with an almighty bang and like many others before us were saved by those many visits to the dunker. The flotation gear had been ripped off and the aircraft rolled to the right and swiftly sank. Fortunately, at least for me, and despite feeling uncomfortable around the lumber regions (which proved to be a classic "ejection seat fracture" in reverse), I just floated out and inflated my Mae West and then had perhaps the bleakest few seconds of my life; the aircraft had gone and apparently my three colleagues with it. Little did I know the struggles going on beneath the surface as Dave the pilot, with a far worse spinal thoracic fracture, had to go down before coming up while, with incredibly cool thinking, Gary the crewman managed to untangle the captain from the rescue winch and get him clear of the sinking aircraft before escaping himself. They both, like me, turned out to have lumbar fractures. Huge was the relief as all three popped to the surface, although clearly in some discomfort. *Avenger*, meanwhile, had weighed anchor and was racing towards us with that famous Type 21 frigate acceleration and we were swiftly hauled over the side of the whaler. Just what you need with spinal fractures! The ship headed swiftly for Muscat where we were transferred to the Sultan's hospital at Seeb before being casevaced to Haslar a few days later by the RAF. We all returned to duty in due course, although it took Dave a very long acquaintance with hospital at Headley Court. The captain, Gary, and I, rejoined the ship in Sri Lanka a couple of months later. In due course, I'm delighted to say, Gary was presented with a Royal Humane Society award for his actions on that day.

'The aircraft was subsequently recovered in one piece from the sea bed and we were reacquainted in the investigation hangar at Fleetlands. The blades were still fairly intact, not a lot of rotor revs on impact! While the front seats had punched through the floor. Someone had calculated a force of minus 14G, but all a tribute to the inherent strength of the Lynx design. It turned out that part of the tail rotor pitch change mechanism had been milled out too far by Westlands and the inherent weakness had twisted before breaking, putting the tail rotor into full coarse pitch. I suspect the Board of Enquiry said a lot of other things, but I don't recall reading it – we had a life to get on with!'

Authors note: This accident, apart from making Dave Midgely half an inch shorter, caused some concern, as it seemed to take forever to find the cause. In the end, six months later, a Westland WG 30 in America suffered a similar failure (it was the same design of tail rotor system). Luckily, once again, everyone survived. However, the culprit was found to be, as Barry Bryant says, the failure of the pitch change link on top of the tail rotor gearbox. The failure was due to metal fatigue caused by a combination of wear on the hydraulic jack mounting and high vibration. The solution was to re-engineer the link, and in the meantime a routine inspection and remote monitoring system was installed on all aircraft. The real concern over this was that the tail rotor threw on pitch and so the aircraft rotated in the opposite direction to that covered in all tail rotor emergency procedures up until then. Afterwards, Dave Midgely recalled that, as he didn't have a clue what was going on, he simply did the crash checks, shut down the engines and pulled up on the collective at the last minute. That they all survived is a tribute to the strength of the aircraft and the skill of the pilot. Once again time would solve the problem when the system was redesigned to make the tail rotor rotate in the opposite direction and a force gradient spring fitted into the control run. This spring system ensured that the blades would not go to full pitch in the event of a control failure.

222   The Royal Navy Lynx

The following two stories were provided by Lieutenant Alun Read. After reading them it might be clear why his nickname is 'Lucky Al':

APRIL 1992 – Formation tip strike

'Having recently joined 702 Squadron to become the training officer I was tasked to learn the "Pairs Display" routine which was part of my Terms of Reference.

'This first sortie was the first flight after Easter leave and was authorized despite formation flying being a shortfall on my Lynx conversion and was flown solo in both aircraft.

'The lead was Lieutenant Mike Holloway in 635 and myself as No 2 in 636.

'The weather was fine and we flew to Merryfield (Yeovilton's satellite airfield) for about fifty minutes practice before returning to Portland. As I remember, we were authorized to half a rotor span distance for formation. All went well until about eight miles from Portland on the return.

'I elected to remain in formation (echelon port) whilst conducting pre-landing checks and stayed close, as it appeared easier than my previous experience in a Sea King at one rotor span. I decided to do the checks two at a time for safety; none of this was discussed at the brief.

'Just before I had completed the checks there was a sound similar to a 7.62 machine gun report and as I looked up, the air was full of dark "confetti" like a cloud. I watched 635 roll right and invert completely, diving rapidly from our 1000ft rejoin height. It disappeared within a second, behind and well below me. At this point I put out a PAN call on the radio to Air Traffic, who asked if it was for exercise (they had previously asked for a practice emergency on the approach frequency).

'The aircraft had already started descending quite quickly despite me not lowering the lever. I pulled to restore level flight but got to the top limit of movement with only about 65% Torque and had to slow down to get level.

'(A couple of weeks earlier, Lieutenant Commander Peter Palm had diverted into Exeter with a vibration. When the second aircraft arrived with engineers, one of the main rotor blades lifted from about half way down the blade in the downwash by about 30 degrees, as the main spar had cracked almost all the way through.)

'I knew exactly what had happened almost immediately and aware of the fragility of the blades, wanted to land with the minimum of control input. Vibration was enormous and I was bracing my foot against the instrument panel regularly so as to read the instruments at all. I picked a field next to the Moonfleet

Hotel (which was already in my 12 o'clock and into wind) and the aircraft, almost without input, got me there. I elected for a zero/zero approach without much of a recce and made a pretty good landing considering my heart rate.

'Immediately on landing I heard Mike calling to say that he had landed safely (on 'Hurberry Hill'), albeit his wheels were completely under the turf.

'We both shut down without the rotor brake.

'636 had lost about 3ft of all four main blade aerofoils and all tip caps, the main D spar was intact except where the tip caps had been ripped out! There were several puncture wounds in the tail assembly and the tail rotor blades (small but scary).

'635 had lost a similar amount of lift area, but to only three blades, one had just lost a tip cap so his vibration was extreme.

'636 flew exactly one year later, 635 a couple of weeks after that, almost all rotating parts had been changed, including all four engines. My punishment was running a training programme with two aircraft missing. I got very drunk in the Officer's Club and Mike drove me home. I don't remember ever speaking to him again.'

Authors note: This accident happened with the old metal blades fitted. Had it been the BERP blades, the imbalance and loss of lift would have been much more severe.

OCTOBER 1996 – Slide off HMS *Marlborough*

'It was the day after my thirty-sixth birthday and we were holding at RNAS Culdrose as a second aircraft to support an anti-drug operation in the South West Approaches. Then the operation was stood down for the weekend. I was looking forward to Happy Hour when the call came from Task Group Commander at sea to go to the ship to collect some passengers and take them to Poole. The weather was horrid, sea state 6 or more, with 40–50 knots of wind. Due to the nature of the operation no SAR cover was made available and we were to arrive at the ship some 240 miles south-west of Culdrose as it got dark. We had an overload tank fitted. Despite my concerns, I was persuaded that this mission was an essential operational task and that normal safety/weather considerations were not relevant. We went.

'It turns out that the Flight embarked on the ship (another crew from 815 Squadron), had flown off at 1400 with a load of officers to go to a Mess Dinner at Portland, leaving the Special Forces on board as a way of guaranteeing that we had to come.

'On transit, we passed our Point of No Return (PNR) with about fifteen minutes to run, having only just established UHF communications with the ship. *Marlborough* insisted that the weather was suitable, but didn't really provide any specifics. The sea state was so high that the ship was actually getting damaged internally when trying to achieve a conventional flying course of Red 30 (wind from thirty degrees to port) due to the size and steepness of the waves, so had elected for an R90 wind. This was giving about fifteen degrees of roll, the limit was six degrees.

'A further complication was that the ship had a modified Harpoon Grid, which was too shallow to accept the MK1 Harpoon and our aircraft had not been modified. We had to land swivel and lash down without a Harpoon, in up to 50 knots of wind. It was getting dark and we had no alternate plan so landed, swiveled successfully and took eight lashings and fuel, remaining rotors running.

'I cannot remember now whether we were expecting four passengers and six sneaked in, or six and eight sneaked in, but the buggers definitely sneaked big time and with more baggage than a removals van, they too were very keen to get off the ship for the weekend!

'We considered shutting down as the weather/deck/motion/weight, were all beyond my experience, but still believing this was an "operational" sortie we continued. The aircraft must have weighed more than 5100kg (Mark 3 max was 4875kg) and we had no Harpoon.

'The ship stuck with the Red 90 launch option, so we had to remove lashings, swivel and go. Contrary to the Flying Guide, I did the pre-take off checks whilst the lashings came off, just in case we slipped whilst castoring! You are supposed to wait until into wind apparently.

'Lashings off, we tried to castor the nose wheel, but it wasn't man enough for the weight and was not rotating correctly after about five seconds of trying. At this point the observer, Lieutenant Butch Bowers, called, "full sub min pitch", and something about a bloody big wave. I did as I was told immediately and then listened to his description whilst looking at a huge wall of water. The aircraft had rotated about thirty degrees to port at this stage without the correct indications for the nose wheel, but then started to rotate to starboard despite full left pedal. This was as the roll to starboard was at its maximum. As the ship rolled level the aircraft slowed its rotation and stopped about Green 30 as the second bigger wave arrived. As the ship rolled beyond ten degrees the aircraft rotated to starboard again and started to slide towards the starboard side of the flight deck. We arrived at the edge facing Green 90, at walking pace and still with full sub min pitch applied. I foolishly believed that the four inch spurn water edge would stop us, but we didn't even slow down. As we bumped the nose wheel over the side of the ship I pulled from bottom to top of collective lever movement in less than one second; 70% negative torque to probably 150% up. The Nr (rotor speed) drooped audibly, I took a glance at the gauge and saw below 90% Nr (I think). The aircraft seemed to keep moving horizontally and I felt we were airborne, but certainly not going up. We were downwind in 50kts, well overweight in the dark (pre NVG) between two 40–50ft waves. The Helicopter Controller in the ship said afterwards that as the ship rolled upright the flight deck nets missed the tail rotor by less than a foot, but he was looking at a camera image from the ops room. The ship had rolled to approximately twenty-three degrees as the stabilizers had cut out at fifteen. Whoops!

'I have read "*Chickenhawk*", an account of a Huey pilot in Vietnam and still believe it was this that got me to put in full right (power off pedal) boot to see if it would help. We were at this stage about 10ft off the water still downwind and not going anywhere really.

'As soon as I did this the rotor speed sounded as if it was recovering and the aircraft turned to the right and airspeed arrived from nowhere. The aircraft was clearly flying forward if not upward, Nr was restored and power was at around 140% matched. The lever was no longer at the top of its travel, but all that had happened with no conscious application by me. It took about 500 yards before the aircraft climbed above the tops of the two waves and we had successfully flown down the trough between them at less than 30ft most of the way.

'We did not volunteer to land back on the ship and chose to take our chances in an over torqued helicopter to go back to land.

'Our passengers were less than pleased by their experience and insisted on getting out ASAP. We dropped them off at a closed Predannack (satellite airfield to Culdrose) and continued to Portland, which was open by the time we got there. It took no time at all with a 50 knot tail wind.

'Aircraft undamaged, exceedances logged. My Incident Signal was so badly edited after I had gone home that I didn't recognize the events within it. Due to that an A25 accident form was ordered and the conclusion was that it was all my fault.

'Thank God I did the take-off checks early and read "*Chickenhawk*".'

226   The Royal Navy Lynx

'Lucky Al' managed to get away with this incident, but when you operate aircraft from small ships you are always at the mercy of the weather. The following is an extract from *Cockpit* magazine where they weren't quite so lucky:

HMS Hermione – *unexpected ditching*

'HMS Hermione, *in company with HMS* Juno, *was some seventy miles west of Gibraltar, steaming at high speed towards Cape Saint Vincent on passage for Portsmouth after a two month Mediterranean deployment. This was to be the last period of planned flying before disembarkation. The task was simple but varied: deck landing practice on* Juno, HDS, *and flying one aircrew wearing an AR5 respirator (not donned during the crash). Photography of HMS* Hermione *conducting pre-wetting.*

'The main contributory factor to this accident was the weather. A strong easterly airflow of 30 knots gusting 40 was setting through the Western Gibraltar Straits generating sea state 5. Visibility was good with a thin veil of cirrus cloud. The ship was steering 295 degrees at 25 knots, giving a relative wind outside either the forward facing or into wind limits. An alteration of course was obviously needed before takeoff. Despite the strong wind and sea state, the deck movement was benign and had been for about two hours following a period of officer of the watch manoeuvres in the forenoon. The Flight commander emplaned at 1312 after the lashings were removed and before rotor engagement. He occupied the forward right-hand position in the four-man inflatable seat. The usual pre-flight button crunching, switch switching and HC banter was underway when the two minute to take-off call was made. The rotors were now running but the pre-takeoff checks were outstanding (this is significant because the circuit breaker for the automatic activation of the floatation gear is made during these checks). A flying course of 090 had been passed by the HC and it was apparent that a turn to port had started just prior to the two minute call. The combined effects of the turn, the wind, sea state and considerable bad luck, caused the ship to roll heavily to starboard. The first roll was somewhat alarming causing the port olio to fully extend, but the ship started to recover and a little negative pitch helped to keep the Dunlops firmly grounded; unfortunately the situation rapidly worsened. Before regaining an even keel, the ship experienced a more violent and sharper roll/lurch to starboard. So severe was this roll that the pilot and observer were pushed up and right in their harnesses with sufficient force to operate the inertia reels. At about 23° of roll (witnessed in the ship) the aircraft rolled forward and right about the line joining the nose and starboard wheels. The time between the Harpoon shear pin breaking and the "machine-gun burst" sound of the main rotors striking the starboard flight deck nets* *was so small as to be infinitesimal. There was an estimated two seconds between the start of the fateful roll and the aircraft entering the water.*

'*Reconstruction has revealed that the aircraft first rolled onto the starboard side of its nose, which caused the pilot's windscreen and door to implode, peppering his helmet and right arm with fragments. Immediately prior to this, the main rotor blades struck the starboard nets and it is thought that they were all effectively shed after one revolution. The aircraft, now under the influence of gravity and with the deck still at an angle of twenty-three degrees, fell into the sea, but not before rotating a further ninety degrees and entering the water inverted. During the fall, the rotor head punctured a hole in the ship's side providing the sick bay with a great deal of extra ventilation.*

'*Disorientation for the crew was immediate. Catapulted from a familiar and secure position in the aircraft to a position upside down underwater and a rough sea, gave rise to a rather classic "now get out of that" situation. The aircraft floated for an estimated three minutes lying nose down with initially the bottom of the cargo door visible, but sinking slowly throughout. First clear was the pilot. His helmet had been removed by the inrush of water. Being temporarily confused by the turbulence, he quickly realised that his cockpit door had been swept away, so he undid his harness, his Quick Release and swam clear of his seat, his egress unhindered. The observer was slightly disadvantaged because he experienced the widest turning arc during the roll. He initially watched as the blades struck the nets, but then closed his eyes as the windscreen shattered. He suffered the same disorientation and severe underwater turbulence. Still with his eyes closed, he searched for the door jettison handle but could not locate it. He remembers feeling a kick, which he later realised was the pilot making his escape, this caused him to open his eyes, which confirmed his orientation and he realised that the door was missing. Instinctively locating the grab handle, he released his Quick Release and swam clear, again unhindered.*

'*The Flight commander, who had previously been seated comfortably in the four-man inflatable seat secured by a lap strap, was perhaps even more disadvantaged. The visual references from the back seat are poor, particularly when facing outboard, so disorientation underwater was immediate. He had been slightly winded by the lap strap, but was able to recognise a patch of light assumed to be the cabin door window. The visibility underwater was severely restricted, probably because of the turbulence. This made recognition very difficult with familiar and expected things being featureless. Black and yellow stripes could not be seen underwater. Unable to reach any method of escape while strapped in, he had to release his strap and right himself in the aircraft. A quick look and feel for the window jettison handle was unsuccessful before the need for air forced him to raise his head and, rather thankfully, locate a small air pocket.*

Following a quick gulp of air, which was mainly water, the hunt for the jettison handle continued; "Where is that handle?", "Which way is up for this aircraft?"; "Where are those beta lights?" (Of course it's not dark!) Then a large rush of bubbles and increased turbulence pushed him close enough to see the back of the pilot's seat. Holding onto the inertia reel he immediately located the main cabin door handle, although he could not see it. "Time at last to get out of here," he thought, "running short of breath now." Especially after an attempt to relocate the air pocket failed the final hurdle in what he thought to be a sinking aircraft, was the need to hold the door handle with two hands, then rest both feet on the forward door frame to give enough leverage to open a previously normal door a couple of feet, just enough to swim through. The aircraft had in fact not sunk, but only the tail boom and aft equipment bay door were visible. Thirty seconds after he arrived on the surface, Lynx 475 sank in 650 metres of the Atlantic.

'All three aircrew and all nine personnel on the flight deck survived with only a couple of minor injuries.'

You don't even have to be flying, or even on deck, for the weather to cause all sorts of problems, as Lieutenant Commander Peter Spens-Black recalls:

HMS **Beaver** *and more rough weather*

'It was an average day on Towed-Array patrol on the good ship *Beaver*. The navigation plot indicated that we were somewhat north of Milton Keynes, even north of Prestwick. North of the Shetlands, but somewhat south of Robert Peary's landmark achievement. It was February. It was a cold Tuesday afternoon. Even the weather was average. Wind, force 7; sea state 6 from the port quarter; visibility not exceptional.

'My role in this epic adventure was as the Flight commander. This particular afternoon the single Lynx (XZ 719) was at eight hours' notice and parked on the right hand side of the hangar. There was a general "make and mend" underway and the SMR was catching up with paperwork in the Air Engineering office. I had retired to my cabin to study BR 45(2) and if memory serves, it was to catch up on Chapter XVI, a well written and exhilarating chapter on the Rising and Setting of Heavenly Bodies. (Author's translation – catching a few sneaky Zzzs).

'I was engrossed in this research when I was aware of a distinct momentary aberration in the pitch and roll of the ship. I immediately threw aside my duvet – it is cold work studying astronavigation – leapt into the main drag and proceeded to the back of the boat at an officer-like pace; not wishing to alarm the troops. Although to be fair, the ship's company were taking the make and mend seriously as well. Without passing anyone, I arrived at the airlock into the hangar. The SMR, quite correctly, took a moment to secure-for-sea his plethora of engineering paperwork. Thus I was the first to arrive at the hangar.

'Now, in my career I have, many times, been in situations of uncertainty, fear, danger, abject terror and total mind-numbing paralysis. And one or two of these situations have actually not been of my own making. So I fearlessly opened and closed the two airlock doors (the ones with the eight handles). Then pausing to get my breath back – for some reason the forward squash court had been unserviceable for the last nine months, so the fish-heads had explained to me. Then I stepped boldly, unlike Captain Kirk, into the hangar and took a razor-like view and analysis of the situation.

'Although not a naval architect, I very cleverly interpreted that the fact that forty per cent of the hangar door was peeled back like the lid of a sardine can was not a "good thing". I walked into the centre of the hangar to port of the aircraft, as the SMR came through the airlock. I then made a leadership orientated remark which as I recall was, "I say Chief, this is a bit of a turn-up for the book. We should probably do something." Note that I played down the potential seriousness of the event, in order to ensure that morale was maintained. Then I made a tiny error. I turned and went to check XZ 719 for any damage which might have resulted in an S126 (loss of stores form) coming my way.

'Then the drama unfolded. The next "rogue wave" struck. No, delete that. I have just remembered that our oceanography tutor at Dartmouth told us; "There is no such thing as a rogue wave – there are only Statistically Predictable Large Waves." So obviously this was another SPLW. Well, over my right shoulder this particular SPLW impacted the flight deck, spotted that the hangar door was less than serviceable and, with several tons of water, entered my domain.

'At this point my recollections are somewhat blurred. I can remember the feeling of being gathered up, being "swept off my feet" and projected towards XZ 719. Getting one's head around the fact that I was completely underwater in what normally constitutes a safe place, was somewhat bewildering. My first thought was to react as if I was in the dunker, but rejected that as I believed panicking probably would not help. Then there was a violent impact on my head. My next recollection is my SMR helping me upright on the right-hand side of the aircraft and ascertaining my well-being. "Boss – you OK?" To which I succinctly replied, immediately taking a strategic view, "Ow! My head hurts".

'I stumbled around the aircraft quickly, realising that steaming bats (special naval shoes worn at sea) full of water were uncomfortable and that a sodden

230 The Royal Navy Lynx

woolly pulley and uniform were probably not sartorially advantageous. But at least I was thinking of the important issues.

'As this drama was unfolding in the hangar, the Squadron WEO, who had been nearby, was prompted to investigate. When he arrived, he fearlessly entered the airlock and then decided to check out the inspection window in the inner door. As he explained later, he could see nothing but water, which he rapidly assessed as being in the "Oh, this is different" category. He grabbed the nearest phone and explained the situation to the Officer of the Watch. The ship was turned into wind and Emergency Stations was piped. Meanwhile, the SMR had found the aircraft's VHF aerial (the "bean can") which was rolling around on the deck. After a short assessment it was decided that this was what had impacted my head whilst underwater and under the aircraft.

'I left the rapidly assembling flight team who would soon be maximising the use of PX24, got checked out by the LMA, climbed into dry gear, went to the wardroom for tea and received precious little sympathy for my death defying exploits. Although it was duly recorded in the aircraft engineering log that the VHF aerial was unserviceable, "due to impact from the Flight commander's head"'.

The weather can catch you out in other ways, as Lieutenant Commander Graham Cooke explained in *Cockpit* magazine in 2002:

Hang on a minute, lads. I've got a great idea …

'A few years ago I was a newly qualified Lynx observer anxious to make a good impression in my first appointment. The Flight and ship in question were still recovering from the tragic loss of one of their aircrew after the aircraft crashed into the sea at night. Within days of my joining, the ship was deployed at very short notice and I found myself en-route for the Adriatic for some intensive flying (more than 100 hours in about five weeks, all with warshot missiles). Both the Flight commander and I subsequently became very tired, juggling the demands of operational embarked flying from a ship at sea in defence watches for more than a month (babysitting a French carrier).

'One day we launched for some Instrument Flying Practice (IFP) followed by a short Flyex to continue to work up our relatively inexperienced Command Aviation Team. Visibility was poor and I had forecast intermittent mist patches, but we were confident we could avoid these and get back on-board quickly if needed, due to our proximity to the ship. We dutifully toddled off to spend some quality time lazily chasing clouds, when to our discomfort the ship announced an urgent change in operational tasking

and steamed north, straight into an extensive fog bank. We attempted to recover via a Helicopter Controlled Approach (HCA), but were not visual at the bottom of the glide slope and overshot. The command were keen (understandably as it subsequently turned out) to have us back and, after much discussion, as we still had diversion fuel at this point, we conducted an Extreme Limited Visibility Approach (ELVA) – my first – and landed safely. For the "Trappers" (Standards Flight Instructors) reading, no mention was made of the necessity for an Incident Signal as we could have diverted, but operational requirements meant that was not the preferred option.

'The ship was racing to the north to the assistance of a French Nuclear Submarine that had surfaced just outside Montenegran Territorial waters with an urgent need to disembark someone (never did find out who or why). A French helicopter was inbound to conduct the transfer, but everyone was worried about the possibility of the Serbian Navy sallying forth to ruin everyone's day with a brace of surface-to-surface missiles. A missile capable helicopter was therefore needed to "ride shotgun" as a deterrent.

'Understandably concerned about the pea-souper now totally enveloping the whole area, the Flight commander and I discussed the situation with the captain. I upgraded the forecast to a worst-case scenario of persistent fog and retired to have a brief think about little operational matters such as identification in the fog in a Mk 3 Lynx, Rules Of Engagement, Skua tactics and so forth.

'Keen to help, we briefed, and the wily Flight commander advised the captain he could authorise the sortie if we were to land at Bari. He produced the Bari forecast of "5000mts visibility in mist or haze with scattered cloud at 500ft" that he had obtained by telephone and said that we would of course try to divert back to the ship (fuel dependent). The captain was happy, duly authorised us, and we launched, blundering off into the fog in the late afternoon. On reaching 500 feet, we climbed out of the gloop and into the sun (hooray), only to see the fog below us stretching out as far as the eye could see in all directions (boo).

'The sortie was uneventful from an operational point of view. The fun started when we tried to land somewhere. We went back to Mum and tried an SCA but failed to become visual and had to overshoot. As we turned south-west for the Italian coast, the command now realized that the authorisation they had given meant they would be without an aircraft until the weather improved. They were not happy bears and there was a lot of tense radio traffic as to our intentions. The Flight commander sighed (maybe he had seen this coming) and replied that we were proceeding to Bari, as briefed. There was a pause, some terse questions about any other options before some bright spark had the brainwave of diverting us to an American cruiser further to the north. Hmmm, anyone for an unplanned, unbriefed, unauthorised diversion

232   The Royal Navy Lynx

to an unfamiliar ship in fog without the fuel to do anything subsequently if it all goes wrong?

'*We continued to the south-west. By now it was getting dark, with an accompanying drop in temperature. "Not to worry", we thought, "ten miles from the coast, we'll descend from 1500ft through the clag, get visual with the coast and hop in to Bari airfield". The smooth sounding Italian controller was still assuring us it was, "5000 metres visibility in mist or haze with scattered at 500ft". Imagine our surprise when we duly descended to our 100ft night Minimum Separation Distance (MSD) and were still in the fog. We climbed, and the alarm bells that began ringing at that point, increasing in volume when we found ourselves orbiting at 1000ft with the dull orange glow of Bari filtering weakly through the fog below us. We informed the ship – apparently the ops room went very quiet, given their recent aviation experiences.*

'*There were few options. Gioia Del Colle (one of the two main airfields for the strike aircraft bombing the Balkans) was just reachable inland, but we would have only one shot at a radar assisted approach, insufficient fuel to return to the coast and their forecast was very poor. Bari had no talkdown and we were not exactly blessed with a suite of navigation aids in the Lynx (no ILS, VOR, DME, TACAN – the list goes on). Fighting down the rising panic, we got ourselves to where we thought the airfield was, using GPS positions and a large-scale chart. By this time the helpful Italian controller was sounding less smooth and had his staff outside the tower listening for us. I then caught my first glimpse of a small hole in the fog and saw a busy city centre street packed with cars. The possibility of making it through this without having to ditch at night in fog, just off the coast, now loomed. The next thought was that we would be landing in a dark city street surrounded by people and goodness knows what other hazards, in an armed helicopter, on a Saturday night, on an Italian Bank Holiday weekend. Funny what you think about at crucial times. However, concentrating on the task at hand we thought we could discern a faint light off to the right and, encouraged by the cries over the radio that they could hear us, we made towards it. With the now distinctly ragged controller informing us that, due to their sophisticated aural direction finding equipment, we must be close to the, "very high control tower with a bright light on it and there is nothing below it just to the south-east", we commenced a very sporting towering landing through the fog, using the light, then the tower, as our single reference (with me peering alternately below us and at the instruments) to land safely with about three minutes of fuel remaining above Minimum Landing Allowance (MLA). The Pope has never kissed the Italian soil with as much reverence as we did on clambering out.*

'*Thankfully the ship's agent pitched up and took care of everything (even providing some RAF chaps from somewhere to guard the aircraft overnight). The resulting alcohol fuelled debrief in a restaurant (thankfully not in goon bag, because we had thought ahead) is a bit of a blur, but we thought that although it had been a "challenging sortie" we hadn't done anything illegal.'*

Sometimes aircraft can do funny things and it's not obvious why. Graham Cooke also wrote this for *Cockpit* magazine in 2009:

'So there we were – pitched nose down, ground coming up fast and nothing on the altimeter but the maker's name.

'Whilst modest understatement has its place, in the telling of tales, perhaps it should be mandated that all decent WAFU dits should contain phrases like this (perhaps with some compulsory wild gesticulating). It has in any case served me well when recounting this tale for the odd drink at the bar.

'It was Tuesday, 10 Dec 08, and I was programmed to fly a relatively short notice first wave discretionary task that had come in the day before. The sortie involved a recce of some sites of interest in the local area. As the pilot was a very experienced Lynx operator and even the third crew member was a private pilot, I estimated that there was approximately 6000 hours experience in the aircraft. After a brief discussion, I foolishly said that as the squadron ops officer I would be happy to be aircraft commander and authoriser – a decision that, whilst perfectly reasonable given the nature of the sortie, ended up with me nearly going blind with extra paperwork for the next few weeks.

'Despite a relatively compressed time frame, first thing in the morning, all the necessary preparations were made, including those with respect to briefing, survival equipment and passenger. The Flight was correctly authorised and we launched more or less on time. Two miles north of the airfield boundary, on the way to Glastonbury, at 1000ft and 120kts, we started a gentle left-hand turn to the north-west. That was the last gentle thing we experienced for a little while. Just after the onset of the turn the aircraft experienced an undemanded control input, yawing rapidly and violently over an arc of about 30–40 degrees three or four times. Now, for those unfamiliar with the Lynx, it does have an effective, if slightly sensitive heading hold, with micro switches in the yaw pedals. In the hands of some of our more club-footed pilots there can occasionally be a slight twitch to the aircraft. At this point I can assure you that this was not what we experienced. The motion was sufficiently violent enough to toss me around in my harness and make my blood run cold. I turned to look at the pilot, who had gone white, and was busy stirring the controls, with seemingly little effect. In the second it took me to look back out the front we were already considerably more left wing low and:

'There we were, pitched nose down, ground coming up fast and nothing on the altimeter but the maker's name!

'Looking back, it's funny what you recollect. Time really did seem to stand still and my life really did seem to flash before my mind's eye in a series of images. I distinctly remember two things:

1. B****y Hell (or words to that effect). We're actually crashing here – I might not walk away from this one.

2. Isn't it like the simulator??!!

'Trying to follow the RCSDF pneumonic (Recognise-Control & Contain-Safe Flight Configuration-Diagnose-Further Actions) that is SOP for dealing with emergencies, we had certainly recognised that all was not well and the pilot was trying to Control & Contain the situation. It was reasonably obvious to me that the safest Flight Configuration was to be on the ground. The pilot and I very quickly agreed on the need to put the aircraft down in the nearest suitable field. Whilst looking out to help pick said suitable field, it occurred to me that this situation was potentially serious enough to warrant going straight for a Mayday. I voiced my intent to the pilot, who was still seemingly engaged in trying to wrestle the cyclic into submission and received a grunted acquiescence. I thus put out my first Mayday in thirteen years. Despite the subsequent squadron banter, I don't recall doing so in an unusually high-pitched voice (and this was born out by the ATC tape!). I remember thinking that the approach controller sounded really calm in response and that soothed my furrowed brow somewhat.

'A quick bit of CRM confirmed that we were both looking at the same field (which was partially flooded in the middle) and I had enough time to warn the passenger to brace. It was at about this point that I noticed two sets of domestic wires running through the field – one set parallel and the other at right angles, crossing our approach, and a considerable hazard to our safe arrival in this particular field.

'"Are you visual the wires?", I quizzed the right-hand seat, who by now seemed to have the upper hand in his ongoing struggle with the controls and had the aircraft descending towards the ground in a controlled fashion.

'I think the reply was something like; "Huh? I'm visual with a parallel set. Are there others?" My perception was that my wingman was reaching the limits of capacity in the very compressed time frame.

'"There are some others perpendicular to our approach – can you see them?" I persisted. The pilot then replied that no he couldn't, "where the B****y hell were these wires???!!" I described their location to him and helped con him safely over. I was trying to effectively manage the situation as aircraft commander and monitor the aircraft gauges when I remembered the pre-landing checks with about 30ft to go. Having whistled

through these and told the pilot they were complete, we touched down safely moments later, in the upslope northern half of the field on the edge of a housing estate, to the intense relief of all on-board.

'*Whilst a friendly Junglie circled overhead (very quickly vectored in by ATC) we discussed the next course of action. Informing the approach controller we were safe, we shut the aircraft down and got out. Indicating to our orbiting shepherd we were OK we commenced a walkround of the aircraft. Nothing appeared untoward (much to our chagrin). We had a quick chat then elected to sit on different sides of the aircraft and separately begin individual narratives to assist with the inevitable Post Incident Management (PIM). These proved to be very valuable later. When that was complete the local police arrived, shortly followed by the first press (less than twenty minutes after landing). As aircraft commander I delegated the media aspects to the pilot, who fortunately had previously worked in fleet media and had both nous and experience. A local media stills photographer and then a news camera crew followed in short order. We quickly became a focus for the locals from the estate (although the upside was a welcome cup of tea) and the squadron "Downbird" team arrived by both air and road very shortly after. Our relief at being uninjured manifested itself in amusement as, having landed on a frozen surface on a cold bright crisp morning, we watched the sun thaw the partially flooded field and the aircraft slowly sink ever deeper. I'm told the road move out was also fun to watch, as the same thing happened to both the crane and low loader.*

'*However, our merriment was short-lived, as the full PIM admin (and banter) nightmare kicked in as we returned to the squadron. There was a sortie debrief and then we started on the Incident Signal and were asked to do an A25. We listened to the ATC tapes as well as the cockpit voice and cabin recorders. Once the aircraft was recovered there were extensive (and I really do mean extensive – possibly even exhaustive) engineering checks to be conducted. Ultimately (and perhaps disturbingly for aircrew), despite finding some other issues with the airframe, any number of which might have in some way contributed, the engineering checks were inconclusive. The aircraft was rebuilt, ground run and flown by the Maintenance Test Pilot, who subsequently experienced two similar incidents, albeit less severe. Subsequently, during further testing, elements of the Flight Control System, Compass controller and Heading Hold, failed second line bench testing at the manufacturers. There was a problem with the system synchros, which was assessed as likely to have produced the undemanded attitude changes.*

'*So, whilst overall this was not a particularly serious incident and thankfully there were no injuries, it was still a nasty little occurrence from which I learnt a number of things, particularly post the event. As a wise man once said, "it is sometimes better to learn from the experiences of others rather than go through it yourself".'*

These are just a few incidents from the long life of the aircraft and illustrate just some of the issues with operating aircraft from small ships, in all weathers, all round the globe. In fact, compared to other types, the Lynx has an excellent safety record, which is a tribute to its design and the quality of those who have operated it.

Chapter 9

Rescue

Search and Rescue is always a secondary role for naval helicopters and all aircraft always carry a rescue winch. However, it is not often seen in photographs of a Lynx because it is fitted inside the cabin and can be swung out into position when needed. With the winch stowed in the cabin, it limits the space inside and therefore the aircraft's passenger carrying capacity. With a normal crew, the winch operator is the observer and so he has to leave his seat to operate the winch, although the pilot can also control it with a switch on the collective lever. In a seven man Lynx Flight, one of the maintainers is used as the "winch weight", in other words the crewman to go down on the wire. Although a far from ideal arrangement, it has proved extremely effective on many occasions.

A Mark 8 Lynx conducting winching training. The observer is operating the deployed winch and providing conning information to the pilot. The crewman on the wire has a second rescue strop to put a casualty into. The small wire trailing below him is to make an earth connection, to ground any static electricity. (*Paul Ellerton*)

238   The Royal Navy Lynx

However, one major limitation of the aircraft is that it does not have a night hover capability and therefore does not have a declared night SAR capability. The Sea King has a fully automatic system which can fly the aircraft hands off from a preset cruise height into the hover. This is primarily to allow it to operate its dunking sonar system, but this also means it has the night capability for rescues. The Lynx never had this ASW role and so was never fitted with such a system. However, it does have a Doppler radar which feeds the navigation system and also an automatic height control fed by an accurate radar altimeter. In the cockpit there is a gauge which indicates true ground speed and drift. However, it consists of a digital readout for speed and a left/right needle to indicate drift. One wonders, had this gauge been changed to one similar to that in the Sea King, with two bars to indicate forward and lateral drift, whether a night hover capability could have been developed. Despite this limitation, as will be seen, it didn't stop various crews over the years using their judgement and skill to operate in the dark when needed.

Of course, providing a rescue service can come in many forms. With the Lynx being deployed on small ships all around the world there have been many occasions when both the ship and the aircraft have been able to offer help. In this chapter are various accounts showing just how flexible the aircraft and those who flew it could be.

Maritime Search and Rescue

Here are four representative accounts of rescues conducted by Lynx Flights and, despite not being fully capable of night SAR, all were conducted, at least in part, in the dark.

In 1985, Flag Officer Naval Air Command awarded the Boyd Trophy to HMS *Beaver* Flight. This is the citation:

> '*On 6 October 1985, the Japanese freighter,* Reefer Dolphin, *was struck by a freak wave 400 miles south-west of land's end. One crew member was killed and two others seriously injured. HMS* Beaver *answered the freighter Mayday call and reached the position at 0100 on 7 October. The petty officer medical assistant and Flight aircrewman were transferred to the freighter by boat in marginal weather conditions, but the condition of the injured men demanded an immediate helicopter evacuation.*
>
> '*Beaver Flight launched at 0120 and over the following two hours in total darkness, conducted a hazardous series of stretcher transfers from the midships position of the freighter close to partially lit derricks and aerials. The necessity to maintain an accurate*

hover throughout this period was further exacerbated by the ship corkscrewing violently in a confused sea and in high winds. However, the Flight displayed considerable skill and professionalism in safely securing both casualties under the most adverse conditions.

'The casualties required urgent medical attention and it was decided to fly them immediately to Truro hospital in Cornwall, a distance of 400 miles. A mid-transit rendezvous was arranged with the Dutch ship HNLMS Banckert *for fuel and additional medical assistance. The aircraft eventually reached Truro after dawn. Regrettably one of the casualties died en-route.*

'Throughout this demanding and arduous period of operations, all Flight personnel conducted themselves in the finest traditions of the service, displaying not only professionalism and resourcefulness, but also exceptional skills, perseverance and courage to achieve most commendable results.'

In 1998, Lieutenant Commander Wilson-Chalon was awarded a Green Endorsement by Flag Officer Naval Aviation for his conduct in evacuating an injured Spanish seaman to shore from HMS *London:*

'On 12 March 1998, Lieutenant Commander Wilson-Chalon, Lieutenant Kent and Chief Petty Officer Barrow were embarked in HMS London *for exercise Strong Resolve. At 1230 the ship received a report that a Spanish unit within the force required to evacuate a casualty ashore with serious head, neck and rib injuries. The Lynx was re-rolled to conduct a stretcher lift, but due to the nature of the casualty's injuries, the distance involved and the very poor weather conditions, the Task Group Commander sought the use of an SAR Sea King to complete the task. Indeed the weather conditions had become so poor that the crew was stood down from all flying.*

'At 1500, after the Task Group Commander had been unable to arrange another aircraft for the evacuation, Lieutenant Commander Wilson-Chalon and his crew were tasked to conduct the transfer with the Spanish warship thirty-five miles away. The aircraft was launched in sea state 6 to 7 with winds of 35 to 45 knots and when the crew reached the ship, it was rolling approximately fifteen to twenty degrees and pitching eight to ten degrees. Given the difficult conditions, Lieutenant Commander Wilson-Chalon elected to conduct a Hi-line transfer and Lieutenant Kent lowered Chief Barrow down to brief the deck crew and dress and prepare the casualty and medical assistant. The transfer of the casualty, medical assistant and equipment, including oxygen, took thirty minutes to complete in very challenging conditions, after which Chief Barrow was left with the warship due to the lack of space within the

240   The Royal Navy Lynx

aircraft. With the expectation of a 40 knot headwind, the crew were conscious that they could only just make Lorient airfield; they elected to return to their ship to refuel before commencing the 140 mile transit ashore. Arriving back at mother, the deck motion was out of limits for flying, with occasional waves breaking over the flight deck. With no alternative available, the ship manoeuvred to minimise deck movement before the aircraft was recovered. Flying at low-level due to the nature of the head injury, the aircraft finally arrived in Lorient at 1800 and the casualty was transferred to hospital. Lieutenant Commander Wilson-Chalon decided that the continuing adverse weather conditions, combined with the proximity to sunset and the need to return the Spanish medical assistant to his ship, meant that he would delay the Lynx's return until the following day.

'Throughout this demanding evolution, Lieutenant Commander Wilson-Chalon and his crew demonstrated great composure in both the management and execution of this hazardous evacuation. The flexibility with which the Flight reacted and the logical manner in which this evolution was accomplished, is a tribute to their teamwork and sound decision-making. The successful evacuation of the very seriously injured sailor, who was in urgent need of specialist medical attention, in conditions that were significantly beyond the normal operating limits, is testament to their capabilities.'

Lieutenant Commander Nick Clark provided this account of a rescue in *Cockpit* magazine in 1992:

'Saturday, 18 April 1992, HMS Campbelltown, cruising 100 nautical miles off the coast of Mauritania, a blue sky and 20°C, made an almost perfect Saturday sea routine. Picture our grim faced, lantern jawed, steely eyed, slightly balding Flight commander relaxing in his cabin with a cup of tea, savoring a slice of his wife's fruitcake as he sighs in contentment. Sadly his daydreams about the forthcoming Copacabana run ashore are shattered by a figure sticking his head around the cabin door. "Excuse me sir, the communications office has just picked up a Mayday from a couple of ships on fire..." One thing this bluff old cove has learnt about his Pussers grey warship is that it attracts Casevacs, compassionate cases and disasters like sub lieutenants around a staff officer (when they were pretty and wore blue stripes).

'A gentlemanly stroll to the bridge found the captain and navigation officer trying to make sense of a garbled story. It was soon obvious that this was the real thing and the decision was made to pipe "scramble the Lynx". Needless to say the petty officers mess had just started cooking the flight deck barbecue that evening. Oh what it is to be popular!

Rescue 241

'I left Flobs to brief in detail and made haste to find the SMR in order to cobble together a cunning plan. Amongst other things, we agreed that we would need to keep a firm grip on safety. Although we would need to be flexible, we decided we would follow the book as closely as possible.

'Meanwhile, the Flight were conducting a world record role change: weapon carriers off, sea tray in and extra SAR kit. Flobs arrived with the latest information giving a position 110 nautical miles south and a crew brief with the winchman took place. Last check of weather and we were ready to go. As the final checks were being made there was just time to discuss rigging the hangar for casualty reception whilst the SMR insured that we had the load lifting gear ready for use. We managed to cover all the detail and paperwork before launch, all in a shade over twenty-five minutes!

'After the hectic rush to get off the deck, we discussed the situation as a crew. A firm commitment to caution was the order of the day. Visual search sectors were allocated and Flobs concentrated on giving me some of that observer stuff with the radar. Sure enough, he quickly found two radar contacts in the right area, highlighted by a growing smoke pall on the horizon. At this stage, we started to reap the benefits of the updated radios in the aircraft which enabled us to keep in contact with mother at ninety nautical miles, whilst talking to two civilian ships at the same time on different frequencies. The improved command and control proved to be invaluable for the captain.

'The first ship we found was the **Clipper Pioneer**, a small freighter extensively damaged with a fire burning on the upper deck. It was obvious that they were making no attempt to fight the fire and efforts to talk on the radio failed due to the crew's lack of English. Fortuitously, we were joined by a Soviet trawler who started firefighting and established that no one was missing or injured. They also told us that a large tanker was on fire to the south and a man was in the water, so with a "thank you Tovarich" we went off to search.

'By following the growing smoke trail we found the World Hitachi Zosen, a 260,000 ton tanker burning quite fiercely from a large gash in her bow and with extensive damage down her starboard side. A good firefighting effort had started forward and a very panicky radio operator gave us the Lat and Long of the man overboard and requested help with the fire. We relayed details back to mother whilst we made an initial search for the man in the water.

'Fortunately, we had GPS in the aircraft and now it proved its worth. Not only could we give the ship accurate navigational information, but we went straight to the man overboard datum ten miles from the tanker, where we found two life rafts and some wreckage. Despite no sign of a survivor we lowered the winchman down to check inside the life rafts, which were sadly empty.

242   The Royal Navy Lynx

'With no sign of the man overboard, the next priority was to gain further information about the tanker fire. Despite good radio communication, we were defeated by their operator's poor English. A quick discussion in the cockpit followed. It was obvious that we needed to land someone on the tanker. Normally I would have sent the winchman (a very experienced and capable man), but Flobs, with his better knowledge of seamanship and firefighting, was the better choice in this situation. A recce of the tanker revealed a helicopter winch spot forward on the port side, good for winching but too small for landing. The only problem was that this was within 100 feet of the fire with flames up to 50 feet! Although the winchman was not trained to operate the winch I decided that his years of experience as a maintainer, backed up with a comprehensive brief, made it a safe and acceptable option to winch Flobs down to the tanker. With the winchman doing an excellent job, Flobs arrived back in the aircraft fifteen minutes later with full details of damage and the happy information that the cargo was not petrol (phew!) but light crude. I also took the time to do a comprehensive survey of the tanker, noting all obstructions, as it was now becoming obvious that we were involved in a major firefighting scenario. With night rapidly approaching and aware that any boarding party would need to be winched on board (the only scrambling ladder was badly damaged), I wanted to assess how difficult a night approach and winching would be.

'It was now time for "Billy Big Steps" back to mother for a suck of fuel. Our second pilot (who by now had torn out what little hair he had left) would now need to be included in the crew as the left-hand seat safety pilot. I knew how disorientating a night approach to the tanker deck could be and, with Flobs in the back, the second pilot's assistance in a high workload environment would be invaluable. This turned out to be an excellent idea, increasing the safety margins during the next two arduous and exciting hours. We also took the opportunity to brief the captain, updating him on the tanker's situation and the fact that we felt that, although hazardous, night load lifting and winching to the tanker was a viable option.

'With the ship racing to the tanker's position, we launched for a last search of the missing man in the water. Sadly nothing was found and with last light, we reluctantly gave up and concentrated on the tanker. By now the crew had abandoned all attempts at firefighting, resulting in a rapidly deteriorating situation on board. Flames were billowing over 150 feet into the night sky, illuminating the tanker and creating a thick black cloud of smoke drifting ahead of the ship. With Campbelltown on scene, firefighting facilities were available. As a winch transfer was the only option for boarding, and the tanker and its crew were now in serious danger, the risks involved in a downwind approach (necessary to keep smoke and flame away from the bridge *and winch site) and hover over the burning tanker seemed acceptable. After a full briefing in the cockpit, two dummy approaches were flown, culminating in a safe and sustainable hover over the tanker's deck. Satisfied that the plan was viable we returned to mother.*

'Once on deck, the situation was discussed as a crew and then with the command. Everyone was happy with the plan and the winchman left the aircraft to provide sufficient room for a firefighting team in the back. Command intentions were to take the first lieutenant, deputy engineer, principal warfare officer and chief marine engineering mechanic, followed by any essential equipment. I have to admit I was beginning to feel quite tired and apprehensive at this stage. There was a definite feeling of let's get on with this, which took a conscious effort to control. Even so, in the rough and tumble of the moment, logic escapes me and instead of breaking the passengers down into two sticks of two, we ended up taking one stick of three and one of one. You know it still bugs me that I didn't do two trips of two! The fire was now visibly worsening and pressure increasing, with heightening awareness of the hazards (and legalities) of flying passengers in the Lynx at night (one wasn't dunker trained), particularly as we had to remove the four-man seat to winch. Having weighed the situation up I decided that the emergency made it an acceptable risk. All passengers were made fully aware of the dangers and well briefed on escape procedures.

'As we loaded the firefighting team, we discussed how the approach would be flown. I told the second pilot that I would talk my way down the approach whilst he called heights and speed and followed through on the controls (we had dual controls fitted). Flobs would give a con and I would use the landing lamp to illuminate the now silhouetted tanker.

'The approach went well and with a cool calm con from both the second pilot and Flobs, we felt our way over the deck of the tanker. Despite some nasty turbulence from the fire and the downwind approach requiring up to 95% engine torque, all went well. I won't bore you with the details of the conversations in the cockpit; the full dit can be heard for the price of a beer in the officer's club at Portland! I will never forget the chief stoker's grin in the back of the aircraft and the site of the first lieutenant running across the steaming deck towards a massive fireball billowing over 150 feet above us. It was also very warm in the cockpit!

'The two trips with the initial firefighting team went well; with teamwork in the cockpit developing to make it a relatively easy job the second time. With the first lieutenant calling for urgent supplies of firefighting foam, we then flew over to the RFA Grey Rover, *who did an exceptionally slick job of hooking on a net with twelve drums. This was smoothly transferred to the tanker with us all feeling more confident*

as we saw our heroes starting to get the forecastle hose monitors bearing onto the fire. Further urgent calls for a scrambling ladder saw us recovering to mother. Again, aware of the time constraints, limited assets in the shape of load lifting nets and absence of a trained cargo handler on the tanker, I elected to load the heavy ladder into the cabin and drop it onto the tanker from a low hover. Of all the evening's decisions I feel the most uneasy about this one; it was the most practical and certainly the quickest way to achieve the aim, but should we have used the net? It is easy to sit back now and say yes, but at the time it seemed the right option; the transfer was quick and safe, if not strictly in accordance with regulations.

'To cut a long story short we had stabilised the situation. With firefighting teams now able to board via a ladder, we shut down to conserve the aircraft and rest the crew. The ship did a brilliant job, particularly those who fought the fire on the tanker, including the SMR and Flight, whose flight deck formation firehose firefighting team is now famous. We had flown five hours, two at night. The next day, we flew three hours forty-five minutes searching for the man overboard and recovering equipment.

'In summary, it was some of the most demanding, exciting and, yes, frightening flying I have ever done and despite eight years of experience in the Lynx, I found myself doing things I had never done before. Afterwards, we debriefed and discussed at length whether we got it right. I feel that most of the time we did. Some things we could have done better, but you never stop learning in this game. Ultimately, experience, common sense and learning is what it's all about.'

In 2011 the Honourable Company of Air Pilots awarded The Prince Philip Helicopter Rescue Award to the Lynx crew of HMS *Chatham*. The following is the citation for this award:

'On the 21 May 2010, HMS Chatham *had been responding to a distress call from MV* **Dubai Moon**, *which had become caught in the centre of Tropical Cyclone Bandu. The merchant ship was rolling heavily, unable to manoeuvre, largely at the mercy of the elements, and was sinking. Having remained with the vessel for twenty-four hours as her condition gradually worsened, the Flight commander, Lieutenant Peter Higgins, judged that the weather had abated sufficiently to allow flying operations and HMS* Chatham *launched her Lynx on a mission to recover the twenty-three mariners from the stricken vessel. After conducting a recce of the transfer area, it was clear that the cargo of cars and trucks had shifted, and was causing the* **Dubai Moon** *to roll from the vertical to 30–40 degrees to starboard, and that she was sinking by the bow with a significant pitching motion.*

'In the prevailing conditions of a sea state 6 and 35–40kts of wind, and after close consultation with the commanding officer, bridge team and flight deck, the aircraft launched in an attempt to recover the twenty-three crew, before the stricken vessel capsized or sank. After the initial recce the observer, Lieutenant Craig Castle, RAN, determined that there was a small area immediately aft of the superstructure in which it would just be possible to put the winchman on to the heaving deck. With the aircraft being severely buffeted in the turbulence caused by the impact of the gale force winds against the slab sided superstructure, Lieutenant Higgins fought to maintain a steady hover, using hover references limited by poor visibility, over the transfer point with the aid of a calm, accurate and detailed con from Lieutenant Castle; he was operating at the very edge of the aircraft flying envelope. The oily conditions and angle of the deck on Dubai Moon *meant that a normal winch or hi-line recovery would not be possible, forcing Lieutenant Higgins to reassess the rapidly changing situation and make a series of quick but crucial decisions to ensure he minimised the risk to his crew, whilst still able to carry out the mission. His position as sole pilot and aircraft commander meant he had to make these decisions whilst dividing his attention between flying, maintaining communications, and while reacting to Lieutenant Castle's con as he relayed details of the developing scenario on deck. This required immense concentration, close teamwork and careful prioritisation in a tense and critical situation.*

'The winchman, AET Wilmot, was carrying out his first live winching serial from the aircraft following his qualifying course. On being lowered to the deck it was immediately apparent that it was covered in a thick layer of oil, which, combined with the seawater on deck, meant that it was impossible to stand up. Wilmot attempted to take hold of the windward rail, but was unable to maintain his hold and slid down the steep and oily deck, caught only by the winch wire he was attached to, from where he was recovered into the aircraft. The Flight crew quickly agreed that there were no other suitable winching points and that the only option was to attempt to recover the stricken crew with a modification to the winching technique. The crew of the Dubai Moon *were instructed to lay a rope on deck, secured to the windward rail, and Wilmot was lowered onto the deck in the vicinity of the rope. Once on deck, he managed to take hold of the rope and pulled himself up to where the first of the crewmen to be rescued was located. He secured the crewman in the double-lift strop and then moved down the improvised recovery rope, ensuring they both passed clear of obstructions before being winched back into the aircraft. Due to a combination of extreme physical exertion and sickness which he had previously insisted he had overcome, Wilmot was violently sick on return to the aircraft and assessed unable to continue with the mission. Whilst his role in the rescue was cut short, his work on deck saved the first life but, more*

importantly, established the method and prepared the crew of the Dubai Moon *for the remainder of this hazardous and highly challenging rescue operation.*

'*Due to severe seasickness throughout the preceding thirty-six hours, Wilmot was in a weakened physical condition, but he was undeterred and his actions should not be underestimated. He demonstrated courage, resilience and grit to an extent that is unexpected and highly commendable in someone so junior and with no operational experience as a winchman. Having only flown for five and a half hours prior to the rescue, the manner in which he took control of the situation on the deck of the* Dubai Moon *in extremely challenging circumstances was outstanding and set the conditions for success.*

'*Lieutenant Commander Chesterman was visiting* HMS Chatham, *conducting a Ship Operational Airworthiness Audit on behalf of Navy Command HQ. During the pre-mission planning, one of the contingencies that had been considered was to use Chesterman to stand in as winchman should there be unforeseen problems in this difficult rescue. Due to Wilmot becoming physically exhausted, Lieutenant Commander Chesterman was asked to take over as winchman. Whilst he is a qualified Lynx observer, Chesterman had not flown for fifteen years.*

'*Wilmot provided a thorough brief and handover of the situation that would be encountered on the deck of the* Dubai Moon. *The aircraft relaunched with Lieutenant Commander Chesterman now embarked as winchman to conduct a total of twenty-two difficult and physically exhausting transfers over a period of three hours. His performance was superb, fighting to recover the crew from a deck which was perilously strewn with debris, slick with a thick film of oil and seawater, and rolling by up to forty degrees. This selfless act of bravery and physical endurance was all the more impressive as the leeward guard rails had been destroyed and a mistake on his part would have resulted in the death of one of the seaman, had they fallen over board. Despite considerable aviation experience, it was the first time that Chesterman had acted as winchman in a rescue mission. His fearless composure galvanised the aircraft commander and crew, whilst reassuring the survivors who placed their lives, quite literally, in his hands. Despite the marginal weather conditions, the hazardous state of the deck, and the dangerous pitch and roll of a vessel on the verge of sinking, all crewmembers were safely recovered to* HMS Chatham.

'*The crew's courage, sense of duty, stamina and professionalism in extraordinary circumstances, ensured that the lives of all twenty-three crewmembers were saved. Within ten hours of completing the mission,* Dubai Moon *sank.*'

In addition to the Prince Philip award, Peter Higgins was awarded and Air Force Cross and Graham Chesterman a Queen's Commendation for Bravery in the Air for their parts in the rescue.

Aid to the Civil Power

The Sumatra Tsunami

On 26 December 2004, the third largest ever recorded and longest lasting earthquake was recorded with the epicenter off the west coast of Sumatra. The resulting tsunami caused widespread chaos in the Indian Ocean. HMS *Chatham* was sent to Sri Lanka to offer aid. The following article, written by Lieutenant Turner of the ship's Flight, appeared in *Flight Deck* magazine:

'HMS Chatham *had been deployed on Operation Calash as part of the coalition war on terror off the coast of Africa and the Middle East since the middle of November 2004. Having spent Christmas day at sea on patrol, the whole ship's company were looking forward to some well-earned rest and recreation in Dubai. On 29 December, most of the ships company explored the local area on a typical "first night in". However, during the wardroom party that evening the commanding officer was informed that a tsunami, caused by an earthquake measuring nine on the Richter scale, had devastated many parts of Asia and that it was likely the ship would be required to sail as part of the UK's force for Humanitarian Disaster Relief Operations (HDROs). The following morning, it was confirmed and the ship's company, some of whom had flown loved ones out from the UK, were recalled to the ship. Having completed a whole ship, store ship,* HMS Chatham *sailed in the afternoon for the 2000 mile maximum speed transit towards Sri Lanka for Operation Garron, the codename for the tsunami HDRO.*

'When the ship sailed from the UK two Lynx Mark 8 aircraft were embarked, with just one crew. The intention was to embark a second crew and maintainers in Dubai over New Year to support the anticipated high flying rate for Operation Calash. The short notice instruction to sail from Dubai, however, did not allow sufficient time for these augmentees to be flown out to join the ship. The four day fast cruise from Dubai to the west coast of Sri Lanka therefore involved much planning and preparation. This was not only to get the additional personnel and stores required for twin aircraft operations onto the ship, but also to plan how two helicopters could be best utilised in disaster relief operations. Apart from in HMS Endurance, *the ice patrol ship, twin aircraft operations from single spot ships are still relatively uncommon in the navy and there is very little published information on the subject. Indeed, the last time they were employed in a warship was in HMS* Chatham *during Operation Telic in 2003.*

248   The Royal Navy Lynx

'There were numerous flying related issues: How will the launch cycle work? What is the procedure if the deck is blocked? What is the procedure if both aircraft are airborne and one suffers an emergency? These points and more needed to be resolved prior to the start of operating both aircraft simultaneously. There were also a number of manpower related issues: Will the ship be running a twenty-four hour deck cycle? How can the watches be best organised with the available personnel? How will the role of the SMR change? The list went on...

'Flight safety was paramount. With the tasking likely to take the aircraft into all manner of unprepared landing sites, littered with debris or covered in sand and FOD, the risk management of it would be vital. Everybody understood that scoring an own goal would be unforgivable. Other issues involved the expected high number of passenger transfers, the best use and control of the limited amount of survival equipment held on board while using both aircraft, and the delivery of mass aircraft safety briefs for the whole ship's company. The flying of foreign nationals, including civilians, and gaining the requisite permissions was also a matter to be resolved.

'The nature of the operations we would be likely to perform were obviously very different from those we were used to. Whereas armed search and reconnaissance with the M3M machine gun had been the norm since sailing from Devonport, secondary roles such as load lifting, winching, and passenger transfers, would be the new order of the day. Consequently, on the transit from Dubai all forms of secondary roles were practiced.

'On arrival at the west coast of Sri Lanka, in the vicinity of the capital Colombo, the ship embarked the extra Flight personnel required to sustain twin aircraft operations. The aircrew were borrowed from 226 Flight (HMS Exeter) and the engineers from 204 Flight (HMS Norfolk). We also embarked the Staff Aviation Standards Officer from Fleet. His roles were firstly to ensure that twin aircraft operations were conducted safely and secondly to approve RFA Diligence (operating in company) as an aviation capable platform. Diligence could provide a very welcome spare deck in the event of Chatham's deck becoming unavailable and also an additional refuelling option if required.

'With all the required personnel and equipment on board, it was time to find out what we would actually be doing. After initial briefings from both the operational liaison and reconnaissance team sent from England, and the British High Commissioner in Sri Lanka, it was clear that despite 30,000 Sri Lankans being lost during the tragic natural disaster, much of the country had not been affected by the tsunami. In fact, it became clear that it was only the first 200 to 300 metres inland from the east, south and west coasts which had actually been touched by the tidal wave, although some of the damage and devastation in these areas was horrific.

'One of the main effects of the tsunami was to virtually destroy the country's vital fishing industry and many of its coastal villages. It was obvious that there was much we could do to help, but before it could be decided where HMS Chatham would focus her aid, aerial reconnaissance was required to establish the bigger picture. It was decided to conduct the majority of flying operations during the daylight hours, with the maintainers running a twenty-four hour cycle of maintenance to facilitate the anticipated high flying rate.

'The first twin aircraft sortie was a reconnaissance mission from Colombo to Tang Gallia, a fishing town on the southern coast, with the two aircraft flying in formation over some fantastic jungle scenery, in stark contrast with some of the terrible sites to come. Tang Gallia and the neighbouring town of Hambanboto were surveyed by one aircraft, while the other flew back along the coast towards Galle, a tourist destination on the south-western coast.

'Over the next two days, the southern and eastern coasts were fully surveyed by both air and shore parties. Most of the coastline in this region had been affected to a degree, but many of the locals had been able to kick start the regeneration process themselves, allowing the ship to transit further round the coast to the north-eastern region of the country. It was here that the worst of the devastation was found.'

The devastation was dreadful. (*Graham Cooke*)

'The ship made its base near the town of Batticaloa for the main push. This area and the coastline for about thirty miles to the south towards the village of Kallar and the island immediately to the north of it had been devastated. Whole villages were razed to the ground with an eerie lack of life where whole communities had existed barely a week beforehand. Where buildings remained standing, it was not uncommon to see boats wedged in the first and second floors. It was clear that some of these places were beyond help. Fortunately however, some areas had been hit to a lesser degree and it was here that we concentrated our efforts.

'Much of the early flying involved aerial reconnaissance missions and flying teams ashore to carry out ground reconnaissance. Due to the devastation, particularly in Kallar, there was a distinct lack of acceptable landing sites: most clearings were littered with debris; some were too sandy while others were still waterlogged. Using all the usual techniques for confined area landings it was decided that the best place to land in this village was on one of the two causeways connecting the island to the mainland, these ran from the northern and southern ends of the island, which had been completely cut off from the mainland due to these roads having been all but washed away. These difficult local conditions, the relatively small size of any prospective landing spots on the causeways, and the many intrigued locals who came rushing towards the aircraft, all added to the challenge.'

Approaching the remains of the causeway. (*Graham Cooke*)

'Following these early reconnaissance missions, a couple of sorties were dedicated to establishing RFA Diligence as an aviation capable platform. Once this was achieved it provided the two Lynx with a spare deck and another refuelling platform. This allowed the twin aircraft operations to get into full swing, with the sorties now quickly progressing to include various types of often challenging flying.

'Many sorties involved transferring teams of personnel to sites ashore in order for them to carry out relief work. Apart from Kallar with its causeway landing site, many of the other villages also lacked suitable landing sites. As a result, many landings were confined to metalled roads, though in many ways these were equally as challenging as landing on the causeways. This was particularly true in the Tamil Tiger controlled regions, where there were not only downed trees and telegraph poles to contend with next to roads, but also unknown numbers of landmines which had been scattered indiscriminately by the tsunami.

'Once these initial trials have been overcome, the relief work could start in earnest. Much of the Flight tasking involved transporting teams ashore to carry out work identified from the earlier reconnaissance. These included building bridges, repairing fishing boats, delivering medical stores, pumping out wells, clearing rubble and renovating buildings.

'Once the teams had been delivered ashore each morning, there were many other flying requirements during the day; tasking included the delivery and redistribution of stores from both ship to shore and also from the town of Batticaloa to the areas where they were needed. Stores were carried both internally and externally, with the load lifting of supplies in cargo nets beneath the aircraft often being the most efficient way of transporting them over long transits.'

Delivering stores by underslung load. (*Graham Cooke*)

'Within two weeks, the attitude and outlooks of the locals were significantly improved. The people of Kallar and the other villages were ready to carry out the required rebuilding work without any further assistance from the ship. One of the more rewarding tasks undertaken by the Flight was showing the newly orphaned children of Batticaloa and the surrounding areas around the aircraft. Despite the traumas they had been through, the joy and excitement on the faces of the children as they climbed in the aircraft was magical.

'The fantastic sense of achievement and pride engendered in the whole ship's company for the transformation they had achieved to help the people of Sri Lanka was remarkable. This was echoed by the Minister for the Department for International Development, Hilary Benn, who visited the area towards the end of the operation to witness the outcome of all the hard work.

'During fourteen days of continuous flying operations, the two aircraft had flown ninety-nine hours. This achievement, which would not have been possible without the availability of both aircraft, enabled the rest of the operation to run smoothly by facilitating the timely delivery of both stores and personnel to where they were required. The opportunity to do something so worthwhile in the military is something that many people never experience; let's just hope that there is no similar requirement for the foreseeable future!'

Hurricane Ivan

2004 was a bad year for weather related issues. In September, Hurricane Ivan wound up in the Atlantic and headed west. The unusual factor about this storm was that its track was much further south than normal. The Caribbean island of Grenada had been considered safe from hurricanes, not the least by all the insurance companies that covered yachts in the region, which is why so many were destroyed in the various boatyards. The effect of the hurricane is still talked about on the island today. Just after the hurricane hit, HMS *Richmond* was in the area with the duty of Atlantic Patrol Task (North) or APT (N), which generally means patrolling the area, operating with the Americans with anti-drug operations and providing humanitarian relief, especially after hurricanes. Lieutenant Graham Connell wrote this account of using a Mark 8 Lynx for hurricane relief in *Flight Deck* magazine:

'As a first tourist Lynx pilot, I welcomed the opportunity to take part in HMS Richmond's APT (N) Caribbean deployment. A few drug busts, the odd hurricane, a string of cocktail parties and home in time for Christmas with a suntan, what more could you ask?

'The role of the ship was to support British overseas territories and former colonies of the West Indies, conduct counter drugs operations in support of the US Coast Guard and be prepared for hurricane disaster relief operations. Arriving in theatre, we were immediately struck by the frequency and strength of the tropical storms and hurricanes sweeping in from the mid-Atlantic. Beginning as tropical depressions off the West African coast, these storms often build rapidly in strength, fuelled by the very warm waters of the Caribbean before swinging north-west towards Florida.

'So there I was, on the beach in Barbados, sipping yet another cocktail, when the message came through that we had been recalled from our leave period. Very soon we discovered hurricane Frances was to become the first storm of several to upset the ops officer's carefully crafted programme. Sailing at short notice, leaving tearful wives and girlfriends behind, we raced for the Turks and Caicos Islands, a low-lying British overseas territory sitting right in the hurricane's path. Fortunately, Frances passed clear and miraculously the island suffered no significant damage. Hurricane Ivan, however, was brewing ominously in the Atlantic. Ivan initially tracked south of Barbados heading directly towards Grenada.

'It passed over the island as a Category 4 hurricane with wind speeds of 125 miles an hour, all contact being lost with the island shortly beforehand. Richmond and RFA Wave Ruler followed at a respectful distance, poised to offer assistance if required as soon as the winds had abated.

'From the outset, the Lynx was a vital asset to the ship and we were under much pressure to get airborne for initial reconnaissance as soon as possible. Our task would be to conduct a brief damage assessment and then find somewhere to land in order to try and establish communications with the island's Emergency Operations Centre, which had not been heard from since the hurricane passed. We launched at first light, as Richmond arrived on station, to be met by incredible scenes of devastation. The harbour area around St George's had been badly damaged; many houses had their roofs removed, others had been simply folded flat like packing cases, or had their contents spread over the steep hillsides. I was particularly impressed by the large containers previously stacked in the port ready to be loaded, which appeared to have been thrown around like pebbles, leaving one balanced precariously on the dockside edge. The effects of Ivan were still evident, with strong winds, low cloud and rain, and as we approached, we encountered turbulence from the mountains behind.

'The initial reconnaissance flight was successful, with our photographer taking video and still images to brief Richmond's command team. We then assessed the area around the Emergency Operations Centre for suitable landing sites. The centre was built on top of a steep hill and we opted for an approach to a bowl offering the nearest, clear, safe and flat approach.

254   The Royal Navy Lynx

'We found that the aircraft was not particularly good in typical Caribbean conditions, we consistently operated near the engines temperature limits even at sea level. We were now at 1000 feet and encountering significant updraughting. The mountain flying training I had received from 815 Squadron during my time as a second pilot was absolutely essential in preparing me for such conditions; it is not a skill maritime Lynx crews often have had the chance to practice. I was also fortunate to have practiced hot and high operations in company with army Bell 212's in Belize two weeks previously.

'The approach was made on the updraughting side of the valley as far as possible. We maintained minimum power speed until it became necessary to decelerate, keeping a careful eye on the torque we had established from the power check; again limited by the engine temperatures. The landing site itself was not particularly confined and the bowl provided reasonable escape options should the turbulence become more significant, as well as providing a clear downhill exit route.

'Having put the aircraft down, the Flight commander got out and crawled up the slope to the road, returning fifteen minutes later with the news that the operations centre was full of frightened women and children with nobody in charge. He had met a doctor on the way back who confirmed that there had been some deaths and that the prison had been damaged to the extent that a number of prisoners had escaped. We lifted and subsequently attempted to find the Governor General's house: built on top of the hill it had been completely destroyed from the first floor upwards. We chose the tennis court as a suitable landing site and as with all potential landing sites extreme care had to be exercised. Careful conning by the Flight commander and second observer on a dispatcher harness in the cabin door was essential for a safe landing. On this occasion we were able to find the chief of police and learned the whereabouts of the prime minister, prior to returning to the ship. The following days provided varied and rewarding flying as local personalities were located and the relief effort swung into action. High on the list of priorities was establishing the serviceability of the airport. A modern well-built facility, it had suffered little damage and the runway was surprisingly free of debris. Nevertheless, there was no functioning air traffic control and a sharp lookout was required to avoid the various low-flying patrol aircraft from neighbouring Caribbean states, a French Navy Panther and (eventually) aid relief aircraft, all arriving and unannounced.

'Contrary to expectations, very little load lifting was required: the ship did not have sufficient stores to justify load lifting and often it was easier and faster to load less bulky items in the back of the aircraft. Later operations in Grand Cayman were also limited by the position of the hospital on final approach to the island's very busy airport; the medical stores were not heavy and ultimately became easier to transport by road. Some of the islands we visited were not used to the flexibility of helicopter operations and air-traffic controllers, once reinstalled in their towers, were frustratingly rigid in their *approach. The "join downwind" or "hold" calls were common, despite our requests to join direct at low-level. With our low fuel states in the hot temperatures, holding for ten minutes often meant the difference between achieving the task or not.*

'In pure flying and operating terms, previous training had prepared us well for the situation we faced, although many lessons were learned. The ability to winch was useful in transferring personnel into sites too confined or hazardous to land and we tended to operate with the doors open and the winch deployed, thus not limiting our passenger carrying capability. The operations centre in Grenada was inconveniently situated on top of the hill with no landing sites nearby and we opted for winching the CO down to say goodbye to the rescue organisation. Richmond *had already sailed and again care was needed to ensure we arrived, firstly with the ability to hover and secondly with the ability to return to the ship. Many lessons were also learnt in terms of flight deck operations. Clearly operating at anchor removed the need for a flying course and the sheer numbers of personnel required to be taken ashore meant a significant amount of deck pounding. "Green deck" operations, concurrent with boat routines on the opposite side, became the most expeditious method of coordinating aircraft movements. Keeping track of our passengers for manifest purposes initially proved difficult as the situation developed rapidly ashore. A manpower controller was required on the flight deck to log personnel on and off the ship. Extra training provided additional personnel who proved invaluable to supplement the flight deck team when members of the Flight were required ashore to set up remote landing sites. Authorisation issues also arose. We often found ourselves speaking directly to the ship's commanding officer on telebrief, as tasking changed by the minute in response to the fluid situation; as an aviator himself he was able to fully anticipate our authorisation limits and verbally reauthorise whilst the maintainers re-roled the aircraft.*

'The aircraft was identified as the single most important asset "in the fleet lessons learnt document" and indeed the flexibility, speed and lifting capability offered, even by our relatively heavy Lynx, made its participation essential. The helicopter was also a welcome sight for the people on the islands emerging from their shelters, demonstrating that help was on its way. We generally received a very friendly welcome, although some perhaps resented our interference and security was at times a concern. On one occasion leading to the evacuation of the resident High Commissioner in Grenada.

'The disaster relief operations I experienced in the Caribbean proved a challenging and highly rewarding experience. Initially, the scale of disaster was daunting; I remember thinking, "what impact can we possibly make?" But quickly realised that our role was simply to assist in getting the established local organisation back on its feet in providing highly specialist mobile teams to facilitate this. As always, I was thoroughly impressed by the flexibility and professionalism of the Flight in the face of a challenging engineering environment and numerous last minute changes. The truism, "flexibility is the key to success", was never more evident than during our disaster relief efforts.'

Chapter 10

Around the World

The Antarctic – HMS *Endurance*

There have been two modern naval ships named *Endurance* after Ernest Shackleton's sailing ship for his 1914 expedition. They were both specifically used for Antarctic operations and both carried helicopters. The first was acquired in 1967, and because of her red colour was known as "The Red Plum", as was her successor. Originally, she operated Wasp helicopters and came to fame during the Falklands war when her aircraft fired missiles at the Argentinian submarine the *Santa Fe* [see HMS *Brilliant* entry in Chapter 4]. From 1987 until 1991 she operated specially modified Lynx Mark 3s. In 1989 she struck an iceberg and damaged her hull and in 1991 she was deemed beyond economic repair and decommissioned. Her replacement was originally named *Polar Circle* and was leased from the Norwegian company, Rieber Shipping, but after eight months she was purchased outright and renamed *Endurance*. She also had good aviation facilities and operated two Lynx. In 2008 she suffered a serious engine room flood and almost sank. In 2009 she was decommissioned and her replacement, HMS *Protector*, was chartered and then purchased. Although she has a flight deck, there is no hangarage on board, and so this was the end of Lynx support for Arctic operations.

An account of her last deployment, including her rather ignominious end, is provided by her Flight Commander, Paul Ellerton:

01 Jul 2008 – 20 Dec 2008

815 SQN 212 FLT

Flight Commander   – Lieutenant P. Ellerton
Flight Operations Officer – Lieutenant J. Green
Flight Pilot   – Lieutenant G. Carnell
Flight Observer – Lieutenant B. Jewson

Aircraft: 2 x Mk 3 (ICE) XZ 246, XZ 238

Endurance and Lynx Mk3 (ICE). (*Paul Ellerton*)

'Appointed Flight commander in July 2008 gave me three months (pre-deployment) to adjust from the standard maritime attack mentality to the Ice Patrol role (whatever that meant). As I'd just finished an operational tour in Northern Ireland, flying out of Bessbrook Mill on the winding up of Operation Banner, I confess I was looking forward to the change.

'212 Flt was equipped with three Mk 3 ICE Lynx helicopters, two flying and one in deep maintenance at Fleetlands in Gosport. The two aircraft at 815 were instantly recognisable in their Antarctic livery, with their striking red nose and doors designed to stand out in the monochrome backgrounds of Antarctica and even a king penguin transfer on each door giving it a non-threatening appearance. The aircraft is basically a Mk 3 with all the war fighting kit stripped out. No secure speech, electronic support measures, or any weapon avionics, meant the aircraft were much lighter and more spacious in the back. The additions were modified weapon carriers converted to fit several different types of camera for filming and survey work. The observer had use of a non-military GPS with the aerial routed through his window and the pilot had an extra voltmeter for the camera fit. The belly aerials were relocated so you could perform snow landings without the risk of bending them, the wheel lock hydraulics had special guards fitted for the same reason and troop steps were fitted for easier exit for back seat passengers. The main gearbox oil was replaced with OEP 70 for operation in freezing conditions and that was pretty much it from a release to service aspect. In theatre we flew with downbird survival back packs and a very useful satellite phone. When flying over particular hazardous environments we took a Royal Marine as an Antarctic survival expert if the worst were to happen.

'*Endurance* (the red plumb) herself was halfway through an eighteen month experimental deployment. She had refitted in South Africa and the Flight would meet her in the Falkland Islands. Both ICE Lynx would be flown in an Antonov transporter to MPA in the first week of October. In the meantime our preparations for the deployment included some mountain flying training in North Wales, winter survival lectures at Yeovilton, and receiving several briefs and lectures from what was known as the "shareholders". This involved visits to; Cambridge University, where the HQ of the British Antarctic Survey (BAS) teams gave us the details of how they'd like to employ the Lynx on what was to be known as Antarctic Operating Periods (AOP's), Taunton Hydrographical Centre for mapping surveys and the BBC's Natural History department, as we were going to be involved in the filming of *Frozen Planet*.'

'A sabbatical from the real navy'. (*Paul Ellerton*)

Around the World 259

'The four aircrew took the arduous eighteen hour flight from Brize Norton to MPA via Ascension Island and met the rest of the flight down there, as they had left the week before to prep the aircraft for embarking on the "red plumb" as soon as we could, as a tailored sea training package was required prior to our first AOP. By mid-November the ship had passed all its training requirements and was assessed safe to proceed to Antarctica. My job was to make sure I was content with my crews ability to operate safely in the challenging environment we were about to face. The training package consisted mainly of fine tuning our secondary roles, in particular load lifting, as the BAS teams often required gear shifted and lifted around various parts of the peninsula. Ambitious scientists would invariably ask to be winched to some of the most inaccessible parts of the planet without the slightest concern for his or, in my opinion and more importantly, the safety of the crew that had to conduct the pick-up and drop off. I quickly developed a sense of risk awareness and often informed the enthusiastic BAS scientist, "I'm not doing *that* for a bacterial sample". The survey work was simply flying in a straight line and the filming for the BBC was the most interesting. You could spend eight hours a day flying around one of the most beautiful continents and end up with only a few minutes footage. We quickly learned what the cameraman and producer (who both sat in the back) were after, where the light had to be, what was a good frame with respect to height and speed, and before long I could put the aircraft in the right place to get the right shot without much prompting. On the odd occasion I would have to rein them in and say, "if I put the aircraft there at this height and with this wind we'll fall out the sky… so re-think it". The conditions were never to be taken for granted, especially as they could change from epic to severe in a very short period of time.

'When *Endurance* floundered in the Magellan Straights on 16 Dec, I was airborne in XZ 238 with Lieutenant Green. We were on our return from Punta Arenas after transferring the BBC and CH 5 TV crews so they could catch flights home for Christmas. XZ 246 was shut down and in the hangar after completing the same tasking. At about seventy miles from the ship and enjoying the epic flying through the Patagonian Mountains, we received an HF message saying the ship was taking on water and could we divert back to Punta? Which we duly did.

'All power on board was lost so they could not refuel XZ 246, which had about twenty mins of fuel left in the tanks. As the ship's outcome was somewhat perilous, command made the decision to launch XZ 246 with Lieutenant's

260   The Royal Navy Lynx

Carnell and Jewson and evacuate the contingent of British students we had on board to a nearby lighthouse. Once that was done, the aircraft was recovered to *Endurance* and lashed to the right-hand side of the flight deck to try and counter the list to port that had developed.

'Several hours later an ocean-going tug arrived and the ship was towed into Punta. During the transit, I used XZ 246 to deliver fresh water and diesel pumps to assist the crew. Once the ship was stabilised alongside, I flew XZ 246 to Punta Arenas Airport (Military side), where essential maintenance was carried out to make sure both aircraft were serviceable for the next phase of the plan.

'*Endurance* had been prepared for a cold tow to the Falkland Islands and both aircraft were to be storm lashed in the hangar for the three week transit. They arrived in the islands mid-Jan 2009. Lieutenant Jewson and I flew down from Brize to fly both aircraft the fifteen yards from the flight deck to the harbour so they could be transported back to the UK on a RORO, which took about three weeks. Both aircraft remained with 212 Flt who had now been appointed to the Carrier Strike Group as the HDS asset for Operation Auriga.

'In summary, the whole deployment was akin to a sabbatical from the navy in what has to be one of the more interesting Lynx commands, albeit with a rather sad ending.'

Counter drug operations

Throughout its long operational life, one task that has regularly been conducted by the Lynx is counter drug operations. The author spent some time working with the US Coast Guard early in 1982 and learnt a great deal about the inventive and downright sneaky methods drug smugglers were using then to bring their goods into America. Since then the drug smugglers become increasingly more inventive and the US Coast Guard increasingly more well-equipped. The Royal Navy has a regular presence in the Caribbean. Initially this was known as WIGS or the West Indies guard ship. Now it is known as ATP (N), in either regard, when a British warship is in the area one of its major tasks is to collaborate with the US Coast Guard and be on the lookout for the bad guys.

As an illustration of how successful the combination of ship and aircraft has been over the years, below is an account by Alex Sims of one such deployment in 2008:

HMS *Iron Duke*

Flight Commander – Lieutenant Alex Sims
Flight Pilot – Lieutenant Jim Fraser
Extra crew – Sub Lieutenant William Wales
US Coast Guard – PO (Equiv) Dellavalle
Royal Marine team – Corporal Smith, Lance Corporal Dalton

Aircraft: Lynx HAS 3 (GMS) XZ 733

'HMS *Iron Duke* and her Lynx Flight conducted Operational Sea Training (OST) in the spring of 2008. During this training period, briefings were provided by a US Coast Guard LEDET (Law Enforcement Detachment) officer. British warships, when operating in the counter drug role in the Caribbean, are required to carry a US Coast Guard official in order to be able to make legal arrests on the high seas. There is a Memorandum of Understanding in the area between all the Caribbean countries allowing them to act on their behalf. Before vessels can be stopped and arrests made, clearance must be given both by the US Coast Guard and British government. This may sound cumbersome, but in practice decisions can be made effectively in real-time.

'Having successfully completed training, *Iron Duke* was to conduct operations as the APT (N) ship in the Caribbean and elsewhere in the Atlantic. Her first stop was Lisbon where she arrived at the end of May. The ships staff were briefed by European counter drugs police and made aware of intelligence that a small fast twin-engined speedboat was liable to be making a transatlantic run from South America in the near future. It was known that twelve mother ships had been spaced out across the Atlantic to refuel the "Go Fast", as it was known.

'The ship then sailed for the Caribbean but did not encounter anything during the transit. However, on 27 June, whilst in Barbados, significant intelligence was received. The US Joint Intelligence Agency Task Force had been monitoring high-frequency radios and had heard that the "Go Fast" had suffered an engine failure and was turning around to return home. The boat's radio signals had been picked up by several radio stations and therefore bearings had been plotted to give a reasonably accurate position of where the boat was. In *Iron Duke*, the captain, Flight commander and commanding officer of the LEDET, assessed the information which was approximately twelve hours old. Using dead reckoning from the datum position, a search box 10 x 30 miles in area was plotted and as soon as possible after the ship had sailed the Lynx got airborne to search, using its radar and the crew's "mark one eyeballs". Inside the aircraft, the two crew were joined by two Royal Marines; one with a sniper rifle, the other armed with the M3M machine gun, as well as the LEDET officer. In almost exactly the calculated spot, a radar contact was discovered. The Lynx closed and visually identified a small, fast looking speedboat, but it was traveling slowly westwards.

'There are certain criteria that must be met before a vessel can be stopped and searched on the high seas. In this case it was clear that these criteria were going to be met. Firstly, she had no national flag or other means of national identification. Secondly, it was possible to see inside the cabin where white bales were stacked up. Finally, when asked on Channel 16 VHF what she was doing, the reply was that the crew were fishing. When asked where their fishing gear was they admitted they didn't have any! This was suspicious enough to provide the final criteria. The LEDET commander gave the go-ahead to stop the boat. At this point *Iron Duke* was over the horizon, so the Lynx kept the boat under observation until the ship could launch a sea boat.'

The 'Go Fast' being apprehended and watched over by the Lynx and its imposing machine gun. The same gun sank her the next day. *(Alex Sims)*

Around the World   263

'The four-man crew of the boat were arrested and approximately one ton of cocaine was recovered. Three of the crew were from Venezuela and one was from Sweden and they were detained in a compartment in the quarterdeck of the ship. The next morning, once the boat had been thoroughly searched and all contraband removed, it was decided that it should be sunk as it was a hazard to navigation. The sea cocks were opened. However, in order to finish her off the Lynx launched and fired 400 rounds from the M3M machine gun to hasten her departure. Being made of fibreglass, most of the bullets passed harmlessly through the hull, but eventually the boat sank. The ship then returned to Barbados where the drug smugglers were offloaded. This was a good result all round and the ship had only been on station a few weeks, but more was to come.

'One route used by drug smugglers from South America northwards is to go in a straight line as fast as possible. Unfortunately, with distances of over 600 miles, it is not possible to do this in darkness in one go. One tactic that is used is to stop during the hours of daylight and cover the boat in a light blue tarpaulin in an effort to remain unobserved. On 10 July, an HF radio intercept was made. An unknown radio operator had called to say they had just seen a warship steam past them. It was highly likely that this warship was *Iron Duke*. The Lynx was scrambled and commenced a search. After an hour and a half, radar contact was gained on a vessel going fast to the north. This looked like their quarry, which had been spooked and was now making a run for it. The aircraft closed the "Go Fast", which did not respond to any radio calls, was flying no national flag, had multiple packages and fuel barrels clearly visible, and immediately started evading. Unfortunately, the aircraft was getting low on fuel and the ship was thirty miles away. The Lynx returned to refuel, but when airborne again was not able to regain contact. There was frustration all round.

'On 18 July, whilst conducting a routine surface search with good visibility, a wake was identified going south this time. The Lynx approached from behind and stayed covert until close enough to visually identify the same boat that had been encountered a week before. At this point, the aircraft went overt and called the contact on the radio, who once again refused to respond. Close visual inspection also revealed possible suspicious packages. They then started aggressive weaving, clearly anticipating some form of attack from the helicopter. Approval was requested to conduct non-lethal disabling fire. Although this only took twenty minutes to be provided, it seemed like forever in the aircraft! At this point, the "Go Fast" stopped weaving and went flat out in a straight line. It was about one hour away from Colombian territorial waters, which was clearly their intended destination, and where the Lynx would not be able to intercept them.

'With authority to fire finally provided, the aircraft closed to 200 metres and fired three bursts of twenty rounds from the M3M ahead of the boat. It was ignored. Consequently, the aircraft closed to 100 metres and fired a further sixty rounds, which was once again ignored. At this point, the "Go Fast" clearly anticipated what was about to happen and tried to cut below the Lynx to keep clear of its firing arcs. However, the manoeuvrability of the aircraft was such that it was able to slide sideways and maintain a firing position. It took about five minutes to get a safe firing solution and then the aircraft sniper was authorised to fire his AW50 rifle. Five rounds were all that were required to hit the casing of one of the two outboard engines and the boat came to a stop. The crew all raised their hands in surrender.

'Once again, the aircraft was running low on fuel and returned to the fast closing ship for a record two-minute refuel and then returned to find the boat had moved a couple of miles. However, *Iron Duke* soon arrived on scene, launched the sea boat and arrested the crew. Unfortunately, no drugs were discovered. However, whilst the ship was closing the boat, the crew had been seen throwing things over the side. The aircraft was able to see the objects in the water and directed the ship's sea boat to pick them up. An incredible hall of mobile phones in plastic bags, maps with critical information marked on them, lists of names, rendezvous and telephone numbers were discovered. One has to wonder at the intelligence of the crew. There may not have been any drugs, but the intelligence gained was assessed to be the greatest amount ever gathered on one occasion. Direct action in the US immediately followed and significant arrests were made.

'Twenty-four hours later, the ship was directed to deliver the crew to the Colombian authorities. The Lynx was given the position of a small airstrip in the jungle where the smugglers were handed over to a squad of heavily armed police who arrived in two curtain sided vehicles. It is not known what happened to them after that.

'These were not the only occasions when the Lynx found drugs. Every island that was visited was overflown to try and identify cannabis farms and many were found. For example, on Antigua, a clearing was clearly spotted, hidden by trees on the ground but not from the air, containing 2500 cannabis plants.'

The Antiguan Cannabis farm easily seen from above but not from the ground. (*Alex Sims*)

'In addition, the aircraft helped with hurricane relief work that season after Hurricanes Ike and Gustav hit the Turks and Caicos and Grand Cayman. However, the task of the APT (N) ship is not restricted just to the Caribbean. By October, HMS *Iron Duke* was patrolling the Falkland Islands.

By the author: 'Readers may notice at the start of this article, that an additional crewmember is credited on these sorties. HRH Prince William had just completed his training at Sandhurst and been commissioned as a second lieutenant. He embarked in *Iron Duke* as a sub lieutenant for three months of this deployment and was in the aircraft for all the drug bust sorties. Chalk yet another success up to the Lynx, as on return to the UK he decided that he wanted to be a helicopter pilot as well.'

'Royal Naval Air Station Gibraltar'

For many years, a Lynx was based at North Front, the airfield at Gibraltar. The reasons were mixed. With such a narrow strait of water to patrol, a Sea Skua armed Lynx could have a significant effect on ships making the transit, as well as sending a

266 The Royal Navy Lynx

subtle message to the Spanish authorities. With the straits being such a choke point, it was also in an excellent position to investigate any warships transiting the area and intelligence gathering became a prime role. Despite its limitations in the night SAR role, the aircraft could also provide some coverage in a very busy piece of water. Even with all these different roles it was a fairly pleasant existence. In an article for *Flight Deck* magazine, Lieutenant Rick Anders recalled one incident where his sunbathing was rudely interrupted:

'A ticklish bead of sweat inched its way down the crick of his back. Two seagulls soared overhead, occasionally casting a fleeting shadow over the hot sand. The wavelets beat gently onto the beach with a cool calling and only the cries of anguish from a novice windsurfer disturbed the hot Sunday afternoon tranquillity.

'Suddenly, a painful screeching noise filled the air. The seagulls dispersed in a sweeping arc and several sunbathers nearby grabbed their beach bags with a look of resignation which was soon overtaken by one of relief. It was not their bleeper which had yet again curtailed the weekend's rest. They looked across half smiling. The Flight commander was already making swift tracks towards the nearest telephone, spurred on by the unbearable heat of the sand against his unprotected feet.

'The voice on the telephone reported "Tango – 120 Europa 8 miles" – he had a way with words.

'The Soviet submarine had been expected to pass through the Straits during the weekend and had finally shown his face. He was crying out through the waves of heat and humidity to be photographed as he cruised menacingly westwards. Flight recall was relatively easy that particular afternoon as the weather demanded that everyone should be on one of Gibraltar's few but crowded beaches. Soon, all the Flight were present and assisting in preparing the aircraft for the task. The bird-scaring Land Rover sped upwind of the runway, dispersing a flock of seagulls with two sharp cracks of pyrotechnics. The road bisecting the Northfront runway was closed to traffic and pedestrians as 320 lifted gracefully from dispersal with an increase in engine noise and departed swiftly west about the rock.

'The target was now due south of Europa point and was soon in sight. The leading photographer moved forward into the dispatcher harness and checked his loaded Hasselblad and Nikon. He was particularly excited today as he also carried colour video equipment normally used during PWO firings by HMS Ambuscade *and was itching to evaluate its use for intelligence photography. Airspeed was smoothly reduced and the cabin door opened in preparation for photography.*

'Meanwhile, life in Gibraltar continued at a sedate pace. The Sunday afternoon procession of cars circled the rock time after time, but did not totally subdue the noise

of tennis ball against racket on the Rooke courts, or the sound of leather against willow on the Northfront Square. The distinctive noise of the Lynx was not heard from the squash courts, but the majority of the inhabitants of Gibraltar's west side were aware of the aircraft's departure, but were not really sure the reason. Few would think any more about it.

'Those of the Flight with families on the Rock had mentioned in parting that there was no need to rush off the beach and back to the quarters since it was bound to be about three hours before the aircraft had completed its mission and had been put to bed. The unaccompanied personnel, who resided in the care of the RAF at Northfront made arrangements for late suppers...

'Out at sea, those of the crew who were able to find a place on the cramped bridge of the Tango Class Soviet submarine appeared most cheerful. A half empty bottle of vodka was offered up in a friendly gesture and their own cameras were used in retaliation. Photographs were obtained and goodbyes were exchanged. The aircraft turned back towards Gibraltar with the sun still high in the blue, but slightly hazy sky. The aircraft's return would not be heard on the west side. Slight turbulence was experienced in the Lee of the rock on final approach due to the westerly sea breeze.'

Vodka and smiles all round. (*Flight Deck*)

'*The SMR looked on anxiously for news of any unserviceability. There was none. Relief was apparent on the faces of the attendant ground crew. The aircraft was refuelled, serviced and stowed in the hangar alongside three of the resident RAF Jaguar detachment. It would fly again the next day on a training sortie.*

'*The beaches were no longer full, although the temperature remained high. Beachgoers were changing into night lifers. Some would make the pilgrimage across the border in search of variety and seafood. The Flight would remain rock bound in case of another callout. Although further employment in the intelligence gathering role was not expected until later in the week, SAR was always a possibility. Brief visits to Spain have been enjoyed by the Flight with the occasional luxury of a weekend stay on a rota basis, but most are content with the sporting and social offerings of Gibraltar.*

'*The beeper would go off another two times that evening, but only to notify the Flight of incoming priority signals, otherwise all was quiet.*'

Authors note: The aircraft used for this sortie was XZ 735 and not much later the Flight and aircraft were involved in evacuating civilians from Beirut in Operation Offcut, so life wasn't always so tranquil.

The Indian Ocean

In October 2009, the British yacht '*Lynn Rival*' was captured by Somali pirates. The Royal Navy were involved from on-board RFA *Wave Knight* and significant publicity was generated for quite some time, much of it critical of the navy's response during the initial kidnap.

What was generally not reported were the more successful actions conducted by the Royal Navy as part of operation Ocean Shield in the Indian Ocean. One such action is described here and once again the Lynx was critical to success:

RFA Fort Victoria *(229 Flight)*
Flight Commander – Lieutenant A.J. Thompson
Flight Observer – Lieutenant A.G. Henderson

Aircraft: Lynx Mk 8 SRU – ZF 562

'In 2009 naval operations began under Operation Ocean Shield, which was NATO's contribution to Operation Enduring Freedom – (Horn of Africa), an anti-piracy initiative in the Indian Ocean. Warships from many nations were involved; the British contribution was either a frigate or Royal Fleet Auxiliary with naval personnel and aircraft embarked.

'RFA *Fort Victoria* had sailed from Dubai in September 2011 with 229 Lynx Flight embarked. The ship was commanded by Captain Shawn Jones, OBE, and Captain Jerry Northwood commanded the military element, which included the aircraft and a team of Royal Marines.

'Piracy operations in the Indian Ocean had been rife over previous years. Somali pirate gangs operated from mother ships and would then board vessels from fast moving skiffs. They were normally armed with AK-47 rifles and rocket-propelled grenades. Their aim was to take over the ship and hold the crews and cargo for ransom. Over the years, millions of dollars had been made through the seizing of dozens of ships and hundreds of crew.

'Monday, 10 October 2011 was the day that they attacked the Italian flagged Motor Vessel *Montecristo*. At five in the morning the 56,000 ton bulk carrier put out a Mayday call reporting that they had been attacked by pirates some 600 miles east of Somalia. The ship was new, having been launched in June that year and had been built with all the latest anti-piracy measures as part of her design. She had initially attempted standard anti-piracy tactics by firing water cannon at the attackers and putting barbed wire along the side of the ship's guardrails. However, despite these measures, the pirates succeeded in getting on board. The twenty-three crew then fled to a safe armoured room specifically designed for just such an eventuality inside their engine room. Whilst in the secure room they could continue to steer and control the ship's engines, but all communication was lost when the pirates destroyed the ship's radio equipment.

'*Fort Victoria*, although closest to the hijacked ship, was still 100 miles away. So a plan was made to use the Lynx to carry out an initial reconnaissance. However, care would need to be taken; the weather was hot and humid and visibility poor due to the dust laden atmosphere. The aircraft had many modifications and was considerably heavier than originally designed and with air temperatures of 40°C it would only just be able to launch with two crew and a full fuel load. Care would also have to be taken because *Fort Victoria* was the only available landing site within 500 miles, there would be no diversion capability. However, the aircraft successfully launched and intercepted the hijacked ship. It was soon confirmed that the *Montecristo* was in the hands of pirates. There were clear signs of damage to the ship's bridge caused by rocket-propelled grenades.

'The aircraft immediately relayed the situation by radio to the ship's operations team and then headed back to refuel. It took several hours to plan and position

270   The Royal Navy Lynx

the ship for the next part of the operation. Being a merchant vessel, *Fort Victoria's* top speed was only about 15 knots, but an intercept was calculated and achieved without much difficulty, although it took all night to get into position. Once the target was visual, the Royal Marines boarding team commenced an approach. They used ballistically protected Rigid Inflatable Boats and were accompanied by the helicopter, which was also carrying Royal Marines. As soon as the Marines boarded the vessel they found eleven Somali pirates on board. However, faced with the overwhelming force of the Royal Navy they soon surrendered. Whilst the boarding was going on, the Lynx stood off and covered the Royal Marines with its O.5 inch calibre M3M machine gun and a Marine sniper team. With a grandstand view, the aircraft could see how the pirates quickly realised that the Royal Marines would easily overcome any fight they put up.

'The crew were released from their safe room unharmed and the vessel was then escorted clear of the area for minor repairs to the bridge before continuing on its passage. Because the *Montecristo* was an Italian ship, the pirates were handed over to the Italian Navy and prosecuted for piracy.

'This was not the only success during this period of operations, later on the ship intercepted a large fishing Dhow which was probably the mothership for the piracy attack on the *Montecristo*. On this occasion, *Fort Victoria* teamed up with the frigate HMS *Somerset* and were able to conduct a successful boarding and capture the vessel and suspect pirates.'

It should be noted that little of this operation and others like it appeared in the British press. But once again the Lynx quietly went about its business proving what a valuable asset it was to nearly every sort of naval operation.

Chapter 11

The Author's Story

1980–1986

I first flew a 702 Squadron Lynx on 5 August 1980. From my logbook, the sortie was the standard initial familiarization flight that is always the start of an aircraft conversion course. The aircraft was XZ 231 and my instructor was Lieutenant Commander Rick Sear. The trip lasted an hour. The purpose was twofold. Firstly to give me, the new pilot, a feel for the machine and also to have a look at the local area and basic air traffic procedures.

I already knew Yeovilton reasonably well. Although up until then I had been flying Sea Kings from Culdrose, we often visited our Somerset counterpart and so I was familiar with the area. The aircraft was another matter. One of the good things about an initial familiarization flight is that it is just about the only sortie that is flown on a conversion course that does not involve intensive instruction and a subsequent post flight debrief. Consequently, one is able to relax more than normal. It is the same for the instructor, so he can have a bit of fun as well.

I had already spent time in the aircraft in the hangar learning where all the switches were and going through the startup procedures, as well as some time in the simulator doing more of the same. I remember it was a nice sunny day with only a little broken cumulus at about two thousand feet, perfect for seeing what a Lynx could do.

The cockpit was much smaller than the roomy Sea King, rather like comparing the driving position of a 1950s American muscle car to a modern British sports car and that is how the aircraft felt in the air as well. We lifted off and Rick showed me what it was like in the hover and I had a quick play with it before we transitioned off to the west to Yeovilton's satellite airfield at Merryfield. On the way he showed me how manoeuvrable the aircraft was and also how much it vibrated at the max speed of 150 knots. Everything happened a little faster than in a Sea King. The controls were far more responsive, courtesy of the rigid rotor, and the ground was covered much faster courtesy of a higher cruising speed. When flying with the auto stabilisation system switched off the aircraft was extremely twitchy and it was clearly going to need a great deal of concentration when flying with it switched out. At Merryfield, we flew a few circuits, several autorotations and did some more hover work before transiting away to visit Westland Helicopters airfield at Yeovil. Here there was a landing grid which Rick used to demonstrate the use of the Harpoon restraint system. He also demonstrated how strong the undercarriage was by dropping us onto the ground from 10ft up. By the end of the hour, I realised that this machine was a quantum leap ahead of the Sea King and was going to be an awful lot of fun.

The rest of the conversion course was just that. Not only was the aircraft demanding and very satisfying to learn to fly, but there was an amazing atmosphere on the squadron. The wardroom mess president had stated his aim to make the mess at Yeovilton the best nightclub in Somerset and all of us on 702 Squadron were more than happy to oblige.

Apart from learning to fly a demanding aircraft in a multitude of roles, we were also having to learn how to operate as a single unit, as opposed to being part of a large squadron. One of the duties I would have to undertake would be that of my ships meteorological officer and so at the end of the course in December I spent ten days at Culdrose learning all about forecasting. By this time I had been appointed to be the Flight pilot of the newly recommissioned Leander class frigate, HMS *Andromeda*. My first sight of the ship was when I attended her commissioning ceremony in Devonport on 12 December. It was also the first time that I met up with my Flight commander and observer and very soon my friend Bob McKellar. The ship's commissioning ceremony went extremely well, as did Bob and my small subsequent 'run ashore' (the first of many over the next eighteen months). Flying back to Yeovilton the next day was interesting (I'll say no more).

Andromeda was the first of a new class of Leander. She had been retrofitted with four Exocet missiles, the new Sea Wolf point defence anti-aircraft system, new radars and new sonars. Of course she also carried the navy's latest all singing, all dancing, shiny, new helicopter.

Our first major task with the ship was to attend sea training at Portland. This was a very busy and intense six weeks where the whole ship was put through its paces. Not that it didn't occasionally have its funny side. One standard training serial was known as the 'disaster exercise' (DISTEX). On this occasion the scenario was that the ship was in a foreign port and giving aid to a disaster ashore which involved coping with rioters, casualties, and various other problems that the staff could think up. Once the exercise was underway, the aircraft was tasked to fly ashore to a small landing site. Unfortunately, the site was under attack by 'rioters' and until a shore team could clear them away, we were unable to land. Consequently, I held a high hover clear of the landing site. What I wasn't aware of, was that I was hovering directly over a small fire that had been lit by more rioters. Standing next to them were several nurses from the Sick Bay who were observing the ships company's attempts at first-aid. Within seconds, the downdraught from the Lynx turned the small fire into a raging inferno and the young nurse's pristine white uniforms were quickly rendered a smutty black. They emerged from the smoke looking like casualties from a Benny Hill sketch. The ship's sailors who were there thought it extremely funny, the girls weren't so impressed. Subsequently, I had to go up to Sick Bay and apologise, but luckily, by that time, they had also seen the funny side.

Our final serial was an antisubmarine and surface search exercise in the south-west approaches. On one search, we were extremely lucky and surprised a Soviet Foxtrot class conventional submarine on the surface, along with a support ship. The submarine immediately submerged and *Andromeda* came steaming up and conducted a cat and mouse game with the submarine for several days before having to return home. One could not get better training. The rest of the year was spent operating mainly with the ship, including a short trip to the Mediterranean. In December, the aircraft was fitted with Orange Crop and we spent an intensive period learning how to use it. The next year, on 5 January, we embarked in *Andromeda* for a transatlantic passage to the Bahamas. The passage was interesting, as halfway across the Atlantic we encountered an extremely deep weather depression. For over four hours our wind speed anemometer was jammed against the maximum stop, which was at least 80 knots of wind speed. Of course, as the ships met officer, I got all the blame. The ship however, survived, with little damage.

We were in the Bahamas to conduct trials on the AUTEC range. This is an extremely deep channel of water to the east of Andros Island and is fully instrumented to track submarines and torpedoes. One of *Andromeda's* new systems was the Ship's Torpedo Weapon System Mark 2 (STWS2), which consisted of two launchers with triple barrels capable of launching homing antisubmarine torpedoes, in this case the new Stingray. The trials were to assess the performance of the torpedo when launched from this new system. Flying for us mainly consisted of taking ship's staff ashore to the range facilities and then having to wait at the beach club for the day until they needed to return to the ship. It was a tough job, but someone had to do it.

We also spent some time working with the US Coast Guard on counter drug operations, although unlike the account in the previous chapter, we were not lucky enough to make any interceptions.

When Argentina invaded the Falklands, we were in Baltimore, but soon on the way home. Having already spent several months away from base support, we were not in a position to head south straight away. I have provided an account of what happened to us next in the earlier chapter about the Falklands War.

I joined the navy as an engineer and qualified as an Aircraft Engineer Officer (AEO) before learning to fly. This was because it is deemed a good idea that some AEOs have practical experience of flying and are also best placed to take on the role of a maintenance test pilot after they have been on the front line. Whilst we were still in the Falklands after the war, my SMR had to go home urgently for compassionate reasons. Because I was already qualified as an AEO he was not replaced. Consequently, I am probably the only Lynx Flight pilot who has also been his own SMR. It was an interesting few weeks, but I learnt a great deal about some of the maintenance issues of the aircraft that would stand me in good stead in my next job.

This next job was to be the maintenance test pilot at the air station at Portland, where the Lynx was now based, having moved there while we had been away in the South Atlantic. I spent a very happy four years in this role flying both the Lynx and the Wasp. With the aircraft still in its early stages of development there was much to do and it was an extremely rewarding period in my career. Unfortunately, being an AEO meant that at some point I was going to have to go back to my core profession. My last flight in command of a naval aircraft was on 7 May 1986 and was in Lynx XZ 255. From my logbook this last sortie only lasted five minutes, so something must have gone wrong to curtail it, but for the life of me I can't remember why. My excuse is that it was thirty years ago.

2016

Having decided to write this book about an aircraft that thoroughly deserves its praises sung, I needed to start gathering material. One of the organisations that has been extremely helpful has been 815 Squadron, now based back at Yeovilton; 815 now parents all Lynx flights and provides headquarters functions. 702 Squadron was disbanded some years previously and 829 Squadron now operates the Merlin helicopter. In addition to helping me out with accounts of the aircraft's exploits in its later years as included in this book, they also provided me with the opportunity to engage with the aircraft one more time.

My encounter with a Mark 8 Lynx was in the simulator. The 'Sim' has full day and night visual capability as well as being able to simulate all the systems that the aircraft now has. I was particularly interested to see what the workload would be like in this aircraft with all these new sensors and buttons to press.

My observer for the sortie was Lieutenant Commander Chris Yelland who I had previously bumped into when visiting 815. Chris reminded me that we had flown together many years before and in fact when I checked my logbook it was on 19 February 1986, a mere thirty years previously. Chris had been with the Lynx for most of his career so who better to demonstrate to me the capabilities of the Mark 8.

Climbing into the cockpit, it all seemed very familiar on the right hand side at least. At the observers station I recognised the radar and orange crop, but not much else. The instruments in front of the pilot have hardly changed although the engine gauges are in a slightly different position and the rotor speed indicator has moved, but apart from that everything else was where I remembered. For the sortie we launched from one of the navy's new Type 45 Destroyers. I managed to take off without hitting anything and we settled down in the cruise at a couple of hundred feet. Within five minutes I had already almost flown into the sea. The distractions for the pilot are significant. In the centre cockpit, where there used to be only switches and boxes for controlling the weapons, there is now a large TV screen, the Tactical Display Unit (Graphics) – (TSDG). This screen can show the radar picture, the tactical picture and also the visual image from the PID. The temptation for the pilot to get suckered into watching what is going on there, rather than what the aircraft is doing, is extremely strong. One particularly disorientating factor is that the TV picture from the PID is horizon stabilized. With the aircraft in a steep turn, the PID picture still appears horizontal, which can get extremely confusing.

Below the TSDG are the two Control Data Navigation Units (CDNUs), these two boxes control everything from the radios to the navigation system. I'm sure that once aircrew know their way around the systems, they are much more capable than the simple switch controlled boxes that we used to have. However, in the short time that we had available, all I could do was admire Chris's ability to press a lot of buttons, very fast.

However, it was very clear that the ability to visually identify a target from a long distance using the PID is an enormous step forward. In addition, the system's ability to take data from the radar and automatically track targets is a quantum leap beyond the system originally used. It was interesting to note that, to me, all this new equipment did not seem to make the observer's job much easier. What it actually seemed to do, was allow him to do much more, for the same sort of frantic workload he always had. It was a fascinating experience. However, I did discover one limitation of the simulator. Without visuals in the overhead panels, when I did a 'standard' visual rejoin of the ship at the end of the sortie and when I pulled the aircraft up and turned it almost upside

276 The Royal Navy Lynx

down in a wingover from 150 knots, I wasn't able to see the ship through the roof of the cockpit! At least that was my excuse for a very scruffy return to the ship.

Often, when an aircraft goes out of service, only a few are retained, whether in museums or in private hands, but this will not be quite the case with this machine. The requirement for an effective maritime helicopter to operate from the navy's small ships has not gone away and the new kid on the block replacing the Lynx is called the Wildcat. A much more modern machine in many ways, particularly as regards the avionics, it is in fact still part Lynx. As each Mark 8 was taken away to be retired, over 300 items were removed and are retrofitted in the new machine, this saved money, and why replace things that you already own and that are still fit for purpose? So, unlike on previous occasions, when a Wildcat flies past, not only will you be seeing the design legacy of its predecessor, but in actuality some of its anatomy as well.

Appendix I

Glossary of Terms

Acronym	Translation	Meaning
AEO	AIR ENGINEER OFFICER	The author's profession.
AAW	ANTI AIR WARFARE	A defined role for a warship with area anti-aircraft missiles such as Sea Dart.
AEW	AIRBORNE EARLY WARNING	Any airborne system that can detect attacking aircraft and give warning.
AM39/MM38	Exocet Variants	AM39 was the air launched variant use by Argentinian Super Etendard aircraft. MM38 is the shorter range ship borne variant.
AMCO	AIR MAINTENANCE CONTROL OFFICE	The engineering hub of a squadron or ship's flight.
AOA	AMPHIBIOUS OPERATING AREA	An area of sea designated for amphibious operations.
APT(N)	ATLANTIC PATROL TASK (North)	The area that modern ships are given to patrol which covers the Caribbean and Atlantic.
AS12	An air-to-surface missile	Carried by the Wasp helicopter and used during the Falklands War on the Argentinian submarine *Santa Fe*.
ASUW/ASV	ANTI-SURFACE WARFARE/ ANTI-SURFACE VESSEL	Two terms meaning the same thing that changed over time.
ASW	ANTI-SUBMARINE WARFARE	
ATC	AIR TRAFFIC CONTROL	
AUM	ALL UP MASS	The total mass of an aircraft at any time.
AUW	ALL-UP WEIGHT	The total weight of an aircraft at any time – changed to 'mass' to be more correct.
BERP	BRITISH EXPERIMENTAL ROTOR PROGRAMME	Joint programme between RAE and Westland to develop more efficient rotor blades, particularly for high speed flight.
CASEVAC	CASUALTY EVACUATION	Term used for helicopter sorties to conduct medical transfers. Also MEDEVAC.
CDU/CDNU	CONTROL DATA UNIT/ CONTROL DATA NAVIGATION UNIT	The central control and data processors for the Mark 8 Lynx, two are mounted side by side in the centre cockpit.
CHAFF	Not really an acronym	Tiny strips of aluminium foil cut to specific lengths to form a cloud in the air and make a large radar contact. Launched by hand or from M130 launchers.

278 The Royal Navy Lynx

Acronym	Translation	Meaning
CTS	CENTRALISED TACTICAL SYSTEM	The complete system installed in the Mark 8 that compiles the tactical picture for the observer based on all the aircraft's sensors and controls all weapons and radios.
DAS	DEFENSIVE AID SUITE	An automated system on the Mark 8 Lynx incorporating an IR missile jammer, missile approach warner and chaff and flare dispenser.
DESO	DEFENCE EQUIPMENT SALES ORGANISATION	MOD department that sells all surplus military equipment.
DIDTAC	DELIBERATE IDENTIFICATION TACTIC	More commonly referred to as 'Death in the Dark tactic'. The use of flares to illuminate a target before firing air-to-surface missiles – primarily used by the Wasp.
ESM	ELECTRONIC SURVEILLANCE MEASURES	Any passive radar receiver that analyses a received radar signal. The Lynx system is called Orange Crop.
EYEWATER		The code word for the seeker radar in the nose of an Exocet missile.
FISHHEAD	Slang	A term of endearment used by naval aviators for their seamen officer friends.
Flobs	Flight Observer	Simple abbreviation.
FOD	FORIEGN OBJECT DAMAGE	A generic term for anything going into a gas turbine engine and causing damage.
FOST	FLAG OFFICER SEA TRAINING	The organisation that works up ships when they enter service, now based in Plymouth.
FOTI	FLEET OPERATIONAL TACTICAL INSTRUCTION	Instructions on how to deploy and use various weapons and systems.
FPB	FAST PATROL BOAT	Generic term for any small, high speed and armed military vessel.
GOONSUIT		Slang term for the immersion coverall worn by naval aircrew when the sea temperature is less than 15 degrees – similar to a divers dry suit.
GPMG	GENERAL PURPOSE MACHINE GUN	7.62 millimetre belt fed machine gun used by all the British services and fitted in the cabin door of a Lynx.
GPS	GLOBAL POSITIONING SYSTEM	Satellite based navigation system.
HANDBRAKE		Code word for the radar in an Argentinian Super Etendard aircraft used just prior to launch of an Exocet missile.
HAS	HELICOPTER ANTI SUBMARINE	A title given to an aircraft to identify its primary role, although in the case of the Lynx it was only one of two.
HCA	HELICOPTER CONTROLLED APPROACH	A method of returning to one's ship using the aircraft's own radar.

Glossary of Terms 279

Acronym	Translation	Meaning
HDS	HELICOPTER DELIVERY SERVICE	Generic term for any helicopter Flight delivering stores whether internally or in underslung loads. See also VERTREP.
HMA	HELICOPTER MARITIME ATTACK	A title given to an aircraft to identify its primary role, in this case the Mark 8 Lynx.
HMP	HELICOPTER MACHINE-GUN POD	Half inch calibre cannon fitted into a pod and carried on either inboard weapon station of a Gulf Modified Lynx.
IFF	IDENTIFICATION FRIEND OR FOE	A transponder carried by aircraft to identify themselves. There are several versions, both civilian and military.
IFP	INSTRUMENT FLYING PRACTICE	Generic term for aircrew training and continuation flying to enable them to fly in IMC (see below).
IFTU	INTENSIVE FLIGHT TRIAL UNIT	First unit to be equipped with a new aircraft in the Fleet Air Arm so that it can be evaluated.
IMC	INSTRUMENT FLYING CONDITIONS	Defined conditions when aircrew are flying solely on instruments.
IRG	IRANIAN NATIONAL GUARD	Iranian forces in the Gulf.
LMG	LIGHT MACHINE GUN	Magazine fed 7.62 millimetre machine gun.
M130		Automated dispenser to discharge Chaff and IR flares.
MAD	MAGENTIC ANOMALY DETECTOR	Device fitted to an aircraft to detect the magnetic field of a submerged submarine.
MCT	MARITIME COUNTER TERRORISM	Term used for helicopter sorties to conduct medical transfers. Also CASEVAC.
MEDEVAC	MEDICAL EVACUATION	Generic term for any aircraft sortie to evacuate a medical emergency. See also CASEVAC.
MEZ	MISSILE ENGAGEMENT ZONE	A defined area where there is a threat from a known enemy missile system.
MLA	MINIMUM LANDING ALLOWANCE	The minimum fuel state an aircraft must have at final land on. Going beyond this may result in engines flaming out.
MPA	MARITIME PATROL AIRCRAFT	Normally a modified commercial airliner. The RAF used to operate the Nimrod, based on the Comet airliner, until they were scrapped in the latest Defence Review.
NASU	NAVAL AIRCRAFT SUPPORT UNIT	An organisation at a Naval Air Station that conducts deeper maintenance and modification than can be conducted on a squadron.
NATEC	Naval Aircraft Technical Evaluation Centre	Based at the Air Station at Lee-on-Solent, the NATEC was responsible for many elements of specialist engineering such as vibration and helicopter oil analysis.

Acronym	Translation	Meaning
NATIU	NAVAL AIRCRAFT TRIALS INSTALLATION UNIT	Now defunct – but an organisation based at the Air Station at Lee-on-Solent that managed and conducted trial modifications of aircraft.
NGS	NAVAL GUNFIRE SUPPORT	The act of spotting the fall of shot of naval guns to correct their aim. Can be done by observers from the ground or in aircraft.
ODM	OPERATING DATA MANUAL	A publication relevant to a type of aircraft listing all its performance data.
OOW	OFFICER OF THE WATCH	The officer in charge on the bridge of a warship.
OP	OBSERVATION POST	A military outpost designed to keep surveillance over a given area.
OTHT	OVER THE HORIZON TARGETING	An important role for the Lynx to find and identify targets for surface ships or other aircraft to attack.
PID	PASSIVE IDENTIFICATION DEVICE	The Sea Owl electro optic infra-red sensor fitted to the nose of a Mark 8 Lynx.
PNR	POINT OF NO RETURN	The point in an aircraft's journey when it will no longer be possible to turn around and land elsewhere.
POW	PRISONER OF WAR	
PVA/ELVA	POOR VISIBILITY APPROACH/ EXTREMELY LIMITED VISIBILITY APPROACH	Normally an emergency procedure to recover to one's ship when the visibility has reduced below safe minima. A combination of radar control, flares being dropped into the wake of the ship and other techniques. During the Falklands War it became almost the normal daily procedure used by Lynx crews.
QHI	QUALIFIED HELICOPTER INSTRUCTOR	A pilot who has completed the instructors course. Then employed on a training squadron or as a senior member of a regular squadron.
RAE	ROYAL AIRCRAFT ESTABLISHMENT	The civilian research organisation based at Farnborough and Boscombe Down as well as elsewhere. Changed to become the Defence Research Agency DRA and then privatised and now known as QinetiQ.
RAN	ROYAL AUSTRALIAN NAVY	
RFA	ROYAL FLEET AUXILIARY	Ships used to support the RN Fleet, i.e. oilers, stores, ships, etc. Painted grey but run to Merchant ship rules.
ROE	RULES OF ENGAGEMENT	The rules provided by Command that give the freedom to use weapons at any given time.

Glossary of Terms   281

Acronym	Translation	Meaning
S126	A naval form	Raised to account for lost stores. Not popular!
SAM	SURFACE-TO-AIR MISSILE	
SAR	SEARCH AND RESCUE	
SARBE	SEARCH AND RESCUE BEACON	A small radio fitted to aircrew life vests that produces a radio signal on the emergency frequency to allow survivors to be located.
SAS/SBS	SPECIAL AIR SERVICE/ SPECIAL BOAT SERVICE	The UK's two Special Forces cadres.
SHOL	SHIP HELICOPTER OPERATING LIMITATIONS	The limits to which a particular helicopter can operate to with a specified type of ship. Mainly consisting of ship's pitch and roll limits and wind speed and direction – represented graphically.
SLR	SELF LOADING RIFLE	For many years the UK standard rifle for all three services: 7.62 millimetre and twenty rounds fired single shot.
SMR	SENIOR MAINTENANCE RATING	The Chief Petty Officer in charge of the maintenance of any ships Flight.
SQAVO	SQUADRON AVIATION OFFICER	Frigates and Destroyers are organised into squadrons and the senior ship's staff take on extra responsibility for the ships in their squadron. The Flight Commander of the senior ship is therefore the Squadron Aviation Officer.
STUFT	SHIPS TAKEN UP FROM TRADE	Generic term for any merchant ships chartered by the MOD during operations.
STWS/STWS2	SHIPS TORPEDO WEAPON SYSTEM	Triple barrel launcher for ships to launch homing ASW torpedoes. Original version used the American Type 46; STWS2 was designed for the Stingray.
SUCAP	SURFACE COMBAT AIR PATROL	On call fixed wing assets to be deployed against surface targets.
TANS	TACTICAL AIR NAVIGATIONS SYSTEM	The Doppler radar fed navigation system in the Lynx Mark 2 and 3.
TDSG	TACTICAL DISPLAY UNIT (GRAPHICS)	The core display for the Lynx Mark CTS.
TEZ	TOTAL EXCLUSION ZONE	The 200 mile zone around the Falklands imposed by the British at the start of the Falklands War.
UAA1		The ESM equipment fitted to many RN warships in the 80s and 90s.
UXB	UNEXPLODED BOMB	
VERTREP	VERTICAL REPLENISHMENT	Generic term for transferring stores to ships by helicopter, normally as underslung loads.

Acronym	Translation	Meaning
VMC	VISUAL METEREOLOGICAL CONDITIONS	Define conditions when aircrew are able to operate visually.
WAFU	Slang – and Varied!! Often – 'Wet and Effing Useless'	A term of endearment used to describe aviators.
WIGS	WEST INDIES GUARD SHIP	Until replaced by APT (N) this was the generic term for any ship operating in the Caribbean.

Appendix II

Naval Lynx Variants – Performance Specifications

The following table is a summary with the key points outlined. In particular, the actual development of the Mark 3 into the Mark 8 was a phased process.

	Mark 2	Mark 3	Mark 8
Max take-off weight (Kg)	4420	4876	5330
Basic weight (Kg) including two crew at 91Kg each	2941	3116	3421
Disposable load (fuel and payload) (Kg)	1480	1760	1900
Speed	150 Knots max for 10% of any sortie. Cruise at 120 Knots	150 Knots max for 10% of any sortie. Cruise at 120 Knots	144 Knots, but less depending on ambient conditions and weight. Cruise at 120 Knots
Main rotor gearbox	2 pinion	3 pinion	3 pinion
Transmission rating (SHP)	1380	1600	1840
Main rotor blades	Metal	Metal/BERP Composite	BERP Composite
Tail rotor	Standard	Standard	Reverse direction
Engines	Gem 2 (900 SHP)	Gem 42 (1120 SHP)	Gem 42 (1120 SHP)
Differences		4 bag flotation gear, uprated engines and transmission.	PID, CTS, Digitized radar, GPS, (some Mk 3s had CTS and early secure speech systems)
Weapons	Mk 46 torpedo Mk11 DC Sea Skua 4.5 inch recce flares WE 177a NDB Cabin mounted GPMG	Stingray torpedo Mk 11 DC Sea Skua HMP 4.5 inch recce flares Cabin mounted GPMG replaced by M3M	Stingray torpedo Mk 11 DC Sea Skua Cabin mounted M3M
Sensors and electronics	Sea Spray radar Orange Crop ESM MAD Hampton Mayfair PTR 377 radios	Sea Spray radar Orange Crop ESM Yellow Veil Sandpiper IR imager AD 3400 Lamberton Secure Speech Early version of CTS	Sea Spray radar (Digital processor) Sea Owl PID Orange Crop ESM CTS Saturn radio

Appendix III

A Dummies Guide to Flying a Helicopter

Although this book is about one specific type of helicopter, the detail of how one is flown is generally only really understood by those who actually get to play with them. Whilst it is obviously not possible to teach someone how to fly one from the pages of a book, in this section the author will attempt to provide just a little more in the way of explanation and maybe bust a couple of myths in the process, as well as providing some more detail about the Lynx.

Nomenclature

'Helicopter speak' uses some common phrases that are not at all obvious to the layman.

The use of the letter 'N' has particular significance to helicopter pilots; it means various forms of rotational speed:

Nr – the speed of the main rotors.
Nf – the speed of the Free Power Turbines – these are the turbines at the back of each engine that are connected to the transmission.
Nl or Nh – in the case of the Lynx – the speed of the high and low speed sections of the engine, other engines may use Ng.

Torque – this is a key measurement. The transmission of a helicopter is driven by the power output of its engine/engines. However, for aerodynamic reasons the rotor speed (Nr) of a helicopter needs to be kept fairly constant. It is actually torque that damages a rotating component and so, rather than a power gauge, a helicopter has a Torque gauge (or several – one for each engine) which, as the Nr is constant, is effectively proportional to the power output of the engines. As torque is the damaging factor for the transmission it is the most useful measurement for the pilot to ensure he flies safely.

Collective – this refers to anything that happens to all the rotor blades the same amount. Collective pitch is the amount of pitch applied by the pilot's collective lever. The more applied, the more lift generated, but the more Torque is needed to keep Nr constant.

Cyclic – this refers to anything that happens to the rotor blades as they go round in a circle. The Cyclic stick used by the pilot will change the pitch of the blades where he wants them in order to manoeuvre the aircraft. For example, if he pushes the stick forward, the angle of blades at the rear of the aircraft is increased and that ahead is decreased. The net effect is to tilt the rotor disc forwards and the aircraft will drop its nose.

Yaw – as collective pitch is applied, the fuselage of a helicopter will attempt to turn in the opposite direction to that of the main rotors (torque reaction). This Yaw is counteracted in most helicopters by a tail rotor. The pitch of this rotor is controlled by rudder pedals.

Autorotation – contrary to popular myth, a helicopter will continue to fly without engine power. If the pilot lowers the collective lever to the bottom in forward flight, the aircraft will start to descend (often quite rapidly), but the air now flowing up through the rotors keeps them turning to the extent that the pilot may well have to apply some collective pitch to keep their speed under control. This is called autorotation and consequently all the flying controls will still operate normally. In the case of an engine failure the pilot will enter autorotation and fly the aircraft to a safe area, normally at a speed of about 70 knots or so. When close to the ground he then pulls up the nose to wash off speed, which also has the effect of reducing his rate of descent. When almost down, he then levels the aircraft and pulls the collective lever up to cushion the landing – this will slow down the rotors, but enables a safe and controlled landing to be undertaken. In the Royal Navy this was only practiced in single engine helicopters such as the Wasp and Gazelle. With twin engine aircraft, the autorotation phase is practiced – but only to a powered hover.

Getting it started

One of the worst sins committed by novelists is when the hero jumps into an unfamiliar helicopter and starts it up. Strangely, any experienced pilot put behind the controls of a 'burning and turning' helicopter would almost certainly be able to lift into the hover and fly away. What he would NOT be able to do is get the machine going in the first place. This is because nearly every machine will use a totally different set of switches, cocks, levers, gauges, controls etc. to manage the process. Add into the mix different numbers of engines with differing types of control systems, different stabilisation and flight control systems and one can see how complicated life can become. If you have a set of the startup check lists you could probably figure it out in slow time once all the

286   The Royal Navy Lynx

switches etc. have been located, and you can understand what they do of course. Any idea what an ESSB or Busbar Coupling switch are?

So, given that learning to fire the thing up is going to be an issue which cannot be addressed here, outlined below is a very simplified routine for getting a Lynx 'burning and turning':

Walk around the machine and check all is secure and all blanks have been removed. Then jump in and do up your straps.

Before engine start, signal to ground crew to connect external power, then all the internal switches need to be made, starting at the overhead centre console. Here, you will turn on the battery and then all electrical and fuel services. Then check the engine controls and ensure that the No1 engine is in 'accessory drive' (more on that later). Ensure the rotor brake is on.

Next, the flying instruments and warning panels are checked before moving to the lower centre console to turn on the radios and other electronics.

When ready, signal ground crew that you are ready to start the No 1 (port) engine. Press the switch at the end of the left-hand Engine Condition Lever (ECL) and then move it forward until it clicks into the Ground Idle position. Monitor the engine T6 (Temperature) to see that it lights up and then runs up to idle with good oil pressure. Once steady, advance the ECL forward, watching the Nf until it is at 100%. The No 1 engine is in 'accessory drive', so it is declutched from the main gearbox, but still able to drive the accessories such as hydraulic pumps and electrical generators. Signal to ground crew to remove external power and that you want to start No 2. Start No 2 as per No 1, but leave it at Ground idle as it is physically connected to the gearbox. With the rotor brake on, the rotors do not move.

With power and hydraulics available, you can now check your flying controls for full and free movement with both, and then each of the two hydraulic systems switched out. Then check the AFCS (Automatic Flight Control System) is working and the bar alt and rad alt height holds engage and can be overridden. Meanwhile, your observer is getting his systems on line. When satisfied all is well, centre the cyclic and bottom the collective. Turn on the anti-collision light and signal to the marshaller that you want to start the rotors. Check all is clear and release the rotor brake. Advance No 2 ECL to accelerate the Nr to 100%. Retard the No1 ECL to Ground Idle and make sure that the No1 Nf is slower than the Nr. This is because you are now going to select the No 1 engine to 'Main Drive' and it has to be going slower than the main rotors or there will be a horrible

A Dummies Guide to Flying a Helicopter   287

crunch and loss of career prospects as you crash engage the system and write off the transmission. Once in Main Drive, re-advance the No1 ECL to match it with the Nr and No 2 Nf. Briefly retard the No 2 ECL to ensure that the No 1 engine is actually driving the rotors before putting it back forwards. Finally, push the middle lever (Speed Select lever) forward to set the Nr at 107% ready for flight.

You are now set for the observer to call out the pre-take-off checks and off you go – easy is it not?

Flying a Helicopter

So now you are at a thousand feet flying along at 120 knots. Your three controls are what you use to keep straight, keep level and maintain speed.

The cyclic stick will bank the aircraft and raise and lower the nose. Unlike a fixed wing aircraft, all helicopters are inherently unstable. This means that if you displace the cyclic in any direction the helicopter will continue to diverge in that direction unless corrected by the pilot. In a fixed wing aircraft, it will tend to self-correct without intervention. In addition, when a manoeuvre is initiated in a fixed wing machine, for example a turn, once the aircraft is at the desired angle of bank then the stick is returned to the central position. In a helicopter the stick has to be held into the turn to hold the bank. This is surprisingly intuitive, unlike the instability issue. Nearly all modern machines have some form of automatic stability built in to make life easier. Normally, this uses gyros to sense aircraft movement and feed in corrective signals. The Lynx has this – but can be flown 'stab out' – but is very twitchy, unlike the Wasp where many preferred it out (including the author). Helicopter instructors also like it out to build up piloting skills (and make their students sweat).

The collective lever in your left hand is used to maintain height and, in conjunction with the cyclic, maintain speed. The cyclic is used to select an aircraft attitude and the collective adjusted to maintain height. If the attitude is right then the speed will be also. If not, small adjustments will get it right.

The rudder pedals are used to balance the aircraft when turning and can also be used to make small heading changes.

The Lynx has two other helpful functions from the AFCS. On the rudder pedals are two switches which are closed when the pilot has his 'size tens' on the pedals. When he takes his feet off, the switches make and the AFCS automatically maintains the heading the aircraft was on when his feet were removed.

Situated near the collective are two buttons on the centre console. These are height holds and when pressed will move the collective to maintain whatever height the

288 The Royal Navy Lynx

aircraft was at when selected. One is driven by the radar altimeter, which only reads up to 1000 feet, and the second is driven by the barometric altimeter, which is less accurate, but can work at all heights.

So, our helicopter pilot can now turn, change speed, and climb and descend. Now, he has to learn to hover.

Hovering is literally like learning to ride a bicycle, in that it seems impossible at first and then it suddenly 'clicks'. The previously described controls still work in the same way as in forward flight, but everything is very sensitive and every control input has an effect which has to be countered by one of the others.

For example; if the aircraft starts to descend slightly, the collective needs to be raised. This increases the torque reaction, so the rudder pedals have to be adjusted to keep the heading steady. Unfortunately, the tail rotor is not at the same height as the main rotor, so increasing the thrust from it will tend to make the aircraft roll slightly. This means the cyclic has to be corrected and so not all the lift is working in the same direction and therefore the collective needs adjusting – you can see where this goes! It's quite fun watching a student for the first time (as long as you have already mastered the art) and its quite obvious, even from the outside, when the penny drops.

Now you can fly forwards and hover – you're a helicopter pilot. Nope. That's just the start. Helicopters are complicated and the systems in it will need managing and you will have to learn how. Then you will need to be able to cope with all the emergencies it is liable to throw your way. This is where simulators come into their own, as all sorts of horrible emergencies can be practiced that would be far too dangerous in a real machine. Many hours will be needed in training before anyone is safe to fly a helicopter. The big danger is 'getting behind the machine' i.e. letting it fly you, not the other way around.

A famous quote from an instructor to his student – *'Blogs, you are the safest pilot I've ever encountered. You're so far behind the aircraft, it will have crashed, burned and the fire will have gone out before you arrive at the scene of the accident!'*

So that's what's needed right? Wrong. Once you can fly the beast and cope with all it can do to you on a bad day, you now start to learn how to use it. In a private aircraft, that may simply be learning to navigate from A to B. In something like the Lynx, it is a fighting machine with a plethora of sensors. The pilot's main task will be to fly the aircraft, but crew cooperation with the observer is a key part of being operationally effective. A worked up Lynx crew will work together and share the load of operating the sensors, navigating, using the radios and firing weapons. It is often observed by passengers that a good crew rarely speaks to each other, as they know exactly what

A Dummies Guide to Flying a Helicopter   289

each are required to do before it needs to be said. Of course, in the Lynx and other naval helicopters, there are lots of secondary tasks like deck landing, load lifting, SAR, collecting the mail and getting ashore before anyone else, but some of those are skills that come naturally! Oh, and some 'non aviators' will also say that aviators are expert at using their 'pits' (beds) and they would be right. After all, we need at least eight hours rest a day – and what we get at night is a bonus!